THE LEGACY OF
JONATHAN
EDWARDS

THE LEGACY OF JONATHAN EDWARDS

American Religion and the Evangelical Tradition

Edited by
D. G. Hart
Sean Michael Lucas
and Stephen J. Nichols

 Baker Academic

A Division of Baker Book House Co
Grand Rapids, Michigan 49516

Published by Baker Academic
A division of Baker Book House Company
P.O. Box 6287, Grand Rapids, MI 49516-6287
www.bakeracademic.com

Printed in the United States of America

Library of Congress Cataloging-in-Publication Data
Reformed Bible Conference (2001 : Westminster Presbyterian Church, Lancaster, Pa.)
    The legacy of Jonathan Edwards : American religion and the evangelical tradition / edited by D. G. Hart, Sean Michael Lucas, and Stephen J. Nichols.
        p.   cm.
    Conference held Oct. 26–28, 2001.
    Includes bibliographical references and index.
    ISBN 0-8010-2622-9 (pbk.)
    1. Edwards, Jonathan, 1703–1758—Congresses. 2. Evangelicalism—United States—History—Congresses. I. Hart, D. G. (Darryl G.) II. Lucas, Sean Michael, 1970– III. Nichols, Stephen J., 1970– IV. Title.
BX7260.E3R44 2001
285.8′092—dc21   2002043712

For George S. Claghorn
Evangelical, Scholar, Mentor, Friend

CONTENTS

CONTRIBUTORS

Richard A. Bailey is a Ph.D. student at the University of Kentucky. He is the coeditor, with Gregory A. Wills, of *The Salvation of Souls: Nine Previously Unpublished Sermons by Jonathan Edwards on the Call of the Ministry and the Gospel* (Crossway, 2002).

George S. Claghorn (Ph.D., University of Pennsylvania) is professor of philosophy at West Chester University. He is the editor of the *Letters and Personal Writings* volume (Yale University Press, 1998) for the Works of Jonathan Edwards project.

Charles Hambrick-Stowe (Ph.D., Boston University) is director of the doctor of ministry program at Pittsburgh Theological Seminary and the author of *The Practice of Piety* (University of North Carolina Press, 1982) and *Charles G. Finney and the Spirit of American Evangelicalism* (Eerdmans, 1996).

D. G. Hart (Ph.D., Johns Hopkins University) is academic dean and professor of church history at Westminster Theological Seminary in California. Most recently, he authored *The Lost Soul of American Protestantism* (Rowman and Littlefield, 2002) and *That Old-Time Religion in Modern America: Evangelical Protestantism in the Twentieth Century* (Ivan R. Dee, 2002).

Samuel T. Logan, Jr. (Ph.D., Emory University) is president and professor of church history at Westminster Theological Seminary, Philadelphia. He is the editor of *The Preacher and Preaching* (Presbyterian and Reformed, 1986).

Sean Michael Lucas (Ph.D., Westminster Theological Seminary) is archives and special collections librarian at The Southern Baptist Theological Seminary. He is working on a biography of Robert Lewis Dabney.

George M. Marsden (Ph.D., Yale University) is the Francis A. McAnaney professor of history at the University of Notre Dame. Among his many books is *Jonathan Edwards: A Life* (Yale University Press, 2003).

Gerald R. McDermott (Ph.D., University of Chicago) is associate professor of religion at Roanoke College. He has written three books on Edwards: *One Holy and Happy Society: The Public Theology of Jonathan Edwards* (Pennsylvania State University Press, 1992); *Seeing God: Twelve Reliable Signs of Spirituality* (InterVarsity, 1995); and *Jonathan Edwards Confronts the Gods* (Oxford University Press, 2000).

Stephen J. Nichols (Ph.D., Westminster Theological Seminary) is associate professor of church history and philosophy at Lancaster Bible College. He is the author of *Jonathan Edwards: A Guided Tour of His Life and Thought* (P&R, 2001) and *The Spirit of Truth: The Holy Spirit and the Apologetics of Jonathan Edwards* (P&R, 2003).

K. Scott Oliphint (Ph.D., Westminster Theological Seminary) is associate professor of apologetics and vice president for student affairs at Westminster Theological Seminary, Philadelphia. He is the coauthor of *If I Die before I Wake: Help for Those Who Hope for Heaven* (Baker, 1995).

Michael A. Rogers (D.Min., Westminster Theological Seminary) is pastor of Westminster Presbyterian Church, Lancaster, Pennsylvania.

C. Samuel Storms (Ph.D., University of Texas at Dallas) is associate professor of theology at Wheaton College. He is the author of *Tragedy in Eden: Original Sin in the Theology of Jonathan Edwards* (University Press of America, 1985).

Harry S. Stout (Ph.D., University of Connecticut) is Jonathan Edwards Professor of American Christianity at Yale University. He is the general editor of the *Works of Jonathan Edwards*, published by Yale University Press, and the author of several books, including *The New England Soul: Preaching and Religious Culture in Colonial New England* (Oxford University Press, 1986).

Douglas A. Sweeney (Ph.D., Vanderbilt University) is assistant professor of church history and the history of Christian thought at Trinity Evangelical Divinity School. He served as assistant editor of the *Works of Jonathan Edwards* and is the author of *Nathaniel Taylor, New Haven Theology, and the Legacy of Jonathan Edwards* (Oxford University Press, 2002).

FOREWORD

Michael A. Rogers

The congregation I pastor, Westminster Presbyterian Church (PCA) of Lancaster, Pennsylvania, enfolds more than a thousand members who feed on the same diet of Christ-centered, evangelical Calvinism embraced by the great Jonathan Edwards three centuries ago. Once he survived the severe shock of transition to the twenty-first century, Edwards might even feel physically at home in our eighteenth-century-style, white-paneled sanctuary with its high central pulpit.

Our congregation annually hosts a Reformed Bible Conference on the October weekend that includes Reformation Sunday, featuring the best Reformed preachers of our day. On October 26–28, 2001, under joint sponsorship with Westminster Theological Seminary, Philadelphia, our conference offered the theme "Jonathan Edwards and the Future of Evangelicalism" to more than five hundred registrants. We were delighted to gather Drs. Timothy Keller, Samuel Logan, George Marsden, and Harry Stout as keynote speakers, plus seven others as workshop leaders. Addresses heard that weekend compose the primary contents of the volume you now hold.

In preparation for the conference within our church, I shared in the teaching of a thirteen-week adult Sunday school class introducing the life and writings of Edwards. Not surprisingly, many of our people found samples of his philosophical writings very hard to penetrate. We emphasized reading Edwards' sermons as a user-friendly way to meet him, since he was first and always a preacher of Christ-saturated sermons to ordinary folk. I continue to marvel that the same man whose prose soars into the stratosphere in *Freedom of the Will* can still render striking wounds to the conscience of nonscholarly readers in sermons such as "The Excellency of Christ" or "Pressing into the Kingdom of God."

As I work at the computer in my church study, I can lift my eyes to the wall above my monitor to see framed portraits of two solemn men gazing at me: Jonathan Edwards and D. Martyn Lloyd-Jones. These two giants of the faith have long been my premier mentors in the high calling of the Christian pulpit. Early in his ministry, Lloyd-Jones discovered volumes of Jonathan Edwards' works moldering in a used bookshop. The Welshman, whose expository preaching electrified hearers at London's Westminster Chapel, soon knew he was in the presence of a greater soul, one that endlessly challenged his own. Both men modeled unremitting zeal to preach "Jesus Christ and him crucified." Lloyd-Jones certainly spoke for both when he defined biblical preaching as "logic on fire." How desperately we need men who will strive before God and his Word to bring forth such gospel preaching again in our own time.

Edwards never lost God's unction to convey in both his writing and preaching some of that remarkable spiritual experience he described in his "Personal Narrative" at the time of his conversion: "The sense I had of divine things would often of a sudden kindle up, as it were, a sweet burning in my heart; an ardor of soul I know not how to express." As we continue to ponder the spiritual legacy of God's incomparable servant, Jonathan Edwards, may the Holy Spirit kindle many such blazes today—first in our pulpits—then in pews throughout a land much in need of another great awakening. *Soli Deo Gloria.*

FOREWORD

Samuel T. Logan, Jr.

The academy of theological education in the United States faces many challenges, some with regard to the means of its survival (finances), some with regard to the integrity of its product (distance education), and some with regard to its fundamental purpose (spiritual formation). Jonathan Edwards cannot solve these problems immediately and directly, but he has a great deal to contribute toward clarifying the third challenge of spiritual formation.

Throughout his ministry, Edwards was concerned to distinguish the true from the counterfeit. George Marsden, in his forthcoming biography of Edwards, points out that this concern arose from Edwards' own personal spiritual struggles and created the major agenda for his later work. From his earliest days, Edwards had been "orthodox" and "moral," some would say oppressively so. Using the criteria of doctrinal orthodoxy and godly living, he would have been, without any further spiritual development or change, fully qualified for membership in his grandfather Solomon Stoddard's church. Using these criteria, he also would have been qualified for church membership in most of the English congregations out of which the Puritans who founded the Massachusetts Bay Colony came. But Edwards would not have been qualified for membership either in the "visible saints" churches of post-1640 Massachusetts or in the church that he himself pastored in 1748.

What constituted the difference? For Edwards, it was the difference between the true and the counterfeit. While most American theological schools today would probably shy away from stating the matter in terms quite this stark, it is nevertheless the case that this difference gets at the heart of what is often called "spiritual formation."

13

Once, in speaking to the faculty and board of Westminster Theological Seminary, Daniel Aleshire, executive director of the Association of Theological Schools, described his experience as a seminary faculty member on the occasion of the annual commencement at the school where he was teaching. When hearing the names of some graduates called, Dr. Aleshire and his colleagues beamed. With some other names, the response was more muted but still basically positive. With a few names, however, Dr. Aleshire found himself gazing quite vigorously at the floor. The embarrassment did not arise entirely from the GPAs of those graduating or the uprightness of their lives, though these factors were extremely important. Something else mattered more. We call that something else "spiritual formation"; Edwards called it "genuinely gracious religious affections," and his superb biblical explication of those affections provides profound guidance to theological schools, churches, and Christian individuals today.

The Great Awakening was the most traumatic event ever experienced in the nation that became the United States. If Alan Heimert was correct, without the Great Awakening, there would have been no American Revolution. The Great Awakening was the first "national" event in America's history. Experienced by colonists from Georgia to Maine, it provided the first genuine sense that the colonists were all part of a single cultural, and soon-to-become political, entity. The events of the Awakening were, however, as divisive as they were dramatic—hence, the use of the word "traumatic." Those events led to the first large-scale ecclesiastical splits in the colonial church, as some leaders supported the Awakening and others opposed it.

Edwards became directly involved in revival activities in the fall of 1734. Upon noticing the twin threats of Arminianism and antinomianism in his own parish, he responded with a series of sermons on "justification by faith alone" and watched God's Spirit bring revival to the Connecticut Valley. Throughout the next twelve years, nearly everything that Edwards preached and wrote bore relation in some way to what, by 1740, had become "the GREAT Awakening." His first written work, published in 1737, was *A Faithful Narrative of Surprising Conversions,* and it was just that—a narrative that focused to an unfortunate degree on the unusual (and even unique) events of the 1734 Northampton revival. Edwards' next written discussion of these things was published in 1742 as *Some Thoughts on the Revival.* Here we find a much more mature Edwards, one who had begun to see that distinctions had to be made among the various events that were all being lumped together as evidence of God's direct, supernatural work among his people. In fact, the longest section of *Some Thoughts* was entitled "Showing What Things are to be Corrected or Avoided, in Promoting this Work, or in our Behaviour Under It." It contained the following thematically significant statement: "Though the devil will do his diligence to stir up the open enemies of religion, yet he knows what is for his interest so well, that, in a time of revival of religion, his main strength shall be tried with the friends of it; and he will chiefly exert himself in his attempts to mislead them."

Continued attacks on the Awakening, such as those of Charles Chauncey and distortions of the Awakening by "friends" like James Davenport, led Edwards to produce his most important work, *A Treatise concerning Religious Affections*, in 1746. It was this work that defined Edwards' legacy in both the church and the academy. It was also this work that formed the foundation of all of Edwards' later publications, particularly *A Careful and Strict Inquiry into the Modern Prevailing Notions of That Freedom of Will Which Is Supposed to be Essential to Moral Agency, Virtue and Vice, Reward and Punishment, Praise and Blame*.

Returning to Professor Marsden's observation and in keeping with Edwards' own announced purpose in the preface to *Religious Affections*, Edwards' focus was to help individuals and churches (and theological schools) distinguish true from counterfeit Christianity. The treatise sought to identify both what "true spiritual formation" is and how "true spiritual formation" may be nourished. As such, outside the Bible itself, *Religious Affections* is one of the most useful works for helping theological schools understand their fundamental purpose and for describing what seminary graduates ought to be.

These thoughts on *Religious Affections* hopefully will whet the appetite for the essays that follow. While these essays examine Edwards' legacy from divergent points of view, including some from which we may dissent, all of the authors are united in desiring the same goal as Edwards himself—the development of genuine piety. As evangelicals committed to the gospel of Jesus Christ, these authors examine the thought of a human author with the hope of understanding the thought of the divine author of the Scriptures, our Triune God. And while these essays advance the scholarly discussion of Jonathan Edwards in the academy, they also will be of inestimable value for the church as well. That Edwards' legacy continues on into the twenty-first century in this way is due solely to the grace of our glorious God.

Yet, as worthwhile as these essays are for stimulating thought and discussion about Edwards, the authors would agree that they are no substitute for reading Edwards himself. When asked by a young theological student what he should do to prepare for ministry, Dr. Martyn

Lloyd-Jones, one of the great pastor-theologians of the twentieth century, is reported to have said, "Read Edwards." Having duly recorded this suggestion in his notebook, the student then asked Lloyd-Jones what was next. The same answer came back, "Read Edwards!" This was also written in the notebook, and once more the student asked and once more Lloyd-Jones replied, "READ EDWARDS!!" It is my prayer that these essays will turn our attention to Edwards and to Edwards' God.

ACKNOWLEDGMENTS

This volume of essays began as an idea and a mere outline nearly five years ago. From the beginning, Sam Logan of Westminster Theological Seminary and Michael Rogers of Westminster Presbyterian Church (Lancaster, Pennsylvania) offered unstinting support as the idea first became a conference and eventually this book. Westminster Seminary and Westminster Church, especially its committee for the annual Reformed Bible Conference, graciously allowed the 2001 conference to be overrun by Edwards scholars and enthusiasts, which facilitated the bringing together of these essays. We thank these two institutions and all who contributed to the conference for their support. Particularly, we thank Tim Keller and David Coffin, who also led important sessions during the conference.

A few of the essays in this book did not derive from the conference. We thank Richard Bailey, George Claghorn, Sam Storms, and Doug Sweeney for offering their work for inclusion in this volume. The essays by Sam and Doug were originally presented at meetings of the Jonathan Edwards study group of the Evangelical Theological Society. Bob Hosack and Wells Turner at Baker Academic deserve thanks for enthusiastic support of this project and for shepherding it through to publication. Thanks also to Ken Minkema at the Works of Jonathan Edwards office at Yale University for his gracious assistance under pressure. We acknowledge permission received from Yale University Press and Oxford University Press for use of the Marsden and Sweeney essays.

Our wives, Ann Hart, Sara Lucas, and Heidi Nichols, also receive our grateful thanks for their helpful suggestions, proofreading, and constant encouragement. Finally, we dedicate this book to George S. Claghorn, Ph.D., D.D., whose dedication both to the church and to the academy best reflect Jonathan Edwards, the subject of his research for the past four decades. For two of the editors especially, Dr. Claghorn has served as a model of evangelical piety and academic perseverance. He has influenced us more than he can ever know. To honor Dr. Claghorn in this way is a small payment on the debt we owe to him.

INTRODUCTION

The publication of this volume of essays coincides with the tercentenary of Jonathan Edwards' birth. During the past three hundred years, more attention has been paid to Edwards than to any other figure in American religious history. And, as Harry Stout points out, there are "no signs of abatement."[1] Stephen Stein adds, "The study of Jonathan Edwards—his life, thought and influence—remains a growth industry today. . . . An astonishing amount of scholarly attention is being paid to him today. And there appears to be no end to this stream of publication."[2] While the sheer volume of Edwardsian scholarship is remarkable, it is equally matched by the range of scholarship and interest. Philosophers look to Edwards as he engages perennial questions related to the will, virtue, and beauty. Historians find that Edwards is a seemingly never-ending source of material for understanding the eighteenth century. Theologians find their own work enriched by returning to their Puritan forebear. Yet interest in Edwards extends beyond these disciplines and beyond the academy deep into the church. Pastors and laity from Baptists to Episcopalians—and all points in between—admire, read, study, and even emulate Jonathan Edwards. Indeed, the contributors to this volume represent a variety of disciplines and make their allegiance to no fewer than eight denominations. In short, Edwards has remarkable staying power.

Accounting for this phenomenon (or in Stein's words, "growth industry") begins with the figure at its center. At first glance, Edwards, clad in Geneva bands and powdered wig and graced with a stern countenance, appears quite foreign to contemporary onlookers. Yet,

1. Harry S. Stout, "Introduction," in *Edwards in Our Time* (Grand Rapids: Eerdmans, 1999), ix.

2. Stephen J. Stein, "Introduction," in *Jonathan Edwards's Writings: Text, Context, Interpretation* (Bloomington: Indiana University Press, 1996), ix–x.

his writings betray this initial assumption. Far from being an isolated colonial, Edwards read the latest works from Europe and proved a formidable interlocutor in the intellectual discussions of his own day. His training, deeply rooted in the classic texts of the Augustinian and Calvinist tradition, also included extended forays into Newtonian science and Lockean epistemology. While such divergent strains quickly led to the diversification of the disciplines of academia that pervades the modern university, Edwards managed to weave all of these strains into a cohesive whole. He exegeted Paul in as facile manner as he explored the wonders of the flying spider. His was an active and far-reaching mind, which resulted in a literary legacy that attracts scholars from a variety of fields. In other words, there is a reason that philosophers, historians, and theologians wrestle with Edwards: they all find something worthwhile in his writings.

Yet his writings do not belong merely to the past or to the academy. Edwards addressed ideas and tackled issues that transcended his own day, and he did so with a timeless style. The central issue that engaged his mind throughout the 1740s, the nature of true religious affections, remains crucial to religion and spirituality. To this we could add his discussion of what God is doing in this world in *History of the Work of Redemption*, his discussion of virtue and morality in *The Nature of True Virtue*, and his discussion of the implications of trinitarian dogma in various shorter writings and sermons. In other words, there is also a reason he captures the attention of so many in the church: they also find something helpful in his writings.

If the saying that you can learn a great deal about a person by the company he or she keeps holds true in the case of Edwards, then we stand to learn about him by looking at those who work with him. To be sure, Edwards may not recognize himself in all of the alleged portrayals of him, and he might not appreciate all of the alliances made with him. Nevertheless, looking at those portrayals and alliances is instructive. The interest in Edwards has some rather distinct manifestations. One such manifestation is the Works of Jonathan Edwards office at Yale Divinity School, currently under the leadership of Harry Stout and Kenneth Minkema. Since 1957, the Works of Jonathan Edwards has undertaken the ambitious and monumental task of producing the most comprehensive and scholarly edition of Edwards' writings, which, when finished, will span twenty-seven volumes. As the center of, and more than likely the reason for, academic interest in Edwards, the Works office also has sponsored numerous conferences and assisted the work of countless scholars and doctoral students working on Edwards.

Another distinct manifestation of interest in Edwards is the Banner of Truth Trust, a Reformed publishing house that, along with other such houses, tirelessly promotes and distributes the writings of Edwards through numerous reprints. In addition to the reprints, Banner also publishes Iain Murray's biography, another volume influential in introducing Edwards to the contemporary generation. The Works of Jonathan Edwards and the Banner of Truth Trust are just two of the many centers of Edwards studies and interest. Certainly, they appeal to different audiences and even represent a variety of approaches and historiographies. Yet, the fact that they both take their cue from the same subject bears notice. Among other things, this points to the relevancy and importance of Edwards for scholar and laity alike, for both the academy and the church.

The essays in this volume testify to these observations. They demonstrate that interest in Edwards continues and is not waning. They reveal that Edwards has something to say to a variety of disciplines, including theology, philosophy, and history. They further show that Edwards, even after three centuries, still has something meaningful to say both to the academy and to the church. Not all of the authors of these essays agree, however, in their assessment of Edwards' impact. Some celebrate his ideas and life as having continuing relevance, importance, and even urgency. Others see Edwards' legacy more ambivalently, if not suspiciously. Here Edwards is seen, not as a conveyor of the heritage of Reformed orthodoxy, but as progenitor of a much broader approach, what we call "evangelicalism" today. Both camps of interpretation are likely to meet criticism and disapproval by readers. That does not disconcert us. In fact, we hope that is the case.

Wrestling with Edwards is an important task. It is important from a historical perspective, given Edwards' prominence over the landscape of American religious history. It is also a present and urgent task, given Edwards' engagement of ideas that shaped and continue to shape our identity. So we offer these essays in the ongoing effort of understanding Edwards' place both in the past and in the present.

We have grouped these essays under the categories of vision, theology, legacy, and reflections. Harry Stout's lead essay explores Edwards' tri-world vision of redemption. Edwards used the interwoven histories of heaven, earth, and hell to encompass all the truths of Christianity. Edwards believed these histories could contain all facets of philosophy and systematic theology and present them in a more compelling and popularly accessible way. This narrative of redemption, Stout argues, was the capstone of Edwards' remarkable body of systematic reflection. Stephen Nichols' essay demonstrates that Edwards' vision was not merely abstract or ethereal. Rather, Edwards was profoundly interested in missions to Native Americans, and the opportunity to go to Stockbridge was the fulfillment of a lifelong ambition. Offering a revisionist reading of those seven "missing" Stockbridge years, Nichols believes that Edwards' preaching of redemption to the Native Americans was central to Edwards' life narrative. Richard Bailey also offers a revisionist understanding of Edwards' vision for preaching. Bailey holds that Edwards' preaching was passionate for God's glory and that this passion evidenced itself in his preaching style. Based on a reading of Edwards' sermon manuscripts, as well as Edwards' ministerial reading, Bailey claims that Edwards' preaching was far from staid and boring; rather, it was enlivened by divine passion. Finally, Charles Hambrick-Stowe presents Edwards' vision of spirituality. Edwards attempted to assist his parishioners into a "sweet sense" of Christ. Conversion was only the beginning of life with Christ; Christian spirituality consisted of continued communion with him.

Of course, Edwards' importance was not restricted to his vision. Rather, he is most frequently remembered as "America's theologian."[3] The four essays in the section entitled "theology" seek new directions in the study of Edwards' theology. George Marsden uses the posthumously published *Two Dissertations* to explore the ways Edwards challenged the intellectual presumptions of the age. While Enlightenment thought led some to abandon Christian principles in philosophy and theology, Edwards devoted some of his best thought in *The Nature of True Virtue* and *Concerning the End for Which God Created the World* to challenging the rising tide of materialism. C. Samuel Storms uses Edwards to challenge contemporary presumptions, specifically those of the newly emergent open theism. Those who decry God's exhaustive foreknowledge will find no friend in Edwards, Storms believes. In his seminal *Freedom of the Will*, Edwards defended God's exhaustive foreknowledge from the attacks of eighteenth-century Arminians; Storms seeks to use Edwards to defend the same truth, which is under attack today. K. Scott Oliphint also believes that Edwards has something to teach evangelicals when it comes to apologetics. The core of Edwards' Reformed apologetics wrestles with the pervasiveness of sin upon human understanding and with the necessity of a "divine and supernatural light" in order to illuminate the sinful mind and enable one to come to Christ. In the final essay of this section, Gerald McDermott investigates Edwards' public theology. Edwards perpetuated a longstanding Protestant tradition of interpreting national and public events

3. Robert W. Jenson, *America's Theologian: A Recommendation of Jonathan Edwards* (New York: Oxford University Press, 1988).

from the perspective of God's national covenant with New England. This covenantal approach was an extension of the same kind of interpretation scattered across the pages of the Old Testament. While noting several difficulties with Edwards' approach and stressing the need for humility, McDermott argues for a qualified appropriation of this way of reading providence.

Edwards' theology and vision did not die with him in the cold winter days of 1758. Rather, Edwards' legacy continued far into the nineteenth century, providing fodder for important ecclesiastical debates, as well as serving as the baseline for several theological arguments. D. G. Hart believes that Edwards' legacy is intimately connected with his defense of experimental Calvinism. Yet that legacy is not all positive; rather, Edwards' understanding of conversion—which carried the day among later American evangelicals—actually represented a move away from the older Reformed tradition represented by John Calvin and later revivified by John Williamson Nevin. Setting the stage for evangelicalism's exaltation of the revivalist bench over family-centered catechesis, Edwards' legacy ultimately paved the way for the lost soul of American Protestantism. Douglas Sweeney explores the contested battle over Edwards' legacy that occurred in the first decades of the nineteenth century in Connecticut. The epic duel between the Taylorites, followers of New Haven theologian Nathaniel Taylor, and the Tylerites, disciples of Bennett Tyler and Ashael Nettleton, involved more than political turf. Rather, the contest centered on the cultural authority and theological legacy of Jonathan Edwards and had import not simply for the church but for all New England society. Edwards' legacy, however, was not localized in New England. Rather, as Sean Michael Lucas demonstrates, southern Reformed theologians also wrestled with Edwards' legacy. While the southern Presbyterians, led by Robert Lewis Dabney, paid the New England sage great respect, they were not afraid to critique Edwards and his later New Divinity disciples, particularly in regard to Edwards' teaching on freedom of the will, the imputation of Adam's sin, and virtue. Southern Presbyterians finally distanced themselves from Edwards, leaving the New England divine to the enthusiastic southern Baptists, who were drawn to Edwards' theology of revival.

The final section of reflections offers the observations of George Claghorn, editor of the *Letters and Personal Writings* volume for the Yale edition of Edwards' works. Claghorn reminisces about the thirty-five-year journey that began with Perry Miller's invitation to work on the Yale edition and concluded with the publication of the *Letters* volume in 1998. In addition, Claghorn pastorally examines some of the lessons he learned from transcribing Edwards' difficult hand. The volume concludes with a very different sort of reflection—the intellectual labor of scholars and writers on Edwards. Sean Michael Lucas' bibliographic essay charts evangelical writing on Edwards as well as mainstream academic writing on Edwards from 1994 to 2000.

Ralph Waldo Emerson once said, "Plato is philosophy, and philosophy Plato." Paraphrasing him, one might say, "Jonathan Edwards is American religious history, and American religious history Jonathan Edwards." Edwards captured the attention of his own day and cast his shadow over significant events of the nineteenth and twentieth centuries. Now, as the twenty-first century gets underway, Edwards continues to impact the life and thought of the church. Though a New England Congregationalist, except for a few brief moments as a Presbyterian, Edwards belongs to many—to evangelicals. Perhaps, looking to this figure from the past might help evangelicals of the present navigate the future. This volume is offered toward that end.

PART 1

VISION

1

✸

JONATHAN EDWARDS' TRI-WORLD VISION

Harry S. Stout

P art of Jonathan Edwards' genius can be traced to his obsession with history and his sense that the days of systematic theology were numbered. For theology to survive (that is, orthodox theology), it would need to don new garments. By 1739, Edwards began to suspect that "history" was, in fact, larger than the antiquarian terms by which it was then known; indeed, it was larger than theology itself. In his evolving thought, carefully recorded and organized in reams of notebooks, commentaries, and sermons, history was emerging as nothing less than a container for the synthetic whole of theology and indeed of God's innermost self-revelation.[1] Gone were parochial notions of history as genealogy or the simple chronicle of human achievements and sequential events. Gone was even the larger but still theologically restrained notion, so familiar to Puritans, of history as the chronicle of "God's Wonder-Working Providence" on earth. Edwards had an even grander conception of history, capacious enough to contain all these ideas—and more.

1. Based on his reading of Edwards' "regulatory notebooks," composed in the 1720s, Wilson Kimnach concludes that Edwards "conceived of his life's work at a fairly early age" (in *The Works of Jonathan Edwards*, vol. 10, *Sermons and Discourses, 1720–1723*, ed. Wilson H. Kimnach [New Haven: Yale University Press, 1992], 56).

Earlier Protestant thinkers such as Philip Melanchthon, John Calvin, and William Ames had thought of theology as the ultimate canvas on which to record the being of God and his relationship to his creation. Whatever distance the reformers may have traveled from Rome, they had retained a Thomistic sense of systematic theology as the queen of the sciences. Edwards would substitute history. Edwards' history was not the history of William Bradford or Cotton Mather, a mere recording of New England towns and their ministers under the nationalistic gloss of *Magnalia Christi Americana*. Nor, as Professor John Wilson convincingly demonstrates, was it history in the emerging Enlightenment sense, the "scientific" history of politics and great men based strictly on empirical observation with no recourse to supernatural revelation. By comparison to this, Edwards' history was, in Wilson's terms, a "profoundly unhistoriographical [method] in any modern sense."[2]

Alongside these modern senses of history, however, lies another, more mythic sense of history that is best labeled "metanarrative." The modern model of history, which we might label "ordinary" or "historiographical" or, in Edwards' term, "actual" time, is simple chronology—history measured in minutes and years and recorded in written records. But as anthropologists and biblical scholars remind us, it is also possible to order and understand history in what we might term "mythic" or, in Edwards' terms, "divine" or "virtual" time—history as seen from God's time-transcending, eternal perspective. Central to this model would be separate but overlapping senses of time, as in the creation myths common to all religions. But, as we shall see, Edwards had an even larger story in mind—a narrative of redemption. To frame the metanarrative of redemption, Edwards would employ historiographical time from every source he could lay his hands on, both sacred and profane. But he would also subject it to the most important time in the narrative—divine time. For all of his piety, perhaps *because* of his piety, Edwards was not afraid to see time from God's vantage point. He would take his narrative where others before him were afraid to tread. If a majestic enough story could be constructed, Edwards speculated, it could contain all the doctrines and philosophical underpinnings of systematic theology in a more compelling—and popularly accessible—format. In other words, a metanarrative method could do all that systematic theology, and for that matter historiography, could do and more.

2. In *The Works of Jonathan Edwards*, vol. 9, *A History of the Work of Redemption*, ed. John F. Wilson (New Haven: Yale University Press, 1989), 73.

Edwards' history incorporated philosophy, theology, and narrative as a synthetic whole. Earlier he had established the proposition that "heaven is a world of love," a metaphysical state infused with the innermost being and character of the Trinity. So too, he proposed, earth is a world of pulsating divine energy and hell a perversion of love that set in motion the intergalactic supernatural conflict between God and Satan with earth as the prize. What if the history of all three—heaven, earth, and hell—were integrated into one narrative, a narrative superior to systematic theology for its drama and to earthbound historiography for its prophetic inspiration?

While Edwards was intrigued with the idea of a narrative history, this does not imply that he was uninterested in theology or even that he would not identify himself as a preacher/theologian if forced to choose. In fact, Edwards often referred to his work as "divinity" and produced several treatises, most notably *Original Sin, Concerning the End for Which God Created the World,* and *The Nature of True Virtue,* that take on the aspect of a systematic theology. It is rather to say that Edwards early on came to sense—especially in his sermons—that the most effective way to realize the theologian's goal of knowledge of God was to abandon the synchronic methods of formal theology and "throw" the truths of "divinity" into the diachronic form of a history.

By the eve of his premature death in 1757, the grand vision had formally matured into nothing less than a Descartes-like new "method" for conceiving religion and thinking about God. When, in 1757, the Princeton Board of Trustees invited Edwards to be the school's new president, he hesitated primarily because his history was not completed. In a sense, all of his great treatises, written in six-month bursts between 1750 and 1757, were ingredients to be pasteurized and refitted into the tri-world narrative. Those who see "the end" of Edwards' scholarly career as his all-fronts assault on Arminianism and Deism miss the larger goal. Those treatises were intended only to remove so much heterodox debris from the highway so that the way would be cleared to his true destination: the narrative history of redemption. In his often-cited letter to the Princeton Board of Trustees, he revealed his ambition:

I have had on my mind and heart, (which I long ago began, not with any view to publication,) a great work, which I call *History of the Work of Redemption,* a body of divinity in an entire new method, being thrown into the form of a history; considering the affair of Christian Theology, as the whole of it, in each part, stands in reference to the great work of redemption by Jesus Christ; which I suppose to be, of all others, the grand design of God, and the *summum* and *ultimum* of all the divine opera-

tions and decrees; particularly considering all parts of the grand
scheme, in their historical order.[3]

As he continued to describe his project to the trustees, Edwards
made plain how his new history would differ from prevailing notions
in several particulars. First, it would be a history in which theology
was subordinated to history rather than vice versa. Second, and more
shocking, Edwards went on in his letter to observe that his new history would be one that transcended space and recorded time, a history telling the simultaneous stories of "three worlds"—heaven, earth,
and hell:

> This history will be carried on with regard to all three worlds, heaven,
> earth and hell; considering the connected, successive events and alter-
> ations in each, so far as the scriptures give any light; introducing all
> parts of divinity in that order which is most scriptural and most natural;
> a method which appears to me the most beautiful and entertaining,
> wherein every divine doctrine will appear to the greatest advantage, in
> the brightest light, in the most striking manner, shewing the admirable
> contexture and harmony of the whole.[4]

The word "method" carried with it steep claims, indeed the highest
claims. For redemptive history—and the worlds it described—Edwards' primary source was, of course, Scripture. But even here Scripture would be augmented by the history of heaven and hell as it
evolved from the church fathers, through the Reformers and the Puritans. Heaven and hell, no less than earth, had their histories, as did
their citizens: angels and demons. For Edwards, each of these worlds
was equally real and dynamic, a constantly evolving protean force that
emanated ultimately from the mind of God. Each, moreover, was
equally knowable through creation and the revelation of nature and
through the Scriptures, the revealed self-disclosure of God in his diverse created worlds. Each, therefore, required a history. These histories would not be independent of one another but interconnected and
whole, like a finely spun tapestry. Rather than connect doctrines, Edwards would weave a story—a story that introduced all the major doctrines and philosophical underpinnings of Christian theology—but in
the process, he would introduce a different, dramatic form, one that
he identified as the history of redemption.

3. Edwards to the Trustees of the College of New Jersey, 19 October 1757, in
Jonathan Edwards, *The Works of Jonathan Edwards*, vol. 16, *Letters and Personal Writings*, ed. George S. Claghorn (New Haven: Yale University Press, 1998), 727–28.
    4. Ibid.

Edwards' doctrine of redemption as the central thread of his great project would not have been well suited to a systematic theology. To be grasped in all its completeness, it had to move out of the polemical confines of the schoolmen and theologians and present itself as a narrative story—indeed, the greatest story ever told. It is precisely the epic quality of *History of Redemption,* in its posthumously printed form in the nineteenth century, which gave it its "enormous influence" on "popular culture."[5]

The "scheme" of redemption perfectly fitted Edwards' ambitions to move through two times. At the outset he observed that "the work [of redemption] itself and all that pertained to it, was virtually done [i.e., in divine time] and finished [before creation], but not actually [in historiographical time]."[6] In "virtual" time—God's time—an indivisible divine "present" engulfs earthly past and future. God's time—and only God's time—is eternal. Even heaven is finite. In *A History of Heaven,* Jeffrey Burton Russell makes this important distinction: "Endless life is one thing, but God's ability to comprehend and embrace all time in one moment is another. Endlessness is perpetual, but only the existence of the entire space and time of the cosmos in one moment is eternal."[7] In similar terms, Edwards pointed out that in God's time, every event merges with every other event, not in successive chronological sequence, but "several parts of one scheme . . . in which all the persons of the Trinity do conspire and all the various dispensations that belong to it are united, as the several wheels in one machine, to answer an end, and produce one effect."[8]

Conscious of heaven and eternity, Edwards made clear that redemption *required* the fact of sin to generate the need for salvation (and hence the fall, and not creation, marked the starting point for his narrative in "actual" time); the "scheme" or divine plan was in fact eternal and "virtual." Before creation, "The persons of the Trinity were as it were confederated in a design and covenant of redemption." Indeed, "the world itself seems to have been created in order to it."[9] With the historical metanarrative in mind, he prompted his congregation to expect a personally riveting narrative of what God created them for. It was, Edwards stated, a far more important history than creation, for creation was the means to a greater end. Since God created the world as his stage to dramatize redemption, the "end" of

5. *Sermons and Discourses, 1720–1723, Works,* 10:82.

6. *A History of the Work of Redemption, Works,* 9:117.

7. Jeffrey Burton Russell, *A History of Heaven: The Singing Silence* (Princeton: Princeton University Press, 1997), 10–11.

8. *A History of the Work of Redemption, Works,* 9:118.

9. Ibid.

creation could not possibly be the happiness of his creatures, as "rationalists" and "Deists" were claiming. It had to be God's own self-glorification.[10]

At the conclusion of his 1739 sermon series on the history of redemption (posthumously published and not the larger vision he outlined to the Princeton trustees), Edwards would come full circle to this central thesis:

> This Work of Redemption is so much the greatest of all the works of God, that all other works are to be looked upon either as part of it, or appendages to it, or are some way reducible to it. And so all the decrees of God do some way or other belong to that eternal covenant of redemption that was between the Father and the Son before the foundation of the world; every decree of God is some way or other reducible to that covenant. And seeing this Work of Redemption is so great a work, hence we need not wonder that the angels desire to look into it. And we need not wonder that so much is made of it in Scripture, and that 'tis so much insisted on in the histories, and prophecies, and songs of the Bible, for the Work of Redemption is the great subject of the whole Bible. In its doctrines, its promises, its types, its songs, its histories, and its prophecies.[11]

Edwards would use the history of earth and earthly time as the spine of his narrative and interleaf the worlds of heaven and hell as they intersected, so that the whole resembled "an house or temple that is building, first the workmen are sent forth, then the materials are gathered, then the ground fitted, then the foundation is laid, then the superstructure erected one part after another, till at length the top-stone is laid. And all is finished."[12] In these terms, earth was the foundation, heaven and hell the superstructure. While he never lived to complete the project, we can infer key aspects of the tri-world history, starting with heaven.

10. Edwards treated this theme most fully in his *Dissertation concerning the End for Which God Created the World*, in Jonathan Edwards, *The Works of Jonathan Edwards*, vol. 8, *Ethical Writings*, ed. Paul Ramsey (New Haven: Yale University Press, 1989), 401–536.

11. *A History of the Work of Redemption, Works*, 9:513–14. John Wilson points out that these "sermons" were prepared more as sustained lectures than typical Sunday sermons. In earlier sermons Edwards employed "applications" and "uses" chiefly to arouse the emotions of his listeners. But in contrast to the *Charity* sermons, many of the individual *Redemption* sermons have no hortatory section at all; they simply lay out the facts, in outline-like form, of the massive cosmic history described later in the letter to the Princeton trustees. Throughout, the text is densely packed with historical facts piled on top of facts, many from Scripture. But, as Edwards' catalogue makes plain, he derived significant numbers of his facts from church and "profane" history as well.

12. Ibid., 121.

Heaven

Though earth grounded his narrative project, Edwards would begin with heaven: the creation of the angels and the eternal communications of the deity. Few systematic theologies dwelt excessively on heaven and its citizens, which was one more reason that Edwards could not frame his life's ambition in a formal theology. Heaven could exist only in narrative form, communicated to the church through a series of stories and histories. Heaven transcended formal theology and abstract categories and placed the ordinary person on a level with the most advanced academic.[13] Heaven, no less than earth, was created and not eternal, and it was created for the same end: the work of redemption. Earlier, in his "Miscellanies," Edwards ruminated over invisible worlds: "Heaven is a part of the universe that, in the first creation and the disposition of things that was made in the beginning, was appropriated to God to be that part of the universe that should be his residence, while other parts were destined to other uses."[14]

The entree into this divine residence is love. In a sermon series on *Charity and Its Fruits*, preached in 1738, Edwards described heaven as "a world of love" created "to be the place of [God's] glorious presence: there dwells God the Father, and so the Son, who are united in infinitely dear and incomprehensible mutual love. . . . There is the Holy Spirit, the spirit of divine love, in whom the very essence of God, as it were, all flows out or is breathed forth in love. . . . There in heaven this fountain of love, this eternal three in one, is set open without any obstacle to hinder access to it."[15]

Though not eternal, heaven is older than earth. Like earth, heaven is a place with a physical, social, and spiritual topography. There are gardens, cities, temples, and fountains. If streets are not made of gold (Edwards was ready to concede the metaphoric power of gold), there are nonetheless streets. Likewise, heaven has a spiritual architecture as the abode of the elect, the crown of the martyrs, and the fount of enlightenment. Heaven also has clouds on which Christ will one day descend; heaven radiates a physicality, with material and moral landscapes of inexpressible beauty. At the center of Edwards' Dantean vision of heaven is supernatural light, not unlike the "blazing point" of *Paradiso*, with angels spinning a ring of light.

13. Russell, *History of Heaven*, 16–17.
14. "Miscellanies" no. 743, in Jonathan Edwards, *The Works of Jonathan Edwards*, vol. 18, *The "Miscellanies," 501–832*, ed. Ava Chamberlain (New Haven: Yale University Press, 2000), 379–80.
15. "Heaven Is a World of Love," in *Ethical Writings, Works*, 8:369–70.

Heaven embraces saints, angels, and, of course, the Persons of the Trinity. Among them, the three constituents form a divine "society." Heaven, Edwards believed, is "the only way that ever has been contrived for the gathering together angels and men into one society and one place of habitation."[16] The best human analogy to this heavenly society is the church community in worship.

Modern readers—even Christian readers accustomed to the discourse of theology—might be surprised at how frequently angels appear as central characters in Edwards' tri-world narrative. Edwards repeated themes he first recorded privately in his "Miscellanies," reminding his hearers that "the creating heaven was in order to the Work of Redemption; it was to be an habitation for the redeemed and the Redeemer. Angels [were created to be] ministering spirits [to the inhabitants of the] lower world [which is] to be the stage of the wonderful work [of Redemption]."[17] Some angels have names, such as Michael the warrior, the archangel identified principally with ancient Israel and later, at Armageddon, commanding the celestial armies battling Satan and his demons. In contrast, the archangel Gabriel appears as the messenger of mercy and promise in Daniel and Luke. In Luke, it is Gabriel who informs the Virgin Mary of her coming glory. A hierarchy of powers and angels exist among angels, from archangels and angels at the top, whose activities embrace heaven and earth, to cherubim and seraphim, whose sole residence is heaven surrounding the heavenly throne (Isa. 6:1–6). Satan himself was formerly an archangel and, in popular church teaching, second only to God. With his banishment for rebellion, along with "hundreds" of other rebel angels, the ranks of remaining angels were purified so that, Edwards concluded, "they never will sin, and . . . are out of any danger of it." While only a handful of angelic names are known, and while most are invisible to human eyes, they number in the legions.[18]

Saints and angels interact with the Trinity. In an earlier sermon, Edwards pointed out that "God is a spirit and is not to be seen with bodily [eyes]. . . . 'Tis not any sight with the bodily eyes. For [the] souls of the saints [in heaven], they see God, and the angels [also, who are] spirit and never were united to bodies. . . ."[19] Though citizens of heaven, angels spend considerable time on earth as ministering spir-

16. "Miscellanies" no. 809 (*Works*, 18:515).

17. *A History of the Work of Redemption, Works*, 9:118–19.

18. Ibid., 123; "Miscellanies" no. 442, in Jonathan Edwards, *The Works of Jonathan Edwards*, vol. 13, *The "Miscellanies," a–500*, ed. Thomas A. Schafer (New Haven: Yale University Press, 1994), 490.

19. "The Pure in Heart Blessed," in Jonathan Edwards, *The Works of Jonathan Edwards*, vol. 17, *Sermons and Discourses, 1730–1733*, ed. Mark Valeri (New Haven: Yale University Press, 1999), 62.

its. Indeed, they exist all around true believers in invisible armies. Though rejecting the Roman Catholic belief in "guardian angels" commissioned for children at baptism, Edwards frequently reminded his children listeners that angels were particularly attentive to them. In his sermon "Children Ought to Love the Lord," delivered in August 1740, Edwards consoled his young listeners with these words:

> If you truly love Christ, all the glorious angels of heaven will love you. For they delight in those that love Christ; they love to see such a sight as children giving their hearts to Christ. There will be joy in heaven among the angels that day that you begin to love Christ. And they will be your angels; they will take care of you while you sleep, and God will give 'em charge to keep you in all your ways.[20]

But angels are neither childish nor limited to children. As ever-present realities, they represented for Edwards a possibility in human nature to become like angels; they lent an intensification of being and becoming unavailable to fallen human mortals.

Although peaceful after Satan's expulsion, heaven was never static. Indeed, it is a theater of dramas every bit as consuming as earth's. And unlike those on earth, heaven's inhabitants can participate in their own heavenly dramas and conflicts and, at the same time, can view and even participate in the dramas on earth. Heaven, no less than earth, remains incomplete, in need of "newness," so that "with respect to the saints and angels, all things in heaven and earth and throughout the universe are in a state of preparation for the state of consummation; all the wheels are going, none of them stop, and all are moving in a direction to the last and most perfect state."[21]

Earth

Since redemption lay at the center of actual history, the hinge dates of earth's history were not tied to the rise and fall of the great empires but to the outworking of redemption: in individuals such as Abraham, David, Christ, the apostles, and Constantine; in movements such as the Reformation and the Puritan migration; and—quite soon, again— in places such as Northampton. In like manner, the triggering mechanism for these turning points in actual history would not be wars and conquests but revivals of true religion.

20. "Children Ought to Love the Lord," in Jonathan Edwards, *The Works of Jonathan Edwards, Sermons and Discourses, 1739–1742*, ed. Harry S. Stout and Nathan O. Hatch (New Haven: Yale University Press, forthcoming).
21. "Miscellanies" no. 435 (*Works*, 13:483).

Throughout the history of fallen humanity, interaction among heaven, hell, and earth never ceased, according to Edwards, although it varied in intensity and immediacy. The form of that interaction he frequently likened to a journey or progress. In the artistic manner of Bunyan, Dante, Milton, or, later, C. S. Lewis, Edwards' history portrayed a dramatic contest between good and evil, with confederations within the Trinity itself playing the triumphant role.

Edwards divided his earth history into three major epochs: from the fall of humankind to the incarnation of Christ, the God-man; from the incarnation to the bodily resurrection of Christ; and from the resurrection to the end of time. The briefest yet most important period of interaction between heaven, hell, and earth came during the life, death, and resurrection of Christ. At Christ's birth, the minions of Satan trembled even as the response in heaven was ecstatic: "This appears by their joyful songs on this occasion, heard by the shepherds in the night. This was the greatest event of providence that ever the angels beheld."[22]

Following the resurrection, "Christ entered into heaven in order to the obtaining the success of his purchase. . . . And as he ascended into heaven, God the Father did in a visible manner set him on the throne as king of the universe. He then put the angels all under him, and he subjected heaven and earth under him, that he might govern them for the good of the people that he had died for. . . ."[23] Throughout his preaching, Edwards drew on church history and profane history to integrate the postresurrection history of earth into one divine "conspiracy."

Hell

Of hell, Edwards had no less detail for his history. In contrast to modern avoidance of hell, seventeenth- and eighteenth-century religious culture and art was more attuned to hell than to heaven.[24] If Edwards was more balanced in his preaching, hell was hardly neglected and formed a central component in his redemption narrative. Soon after the world was created, "evil entered into the world in the fall of the angels and man. . . . Satan rose up against God, endeavoring to frus-

22. *A History of the Work of Redemption, Works*, 9:301.
23. Ibid., 361.
24. Like other Puritan preachers, Edwards' thinking about hell and Satan was influenced heavily by medieval glosses on Scripture, as well as Scripture itself. See Edward K. Trefz, "Satan as the Prince of Evil: The Preaching of the New England Puritans," *The Boston Public Library Quarterly* 7 (1955): 3. On the gradual minimalization of hell and Satan outside of the Puritans, see D. P. Walker, *The Decline of Hell: Seventeenth-Century Discussions of Eternal Torment* (Chicago: University of Chicago Press, 1964).

trate his design in the creation of this lower world."[25] Satan's rebellion would introduce the narrative of hell—a place as real and palpable as heaven and earth. Modern readers miss Edwards entirely if they cannot understand the immediacy of Satan in his thought. If removed or glossed over, Satan, Christ, the Trinity, and heaven and hell become an abstraction, and the whole scheme of Edwards' history is lost.

Edwards did not hesitate to introduce young hearers to the horrors of hell at the earliest moments. In a 1740 sermon directed to young children, Edwards spared no detail in describing the evils of hell and Satan, but he then went on to assure them that they were safe in Christ:

> If you love Christ, you will be safe from the devil, that roaring lion that goes about seeking whom he may devour. He will not be able to hurt; you shall be out of his reach. If the devil should appear to you, you need not be afraid of him, but might triumph over him. The devil knows that Christ will subdue him under the feet of such as love him. Christ will bring down that dreadful giant and cause all holy children that love him to come and set their feet upon his neck.[26]

Satan's kingdom is hell, a place without goodness or God; a physicality of pain and suffering, where flames lick at sinners with relentless ferocity. Whereas many medieval writers favored images of hell that played on infinite darkness, Edwards preferred images of furnaces and fire. In a "Miscellanies" entry he wrote: "Hell is represented by fire and brimstone. . . . Lightning is a string of brimstone; and if that stream of brimstone which we are told kindles hell be as hot as streams of lightning, it will be vehement beyond conception."[27] What makes this infinite stream of fire even more agonizing is the fact that God permits the damned to view the alternative paradise of the saints in heaven. And, like Calvin, Edwards' God would allow for no second chances after death. Hell is eternal and irreversible. With relentless logic he would insist that because God hates sin, "it is suitable that he should execute an infinite punishment."[28]

Like heaven, hell's history is intimately connected to earth's and necessary to engage the drama of redemption. In a "Miscellanies" en-

25. "Like Rain upon Mown Grass," in *Sermons and Discourses, 1739–1742, Works,* forthcoming.

26. "Children Ought to Love the Lord," ibid.

27. "Miscellanies" no. 275 (*Works,* 13:376).

28. For a fuller elaboration of Edwards' sense of hell, see Norman Fiering, *Jonathan Edwards's Moral Thought and Its British Context* (Chapel Hill: University of North Carolina Press, 1981), 61–62; and Philip C. Hammond, *Heaven and Hell in Enlightenment England* (Cambridge: Cambridge University Press), 98, 151.

try dating from 1740, Edwards noted that "God hath so ordered it that all the great concerns and events of the universe should be some way concerning of this work [of Redemption], that the occasion of the fall of some of the angels should be something about this." Indeed, he continued, redemption was "why the fall of man was so soon permitted." When the Israelites were enslaved in Egypt, "Hell was as much and much more engaged [than Egypt]. The pride and cruelty of Satan, that old serpent was more concerned in it than Pharaoh's."[29] With deliverance, Israel enjoyed a victory as much over hell as over Egypt.

When earth history, at last, comes to an end in the final climactic battles with Antichrist and Satan, all three worlds will come together, with heaven especially enlisted for the conflict: "At the day of judgment, the Sun of righteousness shall appear in its greatest glory; Christ shall then come in the glory of the Father, and all the holy angels with him." In a sermon on "Millennial Glory," Edwards cautioned that the destructions to accompany this day would exceed the persecutions of the Jews at Christ's death:

> Soon after [the resurrection] he brought the amazing destruction of the unbelieving Jews, terribly destroying their city and country by the Romans. So when he will come in a spiritual sense at the beginning of the expected glorious times of the church, he will come [not only] for the deliverance and healing and rejoicing of his church, but for the amazing destruction of Antichrist and other enemies of his church.[30]

With the toppling of Antichrist, Satan's earthly kingdoms will be utterly abolished. Satan will be banished from earth as he was from heaven. There will be a "new heaven" no less than a "new earth." Indeed, from "Miscellanies" entries it is clear that Edwards believed the "new heavens and new earth" will strictly be located in heaven: "The NEW HEAVENS AND NEW EARTH, so far as a place of habitation, is meant by 'em, are heaven and not the lower world." While the old heaven was corruptible, as evidenced by Satan's fall, the new heaven will be pure and incorruptible, a paradise without end. With Christ's second coming, the saints already in heaven and those joining them will see glories that were previously unavailable even in heaven. Human minds will see universes inside an atom: "'Tis only for want of sufficient accurateness, strength and comprehension of mind, that from the motion of any one particular atom we can't tell all that ever

29. "Miscellanies" no. 702 (*Works*, 18:304, 307); "Miscellanies" no. 176 (*Works*, 13:326).
30. "Christ the Spiritual Sun," in *Sermons and Discourses, 1739–1742, Works*, forthcoming.

has been, [all] that now is in the whole extent of creation . . . and everything that ever shall be. Corol. What room for improvement of reason is there [in heaven] for angels and glorified minds."[31]

Revivals as Millennial Harbingers

Even as he read voraciously in the history of heaven, earth, and hell and sketched their interconnected histories, Edwards eagerly scanned the horizons of his own world for signs of revival and regeneration that would presage the new heavens and the new earth. In a letter to Josiah Willard, a widely connected evangelical and secretary of the Massachusetts Province, Edwards inquired after the state of revivals worldwide. Familiar with Whitefield and the British Isles, he extended his inquiry to Prussia, and in particular to the city of Halle, where a Dr. August Hermann Francke was rumored to have promoted revivals. He also expressed curiosity about the East Indies and Moscovy, adding, "I cannot hope that God is about to accomplish glorious things for his church, which makes me the more desirous of knowing as fully as may be the present state of religion in the world."[32]

From his reading and correspondence, Edwards was able to apprise his congregation of recent events and set them in historical context. At a "private meeting" in December 1739, Edwards reported on "God's Grace Carried On in Other Places." In particular he singled out "a remarkable work of God's grace that has of late appeared in some parts of the British denominations." Even more surprising was the fact that this movement grew out of the Church of England, which, though "sound in its principles in the beginning of the Reformation," fell prey to heresy and corruption, "especially during King Charles the Second's reign." With mounting excitement and recalling Northampton's great revival of 1734, he informed his listeners that "God has raised up in England a number of younger ministers . . . called, by way of derision, the New Methodists."[33] Soon this British revival would land on colonial shores with hurricane force.

On October 17, 1740, Whitefield arrived in Northampton and preached to Edwards' congregation and in the parsonage later that evening. The next day he preached twice more. All correspondents agreed that something dramatic had happened. Whitefield himself re-

31. "Miscellanies" no. 809 (*Works*, 18:516); "Miscellanies" no. 710 (ibid., 336–38); and "Miscellanies" no. 272 (*Works*, 13:374).

32. Edwards to Josiah Willard, 1 June 1740, *Letters and Personal Writings*, *Works*, 16:83.

33. "God's Grace Carried On in Other Places," in *Sermons and Discourses, 1739–1742*, *Works*, forthcoming.

ported great movings, including "Mr. Edwards," who "wept during the whole time of the exercise."[34] Edwards reported that "the congregation was extraordinarily melted by each sermon, almost the whole assembly being in tears for a great part of the time."

Northampton after Whitefield

Following Whitefield's visit, Edwards sought to fan the flames by preaching a sermon series on the parable of the sower, enjoining his listeners to be planted in the Word. While pleased that a revival spirit seemed to be thriving, Edwards was careful not to gloat. Recalling the earlier revival, he asked: "Was there too much of an appearance of a public pride, if I may so call it? Were we not lifted up with the honor that God had put upon us as a people, beyond most other people?"[35]

In December 1740, Edwards wrote to Whitefield, describing the state of religion in Northampton as having "been gradually reviving and prevailing more and more, ever since you was here." He noted of special importance "a considerable number of our young people, some of them children, having already been savingly brought home to Christ." Among these young converts was "one, if not more, of my children." In a later account, first written as a letter to Boston's Thomas Prince and later published in Prince's magazine *Christian History,* Edwards happily reported that "in about a month there was a great alteration in the town, both as to the revival of professors, and awakening of others. . . . By the middle of December a very considerable work of God appeared among those that were very young, and the revival of religion continued to increase; so that in the spring, an engagedness of spirit about things of religion was become very general amongst young people and children. . . ."[36]

Edwards had good reason to focus on the young people. From a demographic analysis of Northampton church membership lists, Kenneth Minkema has shown how large a majority of the recalcitrant members who criticized Edwards and eventually dismissed him were older members who had entered the church under the ministry of his grandfather and predecessor, Solomon Stoddard. Many of these members resented Edwards' fame at the expense of their beloved Mr. Stod-

34. Quoted in Arnold A. Dallimore, *George Whitefield: The Life and Times of the Great Evangelist of the Eighteenth-Century Revival,* 2 vols. (Westchester, Ill.: Crossway, 1980), 1:539.

35. "Bringing the Ark to Zion a Second Time," in *Sermons and Discourses, 1739–1742,* forthcoming.

36. Edwards to George Whitefield, 14 December 1740, *Letters and Personal Writings, Works,* 16:87; Edwards to Thomas Prince, 12 December 1743, ibid., 116–17.

dard and his criticism of Stoddard's lax admission policies. But by then, Edwards was not innocent. In retaliation he berated the aged as too old for conversion and held the youth up as role models of faith.[37]

The youth were Edwards' best hope and the ones he would especially cultivate for conversion. Signs of "young people" and even "children" converting appeared throughout his reports as a special providence. Following the drowning of a young man named Billy Shelden in February 1741, Edwards pressed home the mortality of youth. The lesson he enjoined was familiar: "Don't set your heart on youthful pleasures and other vain enjoyments of this world." Instead, prepare for eternity. Even now, Edwards warned another youth was presently dying of consumption and "on the brink of eternity . . . therefore lose no more time."[38]

In another sermon, delivered in July 1740, Edwards again directed his young listeners' attention to a different world, but this time to heaven rather than hell. He was particularly concerned about the consequences of conversion in respect to youthful conversation. In place of mundane or vulgar conversation, he enjoined his young listeners to move their thoughts and communications toward "the great things of another world." Such a subject matter would be infinitely rewarding and encouraging in contrast to the sorrows of life in this world. Young people everywhere, but especially in Northampton, "should be much in speaking of the saints' happiness and glory in heaven, where they will be perfectly holy and happy in the full enjoyment of God and Christ, and in perfect love and friendship one with another, forever and ever."[39]

At about the same time that Edwards wrote to Whitefield in December, he penned his "Personal Narrative." In reading it, one sees how the revivals buoyed his sagging spirits and uplifted his soul. He recalled his earlier yearnings with startling immediacy. He now recalled: "My mind was much taken up with contemplations on heaven, and the enjoyments of those there; and living there in perfect holiness, humility, and love."[40] How much of this description pertained to Edwards' youthful experience and how much to his renewed hope in

37. Kenneth P. Minkema, "Old Age and Religion in the Writings and Life of Jonathan Edwards," *Church History* 70 (2001): 674–704.

38. "Youth Is Like a Flower That Is Cut Down," in *Sermons and Discourses, 1739–1742, Works,* forthcoming. In fact, Edwards exaggerated the numbers of youthful converts. See Minkema, "Old Age and Religion."

39. "The Danger of Corrupt Communication among Young People," in *Sermons and Discourses, 1739–1742, Works,* forthcoming.

40. "Personal Narrative," *Letters and Personal Writings, Works,* 16:795. The case for dating the "Narrative" to December 1740 is made by George Claghorn in ibid., 747.

1739 is unclear, but certainly these words expressed Edwards' present state.

Edwards the Awakener

Given Edwards' tri-world perspective, we can see why Whitefield's revivals loomed large in his thinking. Indeed, Edwards was obsessed with Whitefield. In his own way, he would imitate him. By December 1740, unmistakable evidences appear in Edwards' manuscript sermons that he had begun to experiment and perfect his own revival rhetoric in Whitefield-like directions. If Edwards' greatest growth as a preacher occurred earlier in the 1730s, his growth as a revivalist specializing in the new birth came now. Edwards' sermon Notebook 45, begun in 1739, is the largest of three and marks a shift in style that reflects both the effect of Whitefield's revivals and his own turbulent relationship with his congregation.[41] By this time Edwards had adopted the duodecimo sermon books that could be "palmed" in the pulpit, allowing for greater freedom and the appearance of extemporaneity.

Edwards knew he was no orator. His voice, gestures, and memory could not equal Whitefield's dramaturgical style. But he also knew he had one advantage that he intended to exploit for his own glory and the glory of God: rhetoric. Edwards was a genius with words, and he set himself to compose the "perfect idea" of an awakening sermon. To aid in that process, he would modify not only his delivery and gestures but also the balance of ideas and the very structure of the composition in ways that are easily uncovered.

Besides altering the form of his manuscript notes, Edwards shifted his content decisively from heaven to hell. While the history of heaven communicated love—the essence of "the new sense of the heart"—Edwards believed, for a moment anyway, that one could get to life eternal only after first being scared to death.[42]

This rhetorical need demanded the change in emphasis from the history of heaven to the history of hell. In earlier years, sermonic invocations of heaven had easily surpassed hell. But in the 1740s, hell, in all its fury and torture, would have to be enlisted if heaven was ever to be gained. Edwards knew that the indispensable emotional appeal in an awakening sermon was fear, even terror, and it knew no age limits. Children needed to absorb horror no less than adults. Just as children

41. Wilson Kimnach describes these shifts in *Sermons and Discourses, 1720–1723, Works,* 10:62–63.
42. The best treatment of Edwards and hell appears in Fiering, *Jonathan Edwards's Moral Thought,* 200–216.

must be taught to fear fire at the earliest age, so also must they be taught to fear the fires of hell. In a later defense of revival preaching, Edwards would observe: "'Tis no argument that a work is not from the Spirit of God, that it seems to be promoted by ministers insisting very much on the terrors of God's holy law, and that with a great deal of pathos and earnestness."[43]

Edwards' first deliberate attempt to shape a new awakening sermon appeared in his sermon entitled "Sinners in Zion" (December 1740). In examining the composition of "Sinners in Zion," it becomes clear that Edwards was already at work perfecting the style for a White-field-like revival sermon. The form would have to promote and encourage extemporaneous delivery, and the content must shift from heaven to hell, from the joys of redemption to the horrors of the damned. In a further step toward freeing up his speech, Edwards began to include large white space breaks in his notes as a signal to extemporize. In place of fully written out sentences, he also began supplying rhetorical cues.

A Second "Sinners"

Two weeks after preaching "Sinners in Zion," Edwards preached another "sinners" sermon: "Sinners in the Hands of an Angry God." It is not clear what effect "Sinners" had on his own congregation. Probably not much. They, after all, had heard its substance only two weeks before. Awakening sermons require unfamiliar audiences and spontaneous delivery. Certainly, no reports exist of exceptional responses. But in one of his repreachings at Enfield, Massachusetts, on July 8, 1741, the effects were extraordinary. The Reverend Stephen Williams of nearby Longmeadow attended and recorded the event in his diary:

Went over to Enfield, where we met Dear Mr. Edwards of New Haven who preached a most awakening Sermon from those words Deut 32:35—and before ye Sermon was done there was a great moaning and crying out throughout ye whole House. What shall I do to be saved—oh I am going to Hell—oh what shall I do for a christ etc. etc.—so that ye minister was obliged to desist. [The] shrieks and crys were piercing and Amazing. After some time of waiting the congregation were still so that a prayer was made by Mr. W—and after that we descended from the pulpitt and discoursed with the people—some in one place and some in another. And Amazing and Astonishing [was] ye power. God was seen and severall souls were hopefully wrought upon that night and oh ye

43. Jonathan Edwards, *The Works of Jonathan Edwards*, vol. 4, *The Great Awakening*, ed. C. C. Goen (New Haven: Yale University Press, 1972), 246.

cheerfullness and pleasantness of their countenances—that received comfort. Oh that God would strengthen and confirm etc. We sung an hymn and prayed and despersed ye Assembly.

Such was the power—and the fear—generated by this sermon that Edwards apparently never finished preaching it—possibly the only time this had happened. Reflecting on the sermon, Williams wrote that Edwards "seemed affected and moved ready to dissolve in Tears etc., but cant well tell why."[44]

"Sinners in the Hands of an Angry God" is arguably America's greatest sermon. It has been analyzed extensively both in the Yale edition and in other works.[45] But what is interesting for our purposes here is not the final text as it appears in print but the handwritten notes, reproduced in this volume for the first time. At the end of these handwritten notes is a brief two-page outline of the sermon that Edwards prepared, probably for multiple deliveries with minimal notes or prompts.[46] When reading the fragment text, as opposed to the fully written-out text, one can discern an almost perfect awakening sermon:

[Humankind] alwaies exposed to fall
suddenly fall
noting that tis G. that holds em up
no want of power in G.
They deserve it.
They are Condemned to it [hell]
Tis the place they belong to
God is angry with them.
The devil if not Restrained would Immediately fly upon them and seize them as his own
They have those Hellish principles in them that if G. should take off his Restrains

44. Stephen Williams, "Diary," Storrs Public Library, Longmeadow, Mass., vol. 3:375–76, typescript.

45. See, especially, *Sermons and Discourses, 1720–1723, Works*, 10:113–15, 175–78; J. O. Leo Lemay, "Rhetorical Strategies in Sinners in the Hands of an Angry God and Narrative of the Late Massacres in Lancaster County," in *Benjamin Franklin, Jonathan Edwards, and the Representation of American Culture*, ed. Barbara B. Oberg and Harry S. Stout (New York: Oxford University Press, 1993), 186–203; and Edward J. Gallagher, "'Sinners in the Hands of an Angry God': Some Unfinished Business," *New England Quarterly* 73 (2000): 202–21.

46. The dating of the fragment is uncertain; see *Sermons and Discourses, 1720–1723, Works*, 10:145. But whatever the date, it is clear that this outline was intended to promote "spontaneous" rhetoric, leading Kimnach to speculate that "the thought arises that J[onathan]E[dwards], under the influence of Whitefield, might have made an outline of his Northampton sermon for the Enfield performance."

Tis no security that there are no visible means of death at hand.
Their own care and prudence to preserve their own lives.[47]

For all the attention paid to "Sinners," no one has appreciated the significance of this fragment version. It confirms the novelty of the sermon, not only on the level of content and rhetoric in print but also on the level of its extemporaneous abbreviation. Assuming that Edwards delivered this sermon on more than two occasions, we can see this two-page fragment text as the *real* "Sinners" sermon: the highly portable and powerful cue card allowing multiple deliveries—and unprecedented terror. Contained in these two pages was rhetorical dynamite.

To keep his congregation focused on the need to preserve the revival spirit, Edwards returned to the themes of history and the worlds of heaven and hell. If he was obsessed with history, it was not the history of America. Earlier accounts that seek to identify Edwards with an American (i.e., New England) "exceptionalism" miss the degree to which New England and America as a discrete entity hardly figured in his earth narrative. For a brief moment in the height of revivals, he would turn his attention homeward to America as the possible seat of God's "new heavens and new earth" at the end of history. But this proved to be a passing speculation. Not only was America too small for his history, but earth itself had to take its place in a larger cosmos.

In the heat of Whitefield's tour, Edwards dared to hope ("posit" would be too strong a term) that "what is now seen in America, and especially in New England, may prove the dawn of that glorious day: and the very uncommon and wonderful circumstances and events of this work, seem to me strongly to argue that God intends it as the beginning or forerunner of something vastly great."[48] Except for this brief America-centered enthusiasm, Edwards always understood the millennium and the church in universal terms. However optimistic about "God's mighty power" at work, the vast majority of Edwards' pronouncements on the subject of the millennium preclude claims of an American "exceptionalism." In April 1741, he preached a sermon on "Millennial Glory" that was universal in its orientation. From revivals at home and abroad, Edwards proclaimed that "now God seems in his providence, in an especial manner, to be calling us to be ready for those [end] times." But where were they to commence? The answer was, *everywhere*. From letters and magazines, Edwards could document "so remarkable a pouring out of the spirit of God in many places

---

47. "Sinners in the Hands of an Angry God," in *Sermons and Discourses, 1739–1742, Works,* forthcoming.
48. *The Great Awakening, Works,* 4:358.

and the commotion the nations of the world seem to be in."[49] Northampton believers should not be deluded into thinking they were the center of God's plans. They remained too ignorant of the "state of God's church in general."

Conclusion

Even after his dismissal from Northampton, Edwards remained obsessed with history and his tri-world vision. In another age, he may well have been a brilliant novelist. Indeed, if we were to seek a twentieth-century artistic parallel to Edwards, it would be not with theologians but with great Christian storytellers, of which the greatest was C. S. Lewis. In a recent essay, Judith Shulevitz criticizes those who would minimize the centrality of Christian faith in Lewis' *The Chronicles of Narnia*. Lewis, she wrote, can only be understood as an "allegory of faith." She concludes:

> In short, when it comes to Narnia, we are not in the modern world. We're inside Lewis's bookish mind, an archaic universe of extremes—profound evil, inexpressible sweetness and heartstopping dramas of the passage from the one to the other by means of grace. The Narnia chronicles are glorious, and they are also very dark, like the literary traditions they're steeped in. No matter how much their outmoded mores may trouble you, you can't alter them without destroying the soul of Lewis's creation. Embrace Narnia or reject it, but don't bowdlerize it.[50]

So too with Edwards. The tendency of academics is to make Edwards modern and to sentimentalize heaven and deconstruct Satan and hell. But this is not the Edwards of history nor the reality of our world today. September 11, 2001, has intervened and reminded us of the reality of evil and hell. To paraphrase H. Richard Niebuhr, the World Trade Center has compelled us to see evil as Edwards saw it, not because we chose to, but because it was thrust upon us.[51] But providentially, it does not stop here. Along with the narrative of hell is the narrative of heaven, and with it the narrative of redemption. For this we can thank Edwards for helping to shape our vision.

---

49. "Importunate Prayer for Millennial Glory," in *Sermons and Discourses, 1739–1742, Works,* forthcoming.

50. Judith Shulevitz, "Don't Mess with Aslan," *New York Times Book Review,* August 26, 2001, 27.

51. H. Richard Niebuhr, "The Anachronism of Jonathan Edwards," in *Theology, History, and Culture: Major Unpublished Writings,* ed. William Stacey Johnson (New Haven: Yale University Press, 1996), 123–33.

2

★

LAST OF THE MOHICAN MISSIONARIES

Jonathan Edwards at Stockbridge

Stephen J. Nichols

As the year 1758 began, Jonathan Edwards preached his farewell sermon to those gathered in the Congregational church in the frontier town of Stockbridge, Massachusetts. This was not his first farewell sermon. His much more famous one was preached in June 1750 as he was released from his pastoral charge in Northampton, Massachusetts. Only forty miles separated these two towns. But this short distance, which felt much longer to those traveling via horseback, belied the great differences between these two towns. On the one hand, consider Northampton. First settled in 1654 and ideally situated along the Connecticut River, this town had risen to great prominence, largely due to the nearly sixty-year ministry of the crowned "Pope of the Connecticut River Valley," Solomon Stoddard. The Congregational church there had equally risen to renown. Outside of Boston, this was perhaps New England's model town, church, and even culture.[1] When Jonathan Edwards ascended to the pulpit in 1727 as assistant to his

I am grateful to Barbara Allen, Lion Miles, and Kenneth Minkema for their gracious assistance in locating materials and for offering helpful suggestions for this essay.

1. Though dated, James Russell Trumbull's *History of Northampton, Massachusetts: From Its Settlement in 1654*, 2 vols. (Northampton: Press of Gazette Printing Co., 1898, 1902) remains the most exhaustive history of colonial Northampton.

grandfather Stoddard and then in 1729 replaced Stoddard upon his death, he furthered the reputation of both Northampton and its already prestigious pulpit.

On the other hand, there was Stockbridge. This town nestled among the Berkshire Mountains was also ideally situated along a river, the Housatonic. In Edwards' day it was the frontier, an isolated outpost. Stockbridge was settled in 1734 and officially established five years later—just a short time prior to Edwards' 1751 arrival—as a mission to the Native Americans living along the Housatonic River, the so-called River Indians. The self-ascribed name "Muh-he-cunnuk," meaning the people who follow the flowing rivers, has been anglicized as Mahican or, since the idealized and romanticized portrait by James Fenimore Cooper, Mohicans.[2]

By the time Edwards arrived, the town consisted of 250 Mohicans, referred to simply as "Stockbridge Indians," approximately 60 Mohawks of the Six Nations, and a few Brothertons.[3] Of this number, 42 names were listed as communicant members of the Congregational church.[4] Additionally, the colonists numbered but a dozen families, whose minds appear to have been more occupied with the things of this world than of the next. Leading this group was Colonel Ephraim Williams, sometime soldier and relentless land investor. As a Williams, he belonged to the ubiquitous clan of the Connecticut River Valley that caused problems for Edwards back in Northampton.[5] As one piece of anecdotal evidence among the many available, Ephraim Williams, though opposed to Edwards' appointment as minister at Stockbridge, nevertheless resigned himself to Edwards' arrival, noting that

2. The Mohicans, largely seasonal hunters, first settled around the Hudson River. By the mid-1700s, a large part of this original group moved east, settling along the Housatonic in Stockbridge. For an authoritative summary, see T. J. Brasser, "Mahican," in *Handbook of North American Indians*, vol. 15, *Northeast*, ed. Bruce G. Trigger (Washington: Smithsonian Institution, 1978), 198–212.

3. See Jonathan Edwards' letter to Jasper Mauduit, 10 March 1752, in Jonathan Edwards, *The Works of Jonathan Edwards*, vol. 16, *Letters and Personal Writings*, ed. George S. Claghorn (New Haven: Yale University Press, 1998), 449–60. See also Shirley W. Dunn, *The Mohican World, 1680–1750* (Fleischmanns, N.Y.: Purple Mountain, 2000); and Patrick Frazier, *The Mohicans of Stockbridge* (Lincoln: University of Nebraska Press, 1992).

4. The list of church members, beginning with Ebenezer Poohpoonuc in 1734, as given in David Field's *An Historical Sketch of the Congregational Church, Stockbridge* (Stockbridge, Mass.: [The Church], 1888), incorrectly numbers twenty-five Native Americans by 1750.

5. For one account of the controversy at Northampton between Edwards and the Williams family, see Patricia J. Tracy, *Jonathan Edwards, Pastor: Religion and Society in Eighteenth-Century Northampton* (New York: Hill and Wang, 1980), 171–94.

his fame would bring some welcome notoriety to the town and in the process lead to "raising the price of my land."[6]

And then there was the Stockbridge mission school. Intended primarily to train Mohawks in the language, literature, religion, and ways of the colonials, this school struggled throughout its short career, beset with mismanagement and perhaps embezzlement. Complicating matters, John Sergeant, the first missionary at Stockbridge and founder of both the school and the church, had married Abigail Williams, the daughter of Colonel Ephraim Williams. Sarah Cabot Sedgwick and Christina Sedgwick Marquand note of Abigail Williams, "The mission with her, as with her father, was the means to the end of developing the town of Stockbridge, and with it the fortunes of the Williams family."[7] By the time Edwards was granted control of the school in 1753, the sachems, or chiefs, had decided in a tribal council to leave the town altogether.

Given the differences between the two towns, the state of affairs at Stockbridge, and the prospects of exchanging one conflict with the Williamses for another, one might rightly ask why Jonathan Edwards went to Stockbridge. Of course, one vaguely familiar with Edwards would quickly point out that Edwards, who by many accounts of both friends and foes stands as America's greatest theologian and philosopher, had been dismissed by his Northampton congregation. Before we conclude, however, that Edwards merely went to Stockbridge because he had lost his position and desperately needed another one, we need to consider some key evidence. First, Edwards had numerous offers once he was freed from his pastoral charge at Northampton. His Scottish friends extended an invitation for him to cross the Atlantic, and various churches throughout New England also would have welcomed Edwards into their pulpits. A group at Northampton, displeased with the decision to remove Edwards, even petitioned for him to start a new church in the town. In other words, Edwards had other options. Additionally, Edwards had a long-standing interest in Indian missions, beginning in the mid-1730s. He served as a trustee for the boarding school at Stockbridge from 1743 to 1747, and the Northampton congregation, under Edwards' direction, heavily supported the work in the mid-1740s. All of this occurred long before the rum-

6. Colonel Ephraim Williams to Ephraim Williams Jr., 2 May 1751, as cited in Wyllis E. Wright, *Colonel Ephraim Williams: A Documentary Life* (Pittsfield, Mass.: Berkshire County Historical Society, 1970), 61.

7. Sarah Cabot Sedgwick and Christina Sedgwick Marquand, *Stockbridge 1739–1939: A Chronicle* (Great Barrington, Mass.: Berkshire Courier, 1939), 31. Further complicating matters, upon Sergeant's death, Abigail married Joseph Dwight, a trustee of the school who was charged with overseeing his wife's accounts.

blings that would lead to the dismissal.[8] Also, Edwards' use of David Brainerd (missionary to Native Americans) as the model saint and his editing of Brainerd's diary (published in 1749 as *An Account of the Life of the Late Reverend David Brainerd*) further testify to his intense interest in Native Americans.[9] In other words, it would be mistaken to view Stockbridge as Edwards' consolation prize or exile after Northampton.

It is a further mistake to interpret the Stockbridge years merely as an opportunity for Edwards to devote the necessary time to writing the treatises that earned his reputation as America's greatest philosopher-theologian, including *Freedom of the Will* (1754), *Original Sin* (1758), and the *Two Dissertations* (published posthumously in 1765). To be sure, Edwards' literary output greatly increased during these years, but this was probably due to the fact that exchanging his congregation of 400 plus at Northampton, along with all of the strains of being the pastor-in-demand along the Connecticut River Valley, for a congregation of 150 or so allowed for that valuable time he often longed for in his study. To view the time at Stockbridge as merely an occasion to write misses the value of this seven-year period in understanding Edwards' thought and practice, and slights the importance of his work among the Stockbridge natives.

By taking a close look at the Stockbridge years, not in terms of what Edwards wrote while there, but in terms of what he did among, for, and with the Stockbridge Mohicans and Mohawks reminds us that to Edwards' long list of credentials, including theologian, philosopher, revivalist, pastor, college president, and author, we also need to add missionary.[10] In order to assess Edwards' missionary career, this essay outlines Edwards' involvement in the politics of "Indian affairs" in the mid–eighteenth century, his struggles related to the mission school, his sermons at the Stockbridge church, and little-known statements of

8. See George Claghorn's "Introduction," in *Letters and Personal Writings*, *Works*, 16:17–18, and Edwards' letter to Eleazer Wheelock, 13 July 1744, ibid., 145–46.

9. See Jonathan Edwards, *The Works of Jonathan Edwards*, vol. 7, *The Life of David Brainerd*, ed. Norman Pettit (New Haven: Yale University Press, 1985). Before Brainerd pioneered the mission work among the Delawares, he served as a missionary to the Mohicans at Kaunaumeek near Albany for one year. The Society in Scotland for Propagating Christian Knowledge thought Brainerd's efforts would be better spent among the Delawares and instructed him to move. Brainerd counseled the Kaunaumeek Mohicans to move to Stockbridge upon his departure. See *Life of David Brainerd*, *Works*, 7:245, and Margaret Connell Szasz, *Indian Education in the American Colonies, 1607–1783* (Albuquerque: University of New Mexico Press, 1988), 213–17.

10. An extensive discussion of Edwards as missionary may be found in Ronald Edwin Davies, "Prepare Ye the Way of the Lord: The Missiological Thought and Practice of Jonathan Edwards (1703–1758)" (Ph.D. diss., Fuller Theological Seminary, 1988).

faith that Edwards wrote for the Stockbridge converts, whom the colonials referred to as "praying Indians." In closing, it will draw out
some implications of this study for the ongoing enterprise of interpreting Edwards.

Edwards and the Politics
of Native American Affairs

Joseph Paice, a London Christian of financial means, repeatedly
wrote to the Boston commissioners regarding his interests in mission
work with Native Americans. The commissioners relayed the letters to
Edwards, hoping that he would inform Paice of the opportunities at
Stockbridge. Edwards did, although he begins his letter by indicting
the British for their dealings with the natives, complaining that the
British "are complacent, lack initiative, and exploit the Indians."[11] In
the letter Edwards remarks that the English have been both negligent
in their duty and "extremely impolitic." He then bemoans the ill-treat-
ment for financial gain:

> 'Tis true we have traded a great deal, but our trade has been carried on
> with them in a way that has naturally tended to beget in them a distrust
> of us, and aversion to us. Most of our Indian traders, being persons of
> little conscience, the Indians have defrauded. . . . Money is embezzled,
> and used for the advance [of] the private gain of those into whose hands
> it falls; and of that part that is given [to the Indians], 'tis bestowed in
> that which issues [in] no good end, that is in rum to make 'em drunk.[12]

Tensions had run high between the settlers and the Native Americans in New England almost since the first British colonists arrived in
Massachusetts. King Phillip's War and the Seven Years' War offer solemn testimony to this observation. Life between these wars could be
no less hazardous for both parties. Much of what survives in colonial
literature tends to emphasize the horrors that the settlers faced at the
hands of Indians in various raids, slaughters, and captivities.[13] Stock-

---

11. *Letters and Personal Writings, Works,* 16:434–35. Claghorn further observes, "Edwards probably little dreamed that this letter would be brought to the attention of the
Archbishop of Canterbury himself," 435.

12. Ibid., 437.

13. For a sampling of the literature and an exhaustive bibliography on the subject,
see Alden T. Vaughan and Edward W. Clark, eds., *Puritans among the Indians: Accounts
of Captivity and Redemption, 1676–1724* (Cambridge, Mass.: Belknap, 1981). Edwards'
own relatives are the subject of one of the most famous accounts: John Williams, *The
Redeemed Captive Returning to Zion* (Northampton: Hopkins, Bridgeman and Company, 1853).

bridge and its environs were no exception in this regard.[14] There is, however, quite another side to these tragedies, and that concerns the grave injustices and horrors inflicted upon the Indians by the colonials.[15] Sedgwick and Marquand recount an incident in Stockbridge involving two colonials who, while stealing horses, shot and killed Waumpaumcorse, a Schaghticoke. They were arrested and tried in nearby Springfield. One was released, and the other received a slight punishment. To amend for the injustice, the governor and general court authorized the payment of an indemnity. Yet, this payment was not even sent. Aware of the frustration of the Schaghticokes, as well as the growing frustration of other tribes including the Stockbridge Mohicans and Mohawks, Edwards quickly intervened, requesting that payment be sent immediately and that it be quite generous so that it would at least be seen as a token of goodwill by the English to the Native Americans. Eventually, payment was sent, but it was merely twenty pounds, despite Edwards' sage warning that it be significantly more. As Sedgwick and Marquand note, the Schaghticokes "remained in a sensitive frame of mind."[16]

Edwards showed particular insight into the differences between the way the British dealt with the Native Americans and the way the French dealt with them. He keenly felt the tremors that led up to the Seven Years' War, and he also had an acute sense of the stakes the war entailed. In many ways, Edwards' perspective from Stockbridge afforded him a vantage point unshared by the Boston commissioners and other New England political leaders. Writing in 1755 to his longtime friend and frequent Scottish correspondent John Erskine, Edwards, sensing the danger, observed, "It seems to be the most critical season with the British dominions in America, that ever was since the first settlement of these colonies. And all probably will depend on the warlike transactions of the present year. A dark cloud seems to hang over us; we need the prayers of all our friends. . . . Stockbridge is a place much exposed, and what will become of us in the struggles that are coming on, God only knows."[17]

14. Kenneth Minkema offers a vivid picture of the tensions at Stockbridge and life on the frontier by noting that Edwards' removal to Stockbridge served as the catalyst for three of his daughters, Sarah, Esther, and Mary, to marry, for they were "not wishing to move to the frontier and live around 'barbarous wretches'" ("The Edwardses: A Ministerial Family in Eighteenth-Century New England" [Ph.D. diss., University of Connecticut, 1988], 366).

15. For a thorough treatment of this issue, see Karen Ordahl Kupperman, *Indians and English: Facing Off in Early America* (Ithaca: Cornell University Press, 2000).

16. Sedgwick and Marquand, *Stockbridge, 1739–1939,* 73. For Edwards' letter, see *Letters and Personal Writings, Works,* 16:644–45.

17. *Letters and Personal Writings, Works,* 16:664–65.

The work of historians Shirley Dunn and Lion Miles has drawn attention to the ways in which the colonials both subtly and overtly moved the Native Americans out of New England through successive bids for the land. Forced out, the natives "removed" to a new location in New York in 1785, a locale they named "New Stockbridge." Eventually, like most of the eastern tribes, they made the move west in the 1810s and 1820s, migrating all the way to Wisconsin, where the reservation remains to this day. Miles' work in particular, however, offers insight into Edwards' position regarding this. Miles notes that prior to 1750 the English settlers laid out the town and parceled out the land largely apart from the direct involvement of the Indians. The Stockbridge Mohicans informed the "Settling Committee" in Boston that the original, agreed-upon amount of 2,400 acres had doubled to 4,800 acres and that the land that was to be left for the Native Americans was taken by the colonials.[18] Miles then refers to the period from 1759 to 1774 as "the great land grab." The silence of Miles regarding the intervening years of 1751 to 1758, which correspond to Edwards' tenure at Stockbridge, reveals the lack of such a land grab under Edwards' watch and further evidences Edwards' attitude toward and treatment of the Stockbridge Mohicans.[19]

Edwards further demonstrated his commitment to the Native Americans rather visibly by locating his house, not on the mountain above and a mile or so away from the wigwams and crude log cabin dwellings of the natives as did his predecessor John Sergeant and the other colonials, but instead on the plain right in their midst.[20] In doing so, Edwards was the first of the settlers to live with his family among the Indians. This provided the Edwardses with daily exposure to the natives and interaction with them that the other colonials, huddled among themselves, often missed. Jonathan Edwards Jr., in his short work *Observations on the Language of the Muhhekaneew Indians* (1788), recalls how as a six-year-old first arriving at Stockbridge, he never spoke English outside of his Stockbridge home: "The Indians being the nearest neighbors, I constantly associated with them; their boys were my daily school mates and play fellows. Out of my father's

18. Indian Petition, 11 November 1749, Massachusetts Archives, 31:654.
19. See Lion G. Miles, "The Red Man Dispossessed: The Williams Family and the Alienation of Indian Land in Stockbridge, Massachusetts, 1736–1818," *The New England Quarterly* 68 (1994): 46–76. For the work of Shirley Dunn, see *The Mohican World, 1680–1750* and *The Mohicans and Their Land, 1609–1730* (Fleischmanns, N.Y.: Purple Mountain, 1994).
20. John Sergeant's house was built in 1737 on Prospect Hill. Today, Sergeant's house stands on the plain, having been moved there in 1929. Edwards' house no longer stands, but a sundial marks the spot.

house, I seldom heard any language spoken beside the Indian. I knew the names of some things in Indian which I did not know in English, even all my thoughts ran in Indian."[21]

Edwards also repeatedly remarks on the self-interest of his fellow "English inhabitants of the town," which he viewed as "one of their great calamities." In some ways this sentiment that he observed first-hand was deeply rooted in the colonial perspective on Native Americans. The House of Representatives for the Province of Massachusetts approved the establishment of a committee to initiate missionary activity among the Native Americans. The resolution concerning this act, which passed November 15, 1716, began by referring to "favourable opportunity" afforded by Providence "to instruct the Eastern Indians in Religion and Learning, which has been one professed Intention of our Ancestors, Settling in this Land." And with remarkable candor, the resolution added, "and is the surest way to fix them in our Interest."[22] Seen against this backdrop, Edwards' treatment of the Native Americans at Stockbridge rises to heroic proportions. Unlike his peers and contemporaries, he showed remarkable sensitivity to Native Americans and their interests.

Gerald McDermott also draws attention to the difference in Edwards' estimation of the Indians when compared to his peers. McDermott contends that Edwards "also held a more positive view of their humanity than most of his fellow colonials. Few of them desired anything but the extermination of Indians, and certainly not their salvation." By contrast, McDermott draws attention to Edwards' repeated chastisement of New Englanders in his sermons for the ill treatment of the Indians and to Edwards' belief that there "was no metaphysical distinction between whites and Indians." McDermott concludes that such ideas were "socially dangerous."[23] Edwards expressed these ideas in a rather public format at the signing of the treaty with the Mohawks and the English at Albany in 1751. Here he refers to the shameful behavior of the English, the Dutch, and the French in their treatment of the Indians, and then he declares, "We are no better than you in no respect."[24]

21. Jonathan Edwards Jr., *Observations on the Language of the Muhhekaneew Indians* (New Haven: Josiah Meigs, 1788), preface. These early experiences of the younger Edwards led to his intense involvement in Indian affairs throughout his adult years.

22. *Journal of the House of Representatives,* vol. 1, *1715–1717* (Boston: Massachusetts Historical Society, 1922), 141.

23. Gerald R. McDermott, *Jonathan Edwards Confronts the Gods: Christian Theology, Enlightenment Religion, and Non-Christian Faiths* (Oxford: Oxford University Press, 2000), 201–3.

24. Jonathan Edwards, "To the Mohawks at the Treaty, August 16, 1751," in *The Sermons of Jonathan Edwards: A Reader,* ed. Wilson H. Kimnach, Kenneth P. Minkema, and Douglas A. Sweeney (New Haven: Yale University Press, 1999), 107–8.

Edwards' handling of the "Indian School" at Stockbridge further reveals a distinction from his peers. Isaac Hollis, a "Baptist minister of
means," was the chief patron of the school designated primarily to instruct Mohawks in both the English language and the gospel. The
boarding school for boys was part of the larger mission work at Stockbridge led by the Society for the Propagation of the Gospel in New England, also known as the New England Company. This work also entailed the church at Stockbridge, routine trips west to various Native
American settlements in New York, and the never-executed plans for a
boarding school for girls.[25] The correspondence of Edwards with
Isaac Hollis, William Pepperell, John Erskine, Joseph Paice, Thomas
Hubbard, the Boston commissioners, and others overflows with his
observations of the problems plaguing the school, his pleas to rectify
the situation, and his repeated appeal to be given charge of the enter-
prise.[26] From his initial involvement, Edwards saw the principal aim
of the school as being "to prosecute the design of instructing [the Indi-
ans] thoroughly in the Protestant religion." Edwards accuses Ephraim
Williams and Martin Kellogg, Williams' ally who held the position of
schoolmaster, of embezzlement, a charge that eventually proved to be
true. Kellogg, himself illiterate, mainly used the Mohawk and Mohican boys in his charge to "cultivate his own land," a practice that historian Jean Fritz Hankins demonstrates to be quite prevalent among
the colonial schools.[27] Hankins records the letter of John Daniel, a
Narragansett who sent his son to study at Eleazer Wheelock's Dart-
mouth. Daniel intones:

> I always tho't your School was free to the Natives; not to learn them
> how to farm it, but to advance in Christian Knowledge, which were the
> chief motive that caus'd me to send my son Charles to you; not that
> against his Labouring some for you, when Business lies heavy on you;
> but to work two Years to learn to Farm it, is what I don't consent to,
> when I can as well learn him that myself and have the profit of his La-
> bour, being myself brought up with the best of Farmers.[28]

25. See Claghorn, "Introduction," in *Letters and Personal Writings, Works,* 16:17–25.
See also William Kellaway, *The New England Company, 1649–1776: Missionary Society
to the American Indians* (London: Longmans, 1961), 271–73; and Samuel Hopkins, *Historical Memoirs relating to the Housatonic Indians* (Boston: S. Kneeland, 1753).
26. See *Letters and Personal Writings, Works,* vol. 16.
27. Jonathan Edwards to Isaac Hollis, 17 July 1752, *Letters and Personal Writings,
Works,* 16:494–509. See also Kenneth Minkema, "The Edwardses," 361–65.
28. John Daniel to Eleazer Wheelock, 30 November 1767, as cited in Jean Fritz
Hankins, "Bringing the Good News: Protestant Missionaries to the Indians of New England and New York, 1700–1755" (Ph.D. diss., University of Connecticut, 1993), 234.
The mission schools were not very successful on the whole. Their failure was some-

At Stockbridge such use of the Mohican and Mohawk boys brought a similar response from the parents, causing a great deal of mistrust and, in Edwards' words to the school's benefactor Isaac Hollis, leaving them "extremely uneasy."[29] After two long years of bringing the matter to the attention of the officials in Boston and in Scotland, action was taken and Edwards' advice regarding the situation was followed.[30] Before Edwards was named schoolmaster, however, the Mohawk chiefs resolved to leave Stockbridge. When the official word finally reached Stockbridge that Edwards was now in charge of the school, it had no pupils. Edwards reluctantly, but without any other choice, closed the school.

During this time, Edwards attempted at great risk to his personal reputation to do all that he could for the school and the Mohawks. He frequently housed Mohawks, teaching them himself, in addition to his pastoral duties and without remuneration. He even opened his home to the Mohawks for tribal councils. He pleaded with the Mohawks to leave some of their children in his care when they left Stockbridge. He recalls the event, noting that when he told them of the care that he would take of their children, they only replied "that they heard such promises concerning the school so often, and so often disappointed that they were discouraged." The Williamses—Ephraim Sr., Ephraim Jr., and Elijah—were largely responsible for these problems at Stockbridge. At one point, Ephraim Sr. frantically went about the town "offering very high prices and cash in hand" to buy out the other residents in order to gain control of the town and rid himself of Edwards.[31] Williams' motives were tied to his land and monetary interests. Lion Miles and others have documented the Williams clan's less-than-ethical dealings with the Stockbridge natives throughout the mid to late 1700s.[32] The tragedy as Edwards saw it, however, lay not in

---

times due to misplaced agendas on behalf of the colonials and at other times due to the lack of interest among the Indians for the work. For an intriguing account that reflects the latter, see William S. Simmons and Cheryl L. Simmons, *Old Light on Separate Ways: The Narragansett Diary of Joseph Fish, 1765–1776* (Hanover: University Press of New England, 1982), a chronicle of the failed school for the Narragansetts in Rhode Island.

29. Jonathan Edwards to Isaac Hollis, 17 July 1752, *Letters and Personal Writings*, Works, 16:494.

30. See Edwards' letter to Thomas Prince, 10 May 1754, ibid., 629–43.

31. Wyllis E. Wright, *Colonel Ephraim Williams*, 66.

32. See Miles, "The Red Man Dispossessed." Upon the death of Ephraim Williams Sr. in 1754, his son Elijah Williams took the helm. Miles documents how Elijah tricked the Stockbridge Mohicans in an election in 1763 in order to get elected as a town select man and then employed underhanded tactics in another election to get himself a seat in the Massachusetts House of Representatives. In response, the Indians charged that "Williams and a party he has made in the town are endeavoring not only to get all the

the attack on his personal reputation throughout the affair but rather in the loss of opportunity regarding the Mohawks and Mohicans.

Edwards and the Ministry at Stockbridge

The school did not constitute Edwards' main duties at Stockbridge. His primary task was pastoring the church, which met with far more successes than the school. In a report to the speaker of the Massachusetts House of Representatives, Thomas Hubbard, Edwards relays the Stockbridge Indians' desire and eventual undertaking of being missionaries themselves. Edwards writes, "Another thing that seems to show a remarkable hand of heaven . . . is this. The last February [1752], the Stockbridge Indians, entirely of their own accord, met together to consider whether they had done their duty to promote the Iroquois coming hither for instruction in Christianity." He notes that the Stockbridge Indians, realizing that "once they were in a state of darkness, but now were brought into light," "earnestly desired" the same for the neighboring Iroquois.[33] Throughout the seven years of his tenure, Edwards, as McDermott observes, "seems to have developed genuine affection for his Indian congregation."[34] Edwards' work at Stockbridge is typically overlooked or even dismissed by most historians or other observers. The chief criticism is that because Edwards never learned the language, his work was of limited impact and importance. Examining the case a little further reveals, however, that such estimates are misguided.

Edwards' extant sermons from this period reveal his concern not to overshoot his audience. At the same time, they are not patronizing. Rather, Edwards demonstrates a remarkable ability within the Stockbridge sermons to communicate clearly and effectively.[35] Many of the sermons from this period are in outline form, though a number of fully manuscripted sermons survive. Edwards preached a few sermon

power but our lands too into their hands," cited in ibid., 62. Additionally, Arthur Perry observes, "His design to obtain a still larger fortune than he was possessed of . . . conspicuously appeared in all of his actions. He endeavored to obtain the manipulation of large monies (mostly English) annually expended in Stockbridge for missionary and educational uses" (*Origins of Williamstown* [New York: Charles Scribner's Sons, 1898], 635).

33. *Letters and Personal Writings, Works,* 16:465.

34. McDermott, *Jonathan Edwards Confronts the Gods,* 203.

35. See the introduction to Kimnach, Minkema, and Sweeney, *The Sermons of Jonathan Edwards,* xxxv–xxxvi. The editors also refer to Edwards' "under appreciated" role as missionary by noting that "none of his Indian sermons has ever been published." They offer a corrective by including two Stockbridge sermons in the reader.

series during this time period, including a series on the parables in Matthew 13, one on the attributes of God, and one on Christology that included a theologically rich sermon on the union of the deity and humanity of Christ.[36] Additionally, Edwards' sermons reflect his sensitivity to his audience by using numerous metaphors and analogies from nature. In one sense, such writing is a mere extension of his previous sermons and writings, for the entire Edwards corpus reflects such devices. He uses such imagery as water and rivers and the motifs of light and darkness profusely. In one of his sermons on God's attribute of mercy, Edwards declares that "God's goodness is like a river that overflows all of its bounds."[37] And, in a sermon from John 15, he notes "that Christ is the original [sic] and fountain of all spiritual life and nourishment."[38] In a sermon to the Mohawks, he likens the Bible to the sun. In fact, he declares, "We invite you to come and enjoy the light of the Word of God, which is ten thousand times better than [the] light of the sun."[39]

Edwards' Stockbridge sermons also contain warnings of God's judgment that rival his famous "Sinners in the Hands of an Angry God" sermon. He stresses the perils and brevity of mortal human life and the coming doom of suffering under God's wrath. But he also trumpets the gospel. His first sermon, as he writes in the top margin, "for the Mohawks at Stockbridge & the St[ockbridge] Ind[ians]," in January 1751 on Acts 11:12–13, illustrates these emphases well as he exposits the account of Peter's encounter with Cornelius. Here Edwards explains, "Now I am come to preach the true religion to you and to your children as Peter did to Cornelius and his family, that you and all your children may be saved."[40] Edwards' sermons at Stockbridge also engage the turmoil caused by the Indian wars. Following a defeat of the French in 1755, Edwards preached a sermon in which he announced, "God is [the one] that orders all things in a time of war just as he pleases and all defense and success in war is from him." He then assures his hearers that God "knows when a people are most in danger," adding "[God] never sleeps."[41]

36. The Stockbridge sermons may be found in boxes 13 and 14 of the Jonathan Edwards Collection, Beinecke Library, Yale University. One of the most thorough studies of the Stockbridge sermons may be found in Rachel Wheeler's "Living upon Hope: Mahicans and Missionaries, 1730–1760" (Ph.D. diss., Yale University, 1998), 161–83.

37. Edwards, MS sermon on Exodus 34:6–7 (January 1753), Beinecke Library, Yale University.

38. Edwards, MS sermon on John 15:5 (n.d.), Beinecke Library, Yale University.

39. *The Sermons of Jonathan Edwards,* 109.

40. Edwards, MS sermon on Acts 11:12–13 (n.d.), Beinecke Library, Yale University.

41. Edwards, MS sermon on 2 Chronicles 20:6 (5 March 1755), Beinecke Library, Yale University.

He preached his farewell sermon in January 1758. Here he can say that his ministry has "come to an happy end." More than likely his mind wandered back to his other farewell sermon at Northampton and its acrimonious occasion. Though under more pleasant circumstances, there is a touch of sadness as Edwards leaves the Stockbridge Indians for Princeton. He closes the sermon on Hebrews 13:7–8 with a series of applications to select groups. One of those groups he identifies as those who "have made it [their] call to live agreeable to the gospel."[42] In many ways, this phrase sums up the intention of his preaching during this seven-year period. The phrase also summarizes a fascinating set of documents, statements of faith that Edwards drafted for Stockbridge Mohicans. Two such manuscripts survive.[43] One is single-sided, containing a full, unedited statement of faith. This statement includes not only one's public confession of commitment to the church but also a succinct statement of the doctrines of grace from the Reformed perspective. Edwards begins by having the Stockbridge congregants affirm their belief in the Triune God:

> I do now appear before God and his People to solemnly & publickly to profess, so far as I know my own heart, the following things; namely that I do believe that there is only one living & true God, who is the Father the Son and the Holy Ghost, who is the great Creatour and Supream Lord of Heaven & Earth; and having been made sensible of his divine Supreme Glory & Excellency, do choose him for my only God and Portion, choosing conformity to Him and his Service and the Enjoyment of him as my highest & sweetest good.

Key themes in Edwards' thought and writings appear in this opening section, such as his emphasis on God's glory and excellency and the response to God of enjoying him as one's "sweetest and highest good." Edwards sought to instruct the Native Americans in the same ideals that he labored to teach others all of his life.

This statement also serves as a primer on basic theology as it continues to offer an exposition of the doctrines of grace:

> I believe that God at first made man in his own Image & entered into a Covenant of life with Him, forbidding Him to eat of the Tree of Knowledge of Good and Evil; but our first Parents fell by eating the forbidden Fruit, exposing themselves & their Posterity to the wrath of God and

42. Edwards, MS sermon on Hebrews 13:7–8 (January 1758), Beinecke Library, Yale University.

43. Edwards, "Profession of Faith," MS, Beinecke Library, Yale University. Though they are not dated, Kenneth Minkema dates the manuscripts to 1751 or 1752, early in Edwards' tenure at Stockbridge.

Eternal Death; But God in mercy sent his Son in our Nature to redeem & save us. . . . I do with all my Heart believe the Truth of the Gospel of Christ; and having been made Sensible of Christ's glorious Excellency & sufficiency as a saviour and the Excellency of the way of Salvation by free grace through his Blood & Righteousness; and by the Holy sanctifying influence of his Blessed Spirit, effectually disposing to holiness of Life, I profess to receive Him as my Savior, my heart cleaving to Him and acquiescing in Him as the Refuge and rest of my soul & fountain of my Comfort and removing all ways of Sin to accept of Christ as my King and great example resolving & promising to follow him and obey him in All things as long as I live, making my Temporal Interest & Pleasure in all things to give Place to this will & honor. I renounce all the Enjoyments of this world from being my Happiness, and choose Heaven for my everlasting Inheritance and Home.

He concludes by having the candidate commit to the duties of church membership:

And as I now desire publickly to join my self to the people of Christ, I profess to be united in Heart unto Them as Brethren in Christ, resolving to serve & follow Christ our common Lord, in union & fellowship with him to the end of my Life, and to perform all those duties that belong to Them as member of the same Family of God and mystical Body of Christ. And as I desire to be admitted to the Lord's supper, that Feast of Love, I profess an universal forgiveness, love & good-will towards mankind; and Promise to be subject to the government of this church during my abode here.

The other statement of faith is two-sided. The one side contains quite rough drafts with various corrections, restarts, and edits. The other side contains a full, apparently unedited, statement that differs slightly from the other manuscript and has one unique feature: the names "Cornelius" and "Mary Munnewaunummuh" appear written in Jonathan Edwards' hand on the bottom. Edwards performed the wedding of Mary Munnewaunummuh to Muttohkaunmun on February 13, 1754. Muttohkaunmun, according to Lion Miles, "was an original Indian proprietor in Stockbridge." Nothing else is known of his wife. There is even less information regarding the identity of Cornelius. The only Cornelius to appear in church records, Cornelius Nouwuhheese, was married to Elizabeth Uhwameen by Edwards on January 2, 1752. It is difficult to pinpoint the exact circumstances of their public profession. The manuscript is undated, and Edwards, as later church records note, did not assign top priority to keeping church records. The statement, which shares themes and phraseology with the previous one, appears below in full:

And I do now appear before God & his People solemnly to give up my self to God to whom my parents gave me upon my Baptism having so far as I know my own Heart chosen Him for my portion & set my Heart on Him as my greatest & sweetest Good. And now would solemnly give up my self to Christ having as I hope seen my need of him being sensible of my sin & misery as I am in myself the insufficiency of my own Righteousness & my unworthiness of any mercy and my deserving that God should cast me off forever and also seen the Sufficiency of Jesus Christ as a Saviour. I now also appear openly to Renounce all the ways of sin which I hope I have seen the hatefulness of sin being made burdensom to me. I desire to spend my life in watching striving & fighting against it. And would give up myself to a life of holiness earnestly to seek & strive after it as what I choose & delight in having hungered & thirsted after it & would ever solemnly give up my life to the service of God & to follow Christ in all his ways & ordinances & to give up my self to the Holy spirit of God to follow his Leading & Guidance humbly depending on his Influence to sanctify me & enable to live an holy Life and I now desire to join my self to the People of Christ as those whom I hope my heart is presently united to as my Brethren in [Christ]. I profess universal forgiveness & good walk to maintain & promise to be subject to the government of this church during my abode here.

Cornelius / Mary Munnewaunummuh

Those familiar with the events surrounding the dismissal at Northampton will readily see the lessons learned from Edwards' prior experience. In some ways, the intensity of commitment required by these statements coheres with Edwards' concerns involving church membership and admittance to the Lord's Supper—the issue at the center of the controversy at Northampton. They also reveal that while requiring an intense commitment, Edwards mainly was insisting on a desire to live a godly life, not a standard of perfection in order for one to partake of the Lord's Supper, as some of his opponents accused him. Neither does he reflect even a hint of antinomianism, again, as some of his opponents accused him.[44] These Stockbridge texts for the Stockbridge natives, as opposed to the published treatises from this period, are worthy of study, for they add important material for estimating and evaluating Edwards.

Other texts reveal Edwards' concern for all aspects of church life at Stockbridge. In a letter to a singing teacher, Edwards asks the teacher to come to Stockbridge because "there is a very great need of some-

---

44. For the full discussion on the "communion controversy," see Jonathan Edwards, *The Works of Jonathan Edwards*, vol. 12, *Ecclesiastical Writings*, ed. David D. Hall (New Haven: Yale University Press, 1994); and Stephen J. Nichols, *Jonathan Edwards: A Guided Tour of His Life and Thought* (Phillipsburg, N.J.: P&R, 2001), 125–37.

body at Stockbridge to teach the Indians to sing. They have good voices and many of them are apt to learn, and I should be glad if I could get you here the next fall or winter to that end."[45] It was typical for the Congregational churches to hire singing teachers to train the congregation in singing. Edwards had done this at Northampton, and his desire to do so at Stockbridge—a desire that probably never materialized—reveals the importance with which he viewed his pastoral charge. The texts from this period reveal that Edwards faithfully performed his pastoral duties and that, while at Stockbridge, he saw himself chiefly as minister in the rather humble First Congregational Church.

Conclusion: Edwards as Missionary

This evaluation reveals that when we consider the various roles of Edwards as philosopher, theologian, apologist, revivalist, pastor, author, and college president, we also need to add the role of missionary. Edwards demonstrated a sensitivity to the issues related to Native American culture and especially to the importance of the land to their identity. He generally avoided xenophobic and ethnocentric attitudes. To be sure, he promoted the learning of English by the Native Americans, and his loyalties to the crown were not entirely obscured. Nevertheless, his tendency to consider the best interests of the Native Americans stands out. Edwards' gesture of living on the plain among the Indians stands as a clear testimony to his respect for them. Further, unlike his peers, he disavowed the exploitation of the Native Americans that became so commonplace during this period. He did so publicly, even chastising those who were his own benefactors. Finally, Edwards perceived the coming problems for both the English and the Indian alike. His acuity, however, largely went unheeded by others.

Two tributes, however, demonstrate that not all of his labor was in vain. Gideon Hawley, Edwards' pick for the position of schoolmaster to replace the problematic Martin Kellogg, apprenticed under Edwards and learned from his example. Given the difficulty that Edwards had in getting Kellogg removed, Hawley eventually left Stockbridge to be with the Oneidas at Onohquaga, New York, for over twenty years. There, unencumbered by the scheming of the Williamses, Hawley witnessed much fruit among the Native Americans. The second tribute is seen in Edwards' long-distance impact on Hendrick Aupaumut. Born in 1757 and probably baptized by Edwards, Aupau-

---

45. Jonathan Edwards to "A Singing Teacher," 4 June 1753, *Letters and Personal Writings*, *Works*, 16:597.

mut was a Mohican chief instrumental in the move to New Stockbridge, New York, in the mid-1780s. Aupaumut wrote a letter to Timothy Edwards, Edwards' son who later settled in Stockbridge as a
merchant, concerning his father's books. While Edwards' *Religious Affections* and especially *Freedom of the Will* tend to stump readers
whose first language is English, Aupaumut requested copies of these
books and eagerly awaited their arrival. Aupaumut translated the
Westminster Shorter Catechism into Mohican in 1795 and has left
quite a legacy regarding the gospel among his people.

In addition to the impact on Hawley and Aupaumut, numerous
names were added to the membership of the Congregational church
at Stockbridge during Edwards' tenure. While Edwards' work at
Stockbridge met opposition, as it did at Northampton, he often met
his goal during these forgotten seven years—proclaiming the gospel
for God's glory among the Mohicans. To be sure, Edwards was not the
last of the Mohican missionaries. Then again, Uncas, James Fenimore
Cooper's legendary character, was not the last of the Mohicans. Like
Cooper's character, however, Edwards demonstrated heroic ideals that
might warrant the accolade.

3

✦

DRIVEN BY PASSION

Jonathan Edwards and the Art of Preaching

Richard A. Bailey

He looked on the bell rope until he looked it off.

Gideon Clark

Although scholars portray Jonathan Edwards in a variety of ways—as a theologian, a philosopher, an exponent of revival, and America's greatest sensationalist—few focus on his passion. Rather, most people depict him much like Gideon Clark's characterization. Nevertheless, Edwards expressed fervor in the one place where it is most often judged absent—in his preaching. An analysis of his pastoral ministry and his ministerial sermons demonstrates that passion drove Edwards in at least three areas of his philosophy of preaching. First, he understood the relationship between divine revelation and human reason differently than many proponents of the Enlightenment. Second, Edwards desired both to encourage the onset of the millennium and to fulfill his divine commission. As a result, he not only used contemporary models to frame his preaching but also modified the prevailing preaching pattern. Third, prompted by his affective

The author would like to thank Paul R. House, C. Ben Mitchell, Amy Plantinga Pauw, Sean M. Lucas, and Ed Blum. Their suggestions greatly improved this essay.

theology, Edwards passionately prepared and proclaimed his message in order to guide his flock to their eternal home.[1]

The Aid to Reason

Though often considered a child of the Enlightenment, Edwards criticized Enlightenment thought where he found it deficient. He specifically critiqued the Enlightenment's emphasis upon reason over revelation. Even though he both knew the work of the great philosophers of his day and affirmed their concept of the important role of human reason, he did not share their conviction of the primacy of human reason. Most advocates of the Enlightenment championed reason over divine revelation. Edwards, however, defended the traditional Protestant notion of revelation both in theory and in practice.[2]

In "Jonathan Edwards, Deism, and the Mystery of Revelation," historian Gerald McDermott demonstrates that Edwards argued against Enlightenment thought in his private notebooks, the "Miscellanies." In particular, he warred against the Deists, asserting the necessity of revelation and the deficiency of reason. From early in his ministry, Edwards understood revelation to serve as the rule of reason in at least three ways. First, he stated that divine revelation provides the means to live morally: "I am of the mind that mankind would have been like a parcel of beasts with respect to their knowledge in all important truths, if there had never been any such thing as revelation in the world, and that they never would have rose out of their brutality." Second, convinced that divine revelation prompts intellectual growth, he maintained that "the increase of learning and philosophy in the Chris-

1. Perry Miller, "The Rhetoric of Sensation," in *Errand into the Wilderness* (Cambridge, Mass.: Harvard University Press, Belknap Press, 1996), 183; Wilson H. Kimnach, Kenneth P. Minkema, and Douglas A. Sweeney, *The Sermons of Jonathan Edwards: A Reader* (New Haven: Yale University Press, 1999), x. Also Wilson H. Kimnach, "Introduction," in Jonathan Edwards, *The Works of Jonathan Edwards*, vol. 10, *Sermons and Discourses, 1720–1723*, ed. Wilson H. Kimnach (New Haven: Yale University Press, 1992), 3.

2. Perry Miller, *Jonathan Edwards* (New York: Meridian Books, 1959), 238; Stephen J. Nichols, "An Absolute Sort of Certainty: The Holy Spirit and the Apologetics of Jonathan Edwards" (Ph.D. diss.: Westminster Theological Seminary, 2000); Gerald R. McDermott, *Jonathan Edwards Confronts the Gods: Christian Theology, Enlightenment Religion, and Non-Christian Faiths* (New York: Oxford University Press, 2000); Gerald R. McDermott, "Jonathan Edwards, Deism, and the Mystery of Revelation," *Journal of Presbyterian History* 77 (1999): 211. Edwards was reported to have read Locke with more pleasure "than the most greedy miser finds, when gathering up handfuls of silver and gold, from some newly discovered treasure" (Sereno E. Dwight, "Memoirs of Jonathan Edwards, A.M.," in *The Works of Jonathan Edwards*, ed. Edward Hickman, 2 vols. [1834; reprint, Edinburgh: Banner of Truth Trust, 1974], 1:xvii).

tian world is owing to revelation: the doctrines of the Word of God are the foundation of all useful and excellent knowledge." Later in the same entry, he proceeded, "Revelation brings nations to rational studious consideration, and there is nothing else will do it; for nothing else will convince them that it's worth the while to be at the pains of it. Revelation does not only give us the foundation and first principles of all learning, but it gives us the end for which [it should be sought], and the only end that would be sufficient to move men to the pursuit." Third, he claimed that divine revelation aids social development: "If it were not for revelation, nations and public communities would see no reason to encourage such speculations, and to uphold an order of men who should make speculation the business of their lives."[3]

Edwards struggled against the Enlightenment understanding of reason not only in his private writings but also in his public addresses. For example, in a May 7, 1740, ordination sermon from 1 Corinthians 2:11–13, he positioned revelation as the guide for human reason and not the other way around: "Hence we learn that rule of interpreting Scripture so much insisted upon by many of late, viz., first to determine by our reason what is agreeable to the moral perfections of God and then to interpret the Scriptures by them, is an unjust and fallacious one." Later, he elaborated on the impossibility of reason's superiority to the revelation of God:

> The supreme legislative authority of a nation don't ask children what laws are just for them to make or what rules are just for them to proceed by, nor do they wait for the judgment and determination of every subject in order to oblige them to submission. Much less does the infinitely great and wise sovereign of heaven and earth wait for the decision of our judgment and reason what laws or rules of proceeding in him are just in order to require our submission to him.
>
> Divine revelation in these things don't go a-begging for credit and validity by approbation and applause of our understanding. On the contrary, the style in which these revelations are often given forth is this: "Thus saith the Lord," and "I am the Lord," and "He that hath an ear to hear, let him hear," and "Who are thou, O man, that repliest against God?"

Edwards believed revelation instructs human reason concerning those things that seem paradoxical and mysterious. He maintained that reason can grasp many things, but for those things reason cannot com-

3. McDermott, "Jonathan Edwards, Deism, and the Mystery of Revelation," 211–24; "Miscellanies" no. 350, in Jonathan Edwards, *The Works of Jonathan Edwards*, vol. 13, *The "Miscellanies," a–500*, ed. Thomas A. Schafer (New Haven: Yale University Press, 1994), 424–25.

prehend, revelation provides the necessary means of explanation. In short, he understood revelation as the brilliant light illuminating "the dark faculties of our present low state."[4]

Believing that revelation contained the key to understanding the mysteries of religion, Edwards saturated almost every sermon, from text to doctrine to application, with Scripture. Given his understanding of revelation as the guide to instruct humanity in its relationship to a holy God, Edwards, almost without fail, interlaced every argument with Scripture. No better way existed than to employ Scripture to explicate Christianity's intricate conceptions and doctrines, because Edwards saw Scripture as the legend to the map of religion.

As Edwards employed divine revelation, he also spoke in a type of "Scripture language." His innumerable allusions to Scripture and his habit of writing in a manner strikingly similar to the Authorized Version illustrate this point. He defended his approach to using Scripture, claiming that "God would have our whole dependence be upon the Scriptures because the greater our dependence is on the Word of God, the more direct and immediate is our dependence on God himself." In fact, modern readers of Edwards' often indecipherable orthography will find an understanding of his reliance on "Scripture language" critical. Often, unrecognizable words can be transcribed only by reading the surrounding passage as part of a scriptural phrase or allusion. His "Scripture language" thus not only reveals his reliance on Scripture to explain the mysteries of the world but also provides a key for modern transcribers.[5]

In sum, rather than use reason like others in the Enlightenment tradition, Edwards relied on Scripture. This insistence on the necessity of divine revelation provides the first glimpse into the passion that permeated his approach to the art of preaching. Even a cursory read-

4. Kenneth P. Minkema and Richard A. Bailey, eds., "Reason, Revelation, and Preaching: An Unpublished Ordination Sermon by Jonathan Edwards," *The Southern Baptist Journal of Theology* 3.2 (summer 1999): 16–33. See also Jonathan Edwards, "Light in a Dark World, a Dark Heart," in *The Works of Jonathan Edwards*, vol. 19, *Sermons and Discourses, 1734–1738*, ed. M. X. Lesser (New Haven: Yale University Press, 2001), 704–33.

5. "Miscellanies" no. 535, in Jonathan Edwards, *The Works of Jonathan Edwards*, vol. 18, *The "Miscellanies," 501–832*, ed. Ava Chamberlain (New Haven: Yale University Press, 2000), 80. Concerning these manuscripts, Helen Westra remarked, "Thus the sermons reveal their contents only to readers possessed of prodigious blocks of time, the strongest of eyesight, and a perverse willingness to be infected by the challenge of punctuationless sentences, erratic capitalization, minute interlineations, and a handwriting which Schafer rightly calls 'exasperatingly formless.' Edwards' great body of sermons is thus, like the proverbial iceberg, largely hidden from the public eye" (*The Minister's Task and Calling in the Sermons of Jonathan Edwards* [Lewiston, N.Y.: Edwin Mellen, 1986], 49 n. 24).

ing of his sermons demonstrates the zeal he had for what he considered the Word of God. As Edwards ministered to his listeners through the proclamation of the gospel, he enthusiastically employed the Scriptures as the "aid to reason."

"Resolved to Live"[6]

Edwards preached as one influenced by the religious milieu in which he lived, as well as one resolved to leave his mark upon that environment. Adopting the style of colonial preaching modeled to him by his father, his grandfather, and available preaching manuals, Edwards showed great concern for the kingdom of God and his role in that kingdom. He simultaneously asserted his own ministerial personality and gifts because of his desires both for the coming kingdom of God and the conversion of his parishioners.[7]

At least three influences contributed to the character of Jonathan Edwards the preacher. The first, and most important, influence was his father, Timothy Edwards. Young Jonathan sat under the preaching ministry of his father, who served as pastor of the Congregational church in East Windsor, Connecticut. Apparently, Timothy Edwards was an able preacher in his own right, following the traditional Puritan arrangement of sermonic literature: text, doctrine, and application. Wilson Kimnach, the leading authority on Edwards' sermons, claims that this exposure to the classical form and content of Puritan preaching formed Jonathan's conception of the sermon. In addition to shaping his son's understanding of the Puritan sermon form, Timothy influenced Jonathan in several other ways. As historian Kenneth Minkema suggests, Timothy Edwards emphasized the minister's worth, acting as "lord and master" while in the pulpit. Furthermore, by memorizing his sermons and delivering an abbreviated version of his manuscript, a method known as "memoriter," Timothy demonstrated for his son the ideal style of Puritan preaching. Finally, Timothy instilled in his son a concern for the conversion of the people under his charge. Jonathan imbibed Timothy's preaching philosophy and style. Even though he apparently did not inherit his father's constitution, he shared Timothy's opinion of the minister's worth. In one of his first sermons in Northampton after Solomon Stoddard's death,

6. This phrase was taken from Edwards' sixth resolution in Jonathan Edwards, *The Works of Jonathan Edwards*, vol. 16, *Letters and Personal Writings*, ed. George S. Claghorn (New Haven: Yale University Press, 1998), 753.

7. Harry S. Stout demonstrated Edwards' place in the New England Puritan preaching tradition in *The New England Soul: Preaching and Religious Culture in Colonial New England* (New York: Oxford University Press, 1986), 228–31.

Jonathan insisted that "wise & Faithfull ministers of the Gosp[el] are very usefull men. They are use[ful] to a people in those things that Concern their Greatest Interests, even the Eternal salvation of their souls." Moreover, Edwards assumed a semi-extemporaneous delivery similar to that of his father, illustrated by the outline form and rough prose of his extant manuscripts. In addition, he applied his sermons in order to awaken souls, thereby demonstrating a similar preoccupation with salvation. Clearly, Timothy Edwards served "as a living exemplar of the preacher during his son's formative years."[8]

The second major influence on Edwards' preaching was his maternal grandfather, Solomon Stoddard, the so-called Pope of Western Massachusetts. Stoddard was an outspoken critic of much of the preaching of his day. In his 1723 sermon "Defects of Preachers Reproved," he excoriated ministers for reading their sermons, observing:

> Reading sermons is a dull way of preaching. Sermons when read are not delivered with authority and in an affecting way. . . . When sermons are delivered without notes, the looks and gestures of the minister are a great means to command attention and stir up affection. Men are apt to be drowsy in hearing the Word, and the liveliness of the preacher is a means to stir up the attention of the hearers and beget suitable affection in them. Sermons that are read are not delivered with authority; they favor the sermons of the scribes. Experience shows that sermons read are not so profitable as others. It may be argued that it is harder to remember rhetorical sermons than mere rational discourses; but it may be answered that it is far more profitable to preach in the demonstrations of the Spirit than with the enticing words of man's wisdom.

Wilson Kimnach believes that Stoddard would have made similar suggestions to his assistant and chosen successor. While not a certainty, it is highly likely that Edwards graciously took his revered grandfather's advice and followed it in his own preaching. Moreover, like Timothy Edwards, Stoddard taught his young associate to preach with the aim of seeing souls converted. Thus, Edwards' two main ministerial models, Timothy Edwards and Solomon Stoddard, shaped their scion's understanding of the pastoral ministry.[9]

8. Kimnach, "Introduction," in *Works*, 10:11; Kenneth Pieter Minkema, "The Edwardses: A Ministerial Family in Eighteenth-Century New England" (Ph.D. diss., University of Connecticut, 1988), 76, 78, 80–88; Edwards' MS sermon on Isaiah 3:1–2 (1729), Beinecke Library, Yale University.

9. Perry Miller, "Solomon Stoddard, 1643–1729," *Harvard Theological Review* 34 (1941): 278; Solomon Stoddard, "The Defects of Preachers Reproved," in *The Nature of Saving Conversion* (Morgan, Pa.: Soli Deo Gloria, 1999), 127–31, 137–38; Kimnach, "Introduction," in *Works*, 10:15.

Finally, Edwards modeled his preaching after several contemporary preaching manuals, particularly Cotton Mather's *Manuductio ad Ministerium* and John Edwards' *The Preacher*. Both of these books appear early in Edwards' "Catalogue," a list of books documenting his reading interests. The latter manual insisted that a preacher "must be a Linguist, a Grammarian, a Critick, an Orator, a Philosopher, an Historian, a Casuist, a Disputant, and whatever speaks Skill and Knowledge in any Learned Science" while he seeks to construct sermons "like diamonds, Clear as well as Solid." This manual also advised the preacher to enforce every portion of his sermon with Scripture and not "be ashamed of the Scripture Phrase, as some seem to be." Likewise, *Manuductio ad Ministerium* advised preachers to employ natural reason and their own personal style to reach their congregations. Based on Edwards' implementation of the material in these volumes, Kimnach asserts, "It is obvious that the *Manuductio* was repeatedly referred to as a kind of manual, and as for *The Preacher*, there are too many echoes of its individualistic expressions throughout Edwards' notebooks to have doubts about its importance to him." Arguably, Jonathan Edwards realized he could learn from mentors and more experienced ministers. He allowed seasoned preachers, whether he knew them personally or only through their writings, to counsel him in the work to which he felt called.[10]

While Edwards inherited a tradition that shaped him, he also thought diligently about how he could personalize—and possibly remake—this tradition. One way he influenced future generations of preachers was his method of preparing sermons. Expanding on the note-taking system of many preachers of his era, Edwards produced a system of detailed, cross-referenced notebooks that virtually constructed his sermons. He then pulled together all the thoughts and ideas he had meditated upon in the previous days, weeks, and years by turning to these resources.[11]

Edwards also made an effort to connect with both the heart and the intellect of his auditors. In this way, he presaged and influenced future affective preachers such as Asahel Nettleton, Horace Bushnell, and Charles Finney. Early in his career, Edwards focused his attention on a logical, theoretical style of argumentation. As he gained valuable pastoral experience, however, he recognized the importance of appealing to the emotions, or affections, of his listeners as well as to their intellects. In *Religious Affections*, his most complete evaluation of the work

10. Kimnach, "Introduction," in *Works*, 10:16–21.
11. Ibid., 42–129.

of the Holy Spirit, Edwards asserted that "such means are to be desired, as have much of a tendency to move the affections. Such books, and such a way of preaching the Word, and administration of ordinances, and such a way of worshiping God in prayer, and singing praises, is much to be desired, as has a tendency deeply to affect the hearts of those who attend these means." By "affections," Edwards meant "the vigorous and sensible exercises" of the heart. Based upon this understanding of the faculties of the intellect and the heart, as well as the intimate relationship between the two, Edwards was convinced that "if we ben't in good earnest in religion, and our wills and inclinations be not strongly exercised, we are nothing." Thus, he contended that "there never was any considerable change wrought in the mind or conversation of any one person, by anything of a religious nature, that ever he read, heard or saw, that had not his affections moved." Crafting his sermons to appeal to the "mind," meaning both the intellect and the heart, Edwards developed a religious psychology that took the Puritan concern with religious feelings and fervor to a new level.[12]

In his preaching, Edwards passionately led souls through the difficulties of life toward eternal joy. No matter what else he intended, Edwards sought to guide his sheep toward their final destination. He directed those under his ministry to prepare for their future, eternal habitation. Edwards exhorted his listeners to live with an eye always toward heaven. He had two reasons for this. First, he was concerned about the coming of the future kingdom of God. Convinced that history prepared the way for the millennial reign of Christ, Edwards saw the preparation of his flock, while they still resided in history, as a portion of his ministerial responsibility. Thus, he fashioned his sermons in order to prepare souls for that heavenly state. As Gerald McDermott observes in *One Holy and Happy Society*, "His vision of the millennium's realities and his anticipation of the 'glorious work of God's Spirit' that would bring it to fruition so pervaded his thinking that nearly every one of his central doctrines is illuminated by an unfolding of the millennial vision."[13]

12. Jonathan Edwards, *The Works of Jonathan Edwards*, vol. 6, *Scientific and Philosophical Writings*, ed. Wallace E. Anderson (New Haven: Yale University Press, 1980), 192–95. (These pages contain the transcriptions of the "Cover-Leaf Memoranda"—a collection of notes dealing with the subject of writing that Edwards jotted down on the first leaf of his notebook dealing with "Natural Philosophy.") Kimnach, "Introduction," in *Works*, 10:180–85, 198; Jonathan Edwards, *The Works of Jonathan Edwards*, vol. 2, *Religious Affections*, ed. John E. Smith (New Haven: Yale University Press, 1959), 97, 99, 102, 121.

13. Kimnach, Minkema, and Sweeney, *Sermons of Jonathan Edwards*, x; Jonathan Edwards, "Heaven Is a World of Love," in *The Works of Jonathan Edwards*, vol. 8, *Ethical Writings*, ed. Paul Ramsey (New Haven: Yale University Press, 1989), 366–97; Gerald R. McDermott, *One Holy and Happy Society: The Public Theology of Jonathan*

Second, Edwards believed he had both a divine calling and a great responsibility as a minister. In his mind, God actively chose his servants and commissioned them into his service:

> Ministers are only sent on his errand; God han't left it to their discretion what their errand shall be. They are to preach the preaching that he bids 'em (Jonah 3:2). He has put into their hands a Book containing a summary of doctrine, and bids 'em go and preach that word. And what daring presumption would it be for them afterwards to pick and choose among the doctrines contained in that summary, and say, "These are fit for me to preach, and these are not fit; this part of my errand is fit to be done, and this not"?
>
> God don't need to be told by his messengers what message is fit to deliver to those to whom he sends them.

In short, Edwards claimed that God gave his message to those he called into his service. Since this message was nothing less than the gospel itself, he recognized the awful responsibility that accompanied it. Nevertheless, he knew a great reward was promised to those who remained faithful to their task. In a November 17, 1736, sermon in Lambstown, Massachusetts, he testified to this view of the minister's work: "When those ministers of the Gospel that have Been faithfull & successful come to give an account of their success to their Lord that hath sent them, X [Christ] & they will Rejoice together." As a result of this understanding of his task, Edwards preached the gospel with passion to those who struggled in this life.[14]

Both his desire for the coming kingdom of God and his role as a divinely sanctioned minister in that kingdom illustrate yet another aspect of Edwards' passion. Faithfully seeking to complete the commission he felt God had placed before him, Edwards not only learned from those faithful ministers who had preceded him but also cast his own shadow on American evangelicalism as he ardently pursued the millennial reign of Christ.

Edwards (University Park: Pennsylvania State University Press, 1992), 42. While I appreciate the recent assertions made about Edwards' primary concern (e.g., John Piper in *God's Passion for His Glory: Living the Vision of Jonathan Edwards* [Wheaton: Crossway, 1998]), I think this concern for redemption represents his ministerial passion.

14. Minkema and Bailey, "Reason, Revelation, and Preaching," 28–29; Edwards' MS sermon on Luke 10:17–18 (17 November 1736), Beinecke Library, Yale University. See also Edwards' MS sermons on Luke 10:17–18, Romans 12:4–8, Acts 14:23, Zechariah 4:12–14, Micah 2:11, Acts 20:28, 2 Corinthians 4:7, and Acts 16:9, all at Beinecke Library, as well as the published ordination sermons on John 13:15–16 ("Christ the Example of Ministers," in *Works of Jonathan Edwards*, ed. Hickman, 2:960–65), Hebrews 13:17 ("The Watchman's Duty and Account," in *The Works of President Edwards*, 10 vols.,

Religious Affections

By most estimates, Jonathan Edwards hardly provides an example of an externally passionate preacher. Although his contemporaries described his preaching as anything but riveting rhetoric, Edwards sought to be affective in his public ministry. This concern for passion was never simply for passion's sake. Knowing that religious affections go much deeper than outward emotions, he wrote that "if it be as has been proved, that true religion lies very much in religious affections, then it follows, that if there be a great deal of true religion, there will be great religious affections; if true religion in the hearts of men, be raised to a great height, divine and holy affections will be raised to a great height." He continued, "on the other hand," arguing that "'tis no evidence that religious affections are of a spiritual and gracious nature, because they are great. . . . And it is the concurring voice of all orthodox divines, that there may be religious affections, which are raised to a very high degree, and yet there be nothing of true religion." As he defended the revival, Edwards balanced these seemingly contradictory ideas of affections. Without denouncing religious passion, he critiqued enthusiasm and extreme fervor in order to promote what he saw as true religion.[15]

The portrait of Edwards standing before his congregation with his head down, speaking in a monotone voice as he read his sermons line by line, following along with his finger, is the image most have of his pulpit style. Such a picture reinforces the common assumption that he lacked fervor in the pulpit. Where did this image originate? Did Edwards' original hearers see him in the same light as many, if not most, of his later readers? Using the accounts of his primary hearers as a guide, at least two lines of evidence possibly lead to the idea that Edwards' preaching lacked external passion.[16]

Edwards' disciples provide the first line of evidence. For example, Samuel Hopkins recorded that his mentor's "appearance in the desk

---

ed. S. E. Dwight [New York: G. & C. & H. Carvill, 1830], 8:178–96), John 5:35 ("The True Excellency of a Gospel Minister," in *Works of Jonathan Edwards*, ed. Hickman, 2:955–60), Isaiah 62:4–5 ("The Church's Marriage to Her Sons, and to Her God," in *Works of Jonathan Edwards*, ed. Hickman, 2:17–26), and 1 Corinthians 2:11–13 (Minkema and Bailey, "Reason, Revelation, and Preaching," 16–33). For Edwards' unpublished ministerial sermons and a treatment of them, see Richard A. Bailey and Gregory A. Wills, eds., *The Salvation of Souls: Nine Previously Unpublished Sermons by Jonathan Edwards on the Call of the Ministry and the Gospel* (Wheaton: Crossway, 2002).

15. *Religious Affections, Works,* 2:127–31.

16. For an interesting and convincing discussion of Edwards as a "manuscript preacher," see Jim Ehrhard, "A Critical Analysis of the Tradition of Jonathan Edwards as a Manuscript Preacher," *Westminster Theological Journal* 60 (1998): 71–84.

was with a good grace, and his delivery easy, natural and very solemn. He had not a strong, loud voice; but appear'd with such gravity and solemnity." When asked about Edwards' preaching, Stephen West replied, "He had no studied varieties of the voice, and no strong emphasis. He scarcely gestured, or even moved; and he made no attempt, by the elegance of his style, or the beauty of his pictures, to gratify the taste, and fascinate the imagination." An obituary in *New York Mercury* on April 10, 1758, presents a final example of the opinion of his primary hearers:

> As a preacher, he was well known, neither quick nor slow of speech. His language was full, but not ornamented. He regarded thoughts more than words. Precision of sentiment and clearness of diction formed the principal character of his style. In middle life he appeared emaciated (I had almost said mortified) by intense study and hard labour; hence his voice was a little low for a large assembly, but much helped by a proper emphasis, just cadence, and great distinctness in pronunciation.

From these images of his delivery, Edwards appears a dispassionate preacher.[17]

Edwards' reliance on manuscripts supplies a second line of evidence for the conventional image of his preaching. Hopkins described him in the following way: "He carried his notes into the desk with him, and read the most that he had wrote. He was wont to read so considerable a part of what he delivered." If he read his manuscript, tracing each line with his finger, it seems unlikely that he preached affectively. Thus, the claim that Edwards lacked external passion seems a fair assumption. Perhaps he appeared this way to his listeners as a result of invidious comparisons with dramatic figures such as the itinerant George Whitefield. Whatever the reason, such evidence typically leads most to believe that Edwards was a solemn preacher of the Word of God, rather than a passionate pulpiteer.[18]

17. Samuel Hopkins, *The Life and Character of the Late Reverend, Learned, and Pious Mr. Jonathan Edwards, President of the College of New Jersey. Together with Extracts from his Private Writings & Diary. And also Seventeen Select Sermons on Various Important Subjects* (Northampton: Andrew Wright, 1804), 52; Dwight, "Memoirs of Jonathan Edwards," 1:cxc, as quoted in Ralph G. Turnbull, *Jonathan Edwards the Preacher* (Grand Rapids: Baker, 1958), 102–3.

18. Hopkins, *Life and Character*, 52; Sandra M. Gustafson, *Eloquence in Power: Oratory & Performance in Early America* (Chapel Hill: University of North Carolina Press, 2000), 63. For discussions of the oratorical prowess of Whitefield, see Harry S. Stout, *The Divine Dramatist: George Whitefield and the Rise of Modern Evangelicalism* (Grand Rapids: Eerdmans, 1991) and Frank Lambert, *"Pedlar in Divinity": George Whitefield and the Transatlantic Revivals* (Princeton: Princeton University Press, 1994).

But a problem remains: How could a preacher who figured so prominently in the First Great Awakening and wrote so much about the affections possibly be so deficient in emotion? In several areas, Edwards displayed an interest in internal, if not external, passion. First, he apparently desired to preach in a different style. In a letter to Thomas Prince, he confessed some appreciation of Whitefield's style of delivery. Recounting Whitefield's visit to Northampton, Edwards stressed the effect of the itinerant's preaching upon the congregation. Not only was the congregation "extraordinarily melted by every sermon" and "in tears for a great part of the sermon time," but "Mr. Whitefield's sermons were suitable to the circumstances of the town; containing just reproofs of our backslidings, and *in a most moving and affecting manner*, making use of our great profession and great mercies as arguments with us to return to God, from whom we had departed."[19]

Additionally, Edwards desired to do more than read his sermons from the pulpit. Hopkins noted that Edwards judged the reading of his manuscripts as "a deficiency and infirmity; and in the latter part of his life, was inclined to think it had been better if he had never accustomed to use his notes at all." Edwards thought preaching without notes was the best method of carrying out the task at hand; he even claimed that if one must write out his sermon in full, then he should attempt to memorize it before approaching the pulpit. Apparently, Edwards attempted to work this strategy into his preaching. While he continued to write out his sermons, at least until the 1740s, he did not read verbatim from the manuscript but rather followed along, inserting extemporaneous remarks when beneficial. He also used several strategies in an attempt to improve his delivery so that he would not be a "statue-like, inflectionless speaker." For instance, he infused his preaching notes with special symbols and ellipses that allowed him to make better eye contact and to preach more extemporaneously. He also moved to briefer outlines in order to force him toward a more extemporaneous style. Once he implemented an outline format rather than a word-for-word manuscript, reading his sermons became impossible.[20]

19. Edwards to Thomas Prince, 12 November 1743, *Letters and Personal Writings, Works,* 16:116 (emphasis mine). For a compelling discussion of the relationship between Edwards and Whitefield, see Ava Chamberlain, "The Grand Sower of the Seed: Jonathan Edwards's Critique of George Whitefield," *New England Quarterly* 70 (1997): 368–85.

20. Hopkins, *Life and Character,* 52–53; Gustafson, *Eloquence in Power,* 62; Kenneth P. Minkema, "Introduction," in Jonathan Edwards, *The Works of Jonathan Edwards,* vol. 14, *Sermons and Discourses, 1723–1729,* ed. Kenneth P. Minkema (New Haven: Yale University Press, 1997), 12–13. It seems quite unlikely that Edwards could have read his sermons verbatim from his manuscripts, because he did not always write in complete sentences and use punctuation. His manuscripts seem to have served the purpose of directing his

Furthermore, Edwards' disciples testified that his preaching often reached the type of passion and power he desired. Hopkins claimed, "His words often discovered a great degree of inward fervour, without much noise or external emotion, and fell with great weight on the minds of his hearers. He made but little motion of his head or hands in the desk; but spake so as to discover the motion of his own heart, which tended in the most natural and effectual manner to move and effect others."[21] Asked if Edwards was an eloquent preacher, Stephen West replied,

> But, if you mean by eloquence, the power of presenting an important truth before an audience, with overwhelming weight of argument, and with such intenseness of feeling, that the whole soul of the speaker is thrown into every part of the conception and delivery; so that the solemn attention of the whole audience is rivetted, from the beginning to the close, and impressions are left that cannot be effaced; Mr. Edwards was the most eloquent man I ever heard speak.[22]

Finally, Edwards engaged in what Perry Miller called a "rhetoric of sensation." Miller argues that Edwards' "pulpit oratory was a consuming effort to make sounds become objects, to control and discipline his utterance so that words would immediately be registered on the senses not as noises but as ideas." Influenced by his study of Locke's theory of ideas, Edwards was convinced of the power of words and the ideas they represented. Consequently, he crafted his sermons so that his ideas might appeal to his auditors' sensations and thus move their affections toward God.[23]

With this understanding of the connection of words and ideas and their combined impact upon the affections, Edwards diligently prepared his sermons. As he wrote his sermons, he meticulously chose the words he desired. This careful selection of words and phrases, as illustrated in his manuscripts by repeated insertions and deletions, demonstrates the artistic element in the sermons of "America's greatest sensationalist." If this care had been art simply for art's sake, one could overlook it; however, it was not simply for artistic and literary reasons that Edwards went to such pains in his sermon writing. On the contrary, he chose the words most likely to

thoughts in the pulpit. Furthermore, in the early 1740s, Edwards began to employ an extended outline in his regular sermons, making reading the sermons all but impossible.
  21. Hopkins, *Life and Character*, 52.
  22. Ibid., 52; Dwight, "Memoirs of Jonathan Edwards," 1:cxc.
  23. Miller, *Jonathan Edwards*, 158.

convey the images and emotions he deemed necessary from the text. Thus, his preparation betrays his passion.[24]

How, then, does one account for Edwards' apparent lack of external passion in the pulpit? One explanation might have been his health. In a letter to the trustees at Nassau Hall, Edwards described why he preached as he did: "I have a constitution in many respects peculiar unhappy, attended with flaccid solids, vapid, sizy and scarce fluids, and a low tide of spirits; often occasioning a kind of childish weakness and contemptibleness of speech, presence, and demeanor; with a dis-agreeable dullness and stiffness, much unfitting me for conversation." Hopkins also stressed Edwards' health as a detriment to his commu-nication skills: "He was not a man of many words indeed. . . . This was in part the effect of his bodily constitution. He possessed but a com-parative small stock of animal life: his animal spirits were low, and he had not strength of lungs to spare, that would be necessary in order to make him what would be called, an affable, facetious gentleman, in all companies."[25]

Nevertheless, Edwards' failing health did not totally check his passion for preaching. The importance he placed on reaching the affections of his auditors represents a final aspect of his passion. Edwards not only pre-pared his sermons to connect with the "exercises of the heart" but also la-bored to deliver his carefully crafted discourses in a manner most condu-cive to affecting a response from both heart and mind.

Conclusion

As a preacher of the Word, Jonathan Edwards provided an example that continues to deserve investigation, if not some imitation. He was convinced that God had commissioned him to herald the good news in preparation for the coming kingdom of Christ. Thus, he centered his ministry on the flock he believed God had called him to shepherd. In a sense, his life passionately revolved around the Word of God. Cer-tain of the power of the Word to instruct and guide human reason in divine things, Edwards anchored his sermons in what he considered the objective, special revelation of God. Not only did he begin with Scripture, but he also employed Scripture and "Scripture language"

24. Miller, "Rhetoric," 183. This careful selection of words and phrases can be seen by examining the footnotes in practically any of the volumes of sermons in the Yale edi-tion of Edwards' works. The most obvious examples can be seen in the manuscripts themselves. Edwards would often mark out a word to replace it with another word that more adequately expressed the tenor of the passage.

25. Edwards to the Trustees of the College of New Jersey, 19 October 1757, *Letters and Personal Writings, Works,* 16:726; Hopkins, *Life and Character,* 45.

throughout his sermons as he preached the Word to his people. More-over, Edwards was influenced by his father and grandfather, as well as by several important preaching manuals. In light of these influences, he proclaimed to his audience the message of the coming kingdom of Christ. The way to draw men and women into Christ's kingdom, Ed-wards believed, was through his auditors' affections. Thus, though not given to extreme external manifestations of emotion, Edwards exer-cised great care in the preparation of his sermons. Resting on a strong belief in Lockean idealism as well as his own unique view of semiot-ics, he used the preaching event to move his listeners' affections from self-love to love of God. Therefore, though the prevailing picture of Jonathan Edwards is that of a passionless man, the truth is that he yearned for truly religious affections—for God-centered passion—in every part of his life, particularly in the act of preaching. He was a preacher truly driven by passion.

4

⭐

THE "INWARD, SWEET SENSE" OF CHRIST IN JONATHAN EDWARDS

Charles Hambrick-Stowe

On the eve of the Great Awakening and five years after the "surprising work of God" in the local revivals of 1734–35, Jonathan Edwards wrote a spiritual autobiography of about seven thousand words. This widely reprinted "Personal Narrative" (c. 1739), as it has been called in twentieth-century anthologies and in the Yale edition of his *Works*, may have been written by the thirty-six-year-old pastor-theologian as a personal favor to his future son-in-law Aaron Burr. In a March 1741 letter, Burr thanked Edwards and blessed God that by writing "so freely of your own experiences," Edwards had advanced Burr's "spiritual good." This, after all, was Edwards' goal in writing. The "Personal Narrative" was intended not for publication but for limited circulation among friends, especially candidates for the ministry. It was a carefully crafted account of Edwards' spiritual pilgrimage, charting, in the words of one of his earlier sermons, his progress on the "journey towards heaven." He made almost no reference in the "Personal Narrative" to external political, social, or even personal career events, mentioning just a few bare details related to his studies at Yale, his early pastorate in New York City, his move back to New Haven as a college tutor, and his Northampton pastorate. The only thing that mattered here was progress as a saint—coming to a saving knowledge of God, repentance from sin, his relationship with Jesus Christ, meditation on Scripture, experiences of grace by the indwelling Holy Spirit, and obedience to the gospel. Here Edwards set forth a description of his spiritual experience during and following his reception of "that new sense of things" bestowed by God in conversion.[1]

The "Personal Narrative" is a retrospective, somewhat stylized account of young adult religious experiences. Some scholars have suggested that it is *so* stylized that it masked his actual spiritual anxiety, that he was in fact uncertain of his conversion, that his description of religious experiences was in effect an exercise in wishful thinking. But the "Personal Narrative" is in no way inconsistent with extant diary entries that were contemporaneous with those experiences. I would argue to the contrary, that in the "Personal Narrative" Edwards offers a fairly reliable record of his spiritual experience and the practice of his piety.[2]

It is true that in 1722, when he was already preaching in New York City, it bothered Edwards that his experience did not conform to the pattern—the morphology of conversion—prescribed in the classic seventeenth-century Puritan devotional manuals and spiritual autobiographies. In his diary he identified four specific worries: (1) that he could not "speak so fully" about the stages of "preparatory work" in his own life as the pattern required; (2) that he could "not remember"

1. The "Personal Narrative" was first published by Samuel Hopkins as "An Account of His Conversion, Experiences, and Religious Exercises, Given by [Edwards] Himself," in *The Life and Character of the Late Reverend, Learned and Pious Mr. Jonathan Edwards* (Boston, 1765). It is published with editorial notes in *The Works of Jonathan Edwards*, vol. 16, *Letters and Personal Writings*, ed. George S. Claghorn (New Haven: Yale University Press, 1998), 747–52, 790–804. The "Personal Narrative" is also in *Jonathan Edwards: Representative Selections, with Introduction, Bibliography, and Notes*, ed. Clarence H. Faust and Thomas H. Johnson (New York: Hill and Wang, 1935; 2d ed., 1962), 57–72. The September 1733 sermon "The True Christian's Life a Journey Towards Heaven," is in *The Works of Jonathan Edwards*, vol. 17, *Sermons and Discourses, 1730–1733*, ed. Mark Valeri (New Haven: Yale University Press, 1999), 429–46. The most useful collection of Edwards' writings is John E. Smith, Harry S. Stout, and Kenneth P. Minkema, eds., *A Jonathan Edwards Reader* (New Haven: Yale University Press, 1995), which includes the "Personal Narrative," 281–96. Because of its ready availability to the general reader, I will cite this paperback volume whenever possible, using the abbreviation *JE Reader*. A companion paperback is also extremely helpful: Wilson H. Kimnach, Kenneth P. Minkema, and Douglas A. Sweeney, eds., *The Sermons of Jonathan Edwards: A Reader* (New Haven: Yale University Press, 1999). For a discussion of the "Personal Narrative" that mentions the correspondence with Aaron Burr, see Patricia J. Tracy, *Jonathan Edwards, Pastor: Religion and Society in Eighteenth-Century Northampton* (New York: Hill and Wang, 1980), 58–64.

2. Tracy quotes selectively in such a way as to suggest far greater anxiety on Edwards' part, that he was uncertain of his salvation, and that in the "Personal Narrative" he wrote about experiences he only wished he had had as a young man (*Jonathan Edwards, Pastor*, 59–60).

experiencing "regeneration, exactly in those steps, in which divines say it is generally wrought"; (3) that he did not "feel the Christian graces sensibly enough, particularly faith"; and (4) that he continued to be painfully aware of committing sin. Again, in August 1723 diary entries, he reflected on his inability to recount his salvation experience according to "those particular steps, wherein the people of New England, and anciently the Dissenters of Old England, used to experience it." He did not seriously think he was unconverted, however. In his December 1722 exercise, he listed his four concerns as "the reason why I, *in the least*, question my interest in God's love and favor." The tone is positive rather than anxious. Concluding with the question of whether he was guilty of a certain sin, he "resolved, No." Similarly, the 1723 entry identified his conversion's variation from the classic pattern as "the chief thing, that now makes me *in any measure* to question my good estate." He went on to resolve not to doubt his salvation but to discover "the real reason, why they used to be converted in those steps."[3]

In another diary entry that has cast a shadow on his spiritual condition, Edwards wrote in May 1724, "It seems to me, that whether I am now converted or not, I am so settled in the state I am in, that I shall go on in it all my life." But again the tone is positive. The next sentence, rather than exhibiting despondency, contains his resolution not to rest in spiritual complacency. What Edwards recorded in his diary was the normal course of meditative self-examination that Puritan clergy had urged upon believers for well over a century. Edwards may have abandoned the earlier notion of conversion's preparatory stages, but his cycle of repentance of sin and renewal of grace typified the classic devotional pattern. Thus, his confession on Friday, December 21, that he was "exceedingly dull, dry and dead" was followed on Saturday night with the uplift of divine grace: "This day revived by God's Spirit. Affected with the sense of the excellency of holiness. Felt more exercise of love to Christ than usual." Moreover, as he wrote on Saturday, February 16, 1723, "I do certainly know that I love holiness, such as the gospel requires."[4]

Rather than undermine his 1739 spiritual autobiography, Edwards' diary entries actually undergird its credibility as a reliable expression, however stylized to suit its didactic purpose, of his religious experience. The "Personal Narrative" opens a window into Edwards' soul both as a young man in the early 1720s and as a journeyman pastor

3. *Letters and Personal Writings*, Works, 16:759, 779 (emphasis added).
4. Ibid., 16:788, 759, 766.

writing a decade and a half later about the progress of his relationship with God.

In the "Personal Narrative," Edwards described the "new sense" or "new sort of affection" as "quite different from anything I ever experienced before." Although he had had "concerns and exercises about my soul" and even several "remarkable seasons of awakening" as a boy, it was evident to him looking back that his "delight . . . in religious duties"—praying "five times a day in secret," building a hideout in a swamp for prayer with his pals, meditating alone in the woods—was merely "self-righteous pleasure." In a reflection that he would expand more fully in his analysis of religious psychology later in the 1740s when the Great Awakening's fervor had waned, he stated, "I am ready to think, many are deceived with such affections, and such a kind of delight, as I then had in religion, and mistake it for grace." The "lively and easily moved" affections or religious feelings that came naturally to Edwards, and to many others during the revivals, were not necessarily the work of God. In Edwards' case, not until his "last year at college" (after completing undergraduate studies, he continued at Yale as an M.A. student, 1720–22) was he "brought to seek salvation, in a manner that I never was before." These "great and violent inward struggles" began during a serious illness and persisted as "God would not suffer me to go on" when "I fell again into my old ways of sin" after recovering. Without "that kind of affection and delight" he had superficially enjoyed as a youth, young Edwards now "made seeking my salvation the main business of my life . . . to part with all things in the world, for an interest in Christ." The change finally came when he confronted his chief stumbling block, the Calvinist "doctrine of God's sovereignty, in choosing whom he would to eternal life, and rejecting whom he pleased." Although he professed inability to "give an account, how, or by what means," he fully submitted to "God's absolute sovereignty, and justice, with respect to salvation and damnation," even though "for a long time after" he could not say for sure that "there was any extraordinary influence of God's Spirit in it." He did testify, however, "Now I saw farther." Soon after this "wonderful alteration" of his mind on the doctrinal issue, Edwards recalled receiving a spiritual breakthrough while meditating on 1 Timothy 1:17. At the time, he was unaware of any "saving nature in this." He is quite candid that it is only in looking back that he can see God's hand. But Edwards' "new sense" of "inward, sweet delight in God and divine things" enabled him to consider this experience his conversion.[5]

5. *JE Reader*, 281–84.

In order to underscore, at least for his own sense of spiritual assurance, that he was soundly converted, on January 12, 1723, Edwards "made a solemn dedication of myself to God, and wrote it down." This is one of several explicit references in the "Personal Narrative" to his "Diary," "Resolutions," or other written meditations. The young New York City pastor recorded, "I have this day solemnly renewed my baptismal covenant and self-dedication, which I renewed when I was received into communion of the church. I have been before God; and have given myself, all that I am and have to God, so that I am not in any respect my own. . . . I have been to God this morning, and told him that I gave myself wholly to him. . . . And did believe in Jesus Christ, and receive him as a prince and a Savior. . . . That I did receive the blessed Spirit as my teacher, sanctifyer and only comforter; and cherish all his motions to enlighten, purify, confirm, comfort, and assist me." Edwards reiterated, "This I have done." As he confessed in the "Personal Narrative," "Resolutions," and "Diary," he always had "reason to be infinitely humbled" for "how much I have failed of answering my obligation." Good intentions are "all nothing, and to no purpose at all, without the motions of the Spirit of God." This ongoing repentance and even a certain anxious tension were essential parts of his assurance that he was in fact soundly converted. This exercise was, as he stated, a renewal or reaffirmation of what had already taken place in his soul.[6]

Edwards held from the start of his ministry that conversion was the decisive beginning—and only the beginning—of the spiritual life. He preached from John 3:3 in late 1730 or early 1731: "There is in conversion infused a principle of spiritual understanding and spiritual action that is far above any principles that man had before, as the heaven is high above the earth. . . . There is a new principle of will and inclination." In "The True Christian's Life a Journey Towards Heaven," delivered in 1733 just before his first Northampton revival erupted, he insisted, "When persons are converted they do but begin their work, and set out on the way they have to go. They never, till then, do anything of that work which their whole lives ought to be spent in." All prior striving occurred at the natural and human level. He argued in another important 1733 sermon, "A Divine and Supernatural Light," that even God's involvement in all people's lives by "common grace only assists the faculties of the soul to do that more fully, which they do by nature. . . . But in the renewing and sanctifying work of the Holy Ghost, those things are wrought in the soul that are above nature, and

6. Ibid., 268, 274–81, 288; *Letters and Personal Writings, Works,* 16:753–59, 762, 796–97.

of which there is nothing of the like kind in the soul by nature." It was therefore important for Edwards to establish in the "Personal Narrative" that while reading the 1 Timothy passage "there came into my soul, and was as it were diffused through it, a sense of the glory of the Divine Being, a new sense, quite different from anything I ever experienced before." He took pains to show that these new "delights which I now felt in things of religion, were of an exceeding different kind . . . totally of another kind" from his adolescent experiences. His earlier religious feelings "never reached the heart." They lacked "any taste of the soul-satisfying, and life-giving good" of the gospel. As if to signify the turning point, Edwards suddenly began to employ a new vocabulary to describe his experiences. God's sovereignty was no longer just revealed truth but a "bright and sweet doctrine." Religious activity no longer brought Edwards "delight" as before but "inward, sweet delight." Meditation on the enjoyment of God moved to the deeper level of being "as it were swallowed up in him," beyond mere "ideas of Christ" to "the beauty and excellency of his person," and "an inward, sweet sense of these things."[7]

Much is made of Edwards' meditations in and on nature—walking in the woods, gazing at the sky, contemplating thunder, which was formerly "so terrible" but now "so sweet to me" because it led to "sweet contemplations of my great and glorious God."[8] But Edwards most commonly meditated on biblical texts and doctrines when he retreated to such solitary settings. His pen's gushing forth of the word "sweet" (and "sweetness" and "sweetly") in the "Personal Narrative" is

7. *Sermons and Discourses, 1730–1733, Works,* 17:186–88, 441; *JE Reader,* 108, 283–84. Note Edwards' abrogation of seventeenth-century Puritan teaching on God's work in the stages of "preparation for salvation." For a good overview of Edwards' devotional life, see Allen C. Guelzo, "The Spiritual Structures of Jonathan Edwards," *Bulletin of the Congregational Library* (spring–fall 1993): 4–15. For Edwards' "new spiritual sense," see also Conrad Cherry, *The Theology of Jonathan Edwards: A Reappraisal* (1966; reprint, Bloomington: Indiana University Press, 1990), 27–39; Robert Jenson, *America's Theologian: A Recommendation of Jonathan Edwards* (New York: Oxford University Press, 1988), 65–78; Norman Fiering, *Jonathan Edwards' Moral Thought and Its British Context* (Chapel Hill: University of North Carolina Press, 1981), 123–29; William K. B. Stoever, "The Godly Will's Discerning: Shepard, Edwards, and the Identification of True Godliness," in *Jonathan Edwards's Writings: Text, Context, Interpretation,* ed. Stephen J. Stein (Bloomington: Indiana University Press, 1996), 85–99; Michael J. McClymond, *Encounters with God: An Approach to the Theology of Jonathan Edwards* (New York: Oxford University Press, 1998), 37–49.

8. See George Claghorn's introductory comment, *Letters and Personal Writings, Works,* 16:749; W. Clark Gilpin, "The Theology of Solitude: Edwards, Emerson, Dickinson," *Spiritus: A Journal of Christian Spirituality* (spring 2001): 33–35; Conrad Cherry, *Nature and Religious Imagination: From Edwards to Bushnell* (Philadelphia: Fortress, 1980).

itself derived from Scripture. The psalmist rhapsodizes, "My meditation of him shall be sweet: I will be glad in the Lord" (104:34 KJV) and "How sweet are thy words unto my taste! yea, sweeter than honey to my mouth!" (119:103 KJV), and David is referred to as "the sweet psalmist" (2 Sam. 23:1 KJV). More specifically, Edwards' vocabulary of "inward sweetness" derived from a devotional tradition rooted in the Song of Solomon, Canticles as the Puritans called it, and focused on the person of Jesus Christ. Edwards wrote in the "Personal Narrative" that after his conversion, "those words, Cant. 2:1, used to be abundantly with me: 'I am the rose of Sharon, the lily of the valleys.'" Even though the text employs nature imagery for the love it describes and Edwards would sometimes meditate "alone in the mountains, or some solitary wilderness," he made it plain that the "sense I had of divine things" centered on Christ: "The words seemed to me, sweetly to represent, the loveliness and beauty of Jesus Christ. And the whole Book of Canticles used to be pleasant to me; and I used to be much in reading it." Edwards' sense of "inward sweetness" would "carry me away in my contemplations," he wrote, "by a calm, sweet abstraction of soul from all the concerns of the world" to the extent that by "a kind of vision, or fixed ideas and imaginations" he was "sweetly conversing with Christ, and wrapped and swallowed up in God." Such religious affections would suddenly "kindle up a sweet burning in my heart; an ardor of my soul, that I know not how to express." Edwards here stood in a tradition of devotional use of Song of Solomon in which the word "sweet" often appeared with erotic overtones but was understood allegorically in reference to Christ's love. This tradition goes back at least to the medieval mystic Bernard of Clairvaux (1090–1153), whose books *On Loving God* and *The Twelve Degrees* were well known and often quoted in seventeenth-century Puritan sermons. In one of his meditations on Christ as the spiritual bridegroom of the Song of Solomon, Bernard wrote, "Jesu, the very thought of thee / With sweetness fills the breast; / But sweeter far thy face to see, / And in thy presence rest."[9]

This vocabulary of "inward sweetness" dominates Edwards' "Personal Narrative" for about ten pages in modern editions. He describes how his "sense of divine things" continued "in a much higher degree" in New York City, where he focused his meditations on God's holiness. He prayed that his yearning for "holy communion with Christ" would

9. *JE Reader*, 284; Charles E. Hambrick-Stowe, *The Practice of Piety: Puritan Devotional Disciplines in Seventeenth-Century New England* (Chapel Hill: University of North Carolina Press, 1982), 36; Tim Dowley, ed., *Eerdmans' Handbook to the History of Christianity* (Grand Rapids: Eerdmans, 1977), 260.

lead him to "sweet conformity to Christ" as "a complete Christian" living "according to the pure, sweet and blessed rules of the gospel." Spending "many sweet hours" on "the banks of Hudson's River"—sometimes in the company of John Smith in whose home he lived—in "sweet converse with God," Edwards meditated on the "sweet and powerful words" of Scripture and found that "every word seemed to touch my heart," and "every sentence" was like "refreshing ravishing food" for his soul. In the period between his New York pastorate and beginning as a tutor at Yale, his experiences continued along the same line, including "one special season of uncommon sweetness." Even after a time when "I sunk in religion" in New Haven, God through an illness "was pleased to visit me again with the sweet influences of his Spirit." Finally, during the years of his Northampton pastorate, he was able to record, "I have often had sweet complacency in God in views of his glorious perfection" and in contemplation of "the sweet and glorious doctrines" of God's sovereignty and grace and humanity's "absolute dependence on the operations of God's Holy Spirit." Moreover, "it has often been sweet to me to go to God" in adoration and "has often appeared sweet to me, to be united to Christ." Meditation, not on personal experience but on the Persons of the Trinity and on the gospel, brought "the sweetest joys of delights I have experienced." Christ's "blood and atonement has appeared sweet, and his righteousness sweet," and God "in the communications of his Holy Spirit, has appeared as an infinite fountain of divine glory and sweetness . . . pouring forth itself in sweet communications, like the sun in its glory, sweetly and pleasantly diffusing light and Life."[10]

If this heaping up of sweetness seems unbearably cloying to modern sensibilities—he uses the word fifty-five times in ten pages and two more times in his conclusion—it is never just treacly sentimentality. The wonder of God's grace is always bestowed in the face of human depravity. In the "Personal Narrative," Edwards suddenly cuts the sweetness with two full pages of confession of his "own sinfulness and vileness" throughout his Northampton ministry, "the badness of my heart, since my conversion." Counterbalancing his ecstatic "ardency of spirit, and inward strugglings and breathings and groanings that cannot be uttered," which attended his meditations on Christ's mercy, Edwards confides that he was not infrequently reduced to "a kind of loud weeping, sometimes for a considerable time together" in repentance—knowing that "my repentance was nothing [compared] to my sin." Such "turns of weeping and crying for my sins" produced, however, "a more full and constant sense of the absolute sovereignty

10. *JE Reader*, 288–93.

of God . . . and a sense of the glory of Christ as mediator." He refers to several Saturday nights when in his devotions it was once again "sweet beyond all expression, to follow Christ." One recent Saturday night in particular, in January 1739, just months before writing the "Personal Narrative," he records his "sense, how sweet and blessed a thing it was, to walk in the way of duty," to conform to "the holy mind of God." During his exercises that night in preparation for the Sabbath, "it caused me to break forth into a kind of loud weeping"—for joy this time—"which held me some time; so that I was forced to shut myself up, and fasten the doors. I could not but as it were cry out, 'How happy are they which do that which is right in the sight of God! They are blessed indeed, they are the happy ones!'" He concludes his "Personal Narrative," "I rejoiced in it, that God reigned, and that his will was done."[11]

The spiritual journals and autobiographies of many New England Puritans include the Bernard-like language employed by Edwards, in which the holiness of Christ is "ravishingly lovely" and the soul is "like a field or garden of God" or like "a little white flower . . . opening its blossom . . . in a calm rapture; diffusing around a sweet fragrancy." Edward Taylor, whose meditative poetry came to light only in the mid–twentieth century, is the most dramatic example. Taylor was pastor from 1671 until his 1725 retirement in Westfield, Massachusetts, just seventeen miles south of Northampton, where Edwards became his grandfather Solomon Stoddard's assistant pastor in 1726. Taylor, who died in 1729, had been Stoddard's adversary in the controversy over admission to the Lord's Supper and the unconventional Stoddardean view of the sacrament as a converting ordinance. These issues were reignited by Jonathan Edwards, who came to oppose his late grandfather's openness in favor of stricter standards toward the end of the 1740s, leading to his famous dismissal by the Northampton church in 1750. In the tension between the ideals of a pure church and a comprehensive church, Edwards moved after the Great Awakening toward the side of purity, the side exemplified in the Connecticut River Valley a generation before by Edward Taylor.[12]

11. Ibid., 294–96.

12. Ibid., 287–88. For Taylor's opposition to Stoddard, see Norman S. Grabo, ed., *Edward Taylor's Treatise concerning the Lord's Supper* (East Lansing: Michigan State University Press, 1966); Thomas M. and Virginia Davis, eds., *Edward Taylor vs. Solomon Stoddard: The Nature of the Lord's Supper* (Boston: Twayne, 1981); and Mark A. Peterson, *The Price of Redemption: The Spiritual Economy of Puritan New England* (Stanford, Calif.: Stanford University Press, 1997), 157–60. On his change of mind, see Jonathan Edwards, *The Works of Jonathan Edwards*, vol. 12, *Ecclesiastical Writings*, ed. David D. Hall (New Haven: Yale University Press, 1994), especially Hall's excellent "Editor's Introduction."

Taylor's entirely private poems, composed between 1683 and 1725 on Saturday nights before communion Sundays as part of his devotional preparation for the Sabbath, from first to last are preoccupied with the intimate spirituality of the Song of Solomon. One of his earliest poems, on the theme "I am the Rose of Sharon," contains the lines:

> Lord lead me into this sweet Rosy Bower:
>   Oh! Lodge my Soul in this Sweet Rosy bed:
> Array my Soul with this sweet Sharon flower:
>   Perfume me with the Odours it doth shed.
>   Wealth, Pleasure, Beauty Spirituall will line
>   My pretious Soul, if Sharons Rose be mine.

And one of his last—from "Canticles 2:3. His fruit was Sweet to my Tast[e]"—begins:

> Sweet Lord, all sweet from top to bottom all
>   From Heart to hide, sweet, mostly sweet.
> Sweet Manhood and sweet Godhead and ere shall.
>   Thou art the best of Sweeting. And so keep.
>   Thou art made up of best of sweetness brast.
>   Thy fruit is ever sweet unto my tast.

Taylor's regular devotions reached their most sublime level as he wrote these love songs for Jesus Christ. Jonathan Edwards never saw Taylor's poetry. But the two pastors, a generation apart, shared the intensely personal spirituality of evangelical Calvinism in the Puritan tradition. In a manner similar to Taylor, Edwards would, as he recalled, "sing over" the texts on which he was meditating before he "went to prayer, to pray to God that I might enjoy him." He would "sing or chant forth my meditations; to speak my thoughts in soliloquies, and speak with a singing voice." In solitude "it was always my manner . . . to sing forth my contemplations." This intensely personal, almost mystical, evangelical spirituality persisted as an ingredient in the religious culture of Puritan New England as late as the 1730s and early 1740s. It was in that context, and with the hope of renewing that culture in the face of Enlightenment rationalism, that Jonathan Edwards sought to bring the people of his community to a "new spiritual sense" of Christ in the revivals of religion sparked by his preaching.[13]

13. *JE Reader,* 284–88; Donald E. Stanford, ed., *The Poems of Edward Taylor* (New Haven: Yale University Press, 1960), 12, 379. See also Charles E. Hambrick-Stowe, ed., *Early New England Meditative Poetry: Anne Bradstreet and Edward Taylor* (New York: Paulist Press, 1988).

In "A Divine and Supernatural Light," delivered in 1733, Edwards advanced the powerful and controversial doctrine of the Holy Spirit as that "spiritual and divine light, immediately imparted to the soul by God" in conversion. Mark Valeri writes that this lecture-sermon "condensed much of a decade of preaching, rumination, and private writing on the nature of spiritual knowledge into a singular, remarkable effort" and also "set forth many of the themes that undergirded his preaching through the Great Awakening." It was, therefore, a pivotal communication, setting the stage and providing a vocabulary for the widespread experience of the kind of powerful intimacy with God that Edwards knew personally. The first sign of spiritual awakening in Northampton came toward the end of 1733, as Edwards wrote a few years later in *A Faithful Narrative of the Surprising Work of God,* when "there appeared a very unusual flexibleness, and yielding to advice, in our young people." They began actually to listen to his sermons. New converts related personally to him the "glorious work of God's infinite power and sovereign grace" in giving "a new heart, truly broken and sanctified." The revival "increased more and more; souls did as it were come by flocks to Jesus Christ," and in worship many were "in tears while the Word was preached; some weeping with sorrow and distress, others with joy and love, others with pity and concern for the souls of their neighbors." The town's youth gathered regularly for religious meetings to discuss God's "glorious work in the conversion of a soul" and "the sweetness of his perfections," while many already-established church members felt their faith "enlivened and renewed with fresh and extraordinary incomes of the Spirit of God." Over the course of the 1730s, as Ava Chamberlain has shown, Edwards moved only gradually to the position that the believer's "new spiritual sense" by itself was an unreliable indicator of grace and that the spiritual fruits of sustained godly behavior were the best means of assurance. In 1733 and 1734, he emphasized the reality of "spiritual knowledge," the "sense of the heart," the "indwelling vital principle" of the Holy Spirit, which God "imparts . . . immediately, not making use of any intermediate natural causes." His preaching was rewarded for a time with the "surprising work of God in the conversion of many hundred souls."[14]

14. Mark Valeri, introductory note to "A Divine and Supernatural Light," in *Sermons and Discourses, 1730–1733, Works,* 17:406; Jonathan Edwards, *The Works of Jonathan Edwards,* vol. 4, *The Great Awakening,* ed. C. C. Goen (New Haven: Yale University Press, 1972), 128–29, 147–52; *JE Reader,* 108, 121. In both *JE Reader* and *Sermons of Jonathan Edwards: A Reader,* "A Divine and Supernatural Light" is unfortunately dated in 1734, its publication date, rather than 1733 when it was preached. The year is significant for its indication of whether the sermon was delivered before or after the onset of the revival.

Edwards drew upon the theological and spiritual reflections recorded in his private notebooks when he wrote "A Divine and Supernatural Light," cutting and pasting phrases, sentences, and blocks of
material. Chamberlain has argued that these "Miscellanies" should be
understood alongside the "Personal Narrative" and "Diary" as "a record of Edwards' affective inner life," composed "not simply as an intellectual exercise but as a devotional discipline" to express "his
heart's delight in the 'glorious things of the gospel.'"[15] In "Miscellanies" dated by Thomas Schafer to 1729 and 1730, Edwards posited
that "the first act of the Spirit of God . . . is in spiritual understanding,
or in the sense of the mind, its perception of glory and excellency, etc.
in the ideas it has of divine things; and this is before any proper acts
of the will." By this "sense or taste . . . the mind in many things distin-
guishes truth from falsehood." Further, "the Holy Ghost influences the
godly as dwelling in them as a vital principle, or as a new supernatural
principle of life and action." By "the sanctifying work of the Holy
Ghost," God boosts the believer's natural faculties to a new level, and
more importantly, "those principles are restored that were utterly destroyed by the fall." Indeed, "the Spirit of God in the souls of his saints
exerts its own proper nature. . . . The Holy Ghost influences the minds
of the godly by living in the godly."[16] To borrow a sentence from David
Hall's analysis of "Miscellanies" entries during the much later controversy over the meaning of church membership and admission to the
Lord's Supper, Edwards "craved in his parishioners the same intensity
of commitment he felt within himself."[17]

The danger in Edwards' passionate spirituality was the way it
flirted at the edge of what the Puritans had called "antinomianism,"
the giddy spiritual excitement of the Separates who in the Great
Awakening fled "impure" established congregations for higher spiritual ground, the kind of emotion-driven religion then commonly
branded "enthusiasm." Edwards vigorously attacked Enlightenment
rationalism and the movement among rationalist-oriented Congregationalists, especially in the Boston area, toward enthusiasm's polar opposite—"formalism." Formalists not only favored the head over the
heart—they would frown on any tears in the pews—but they also
tended to reduce the life of faith to ethical behavior. Edwards thus
viewed the greatest threat to New England's spiritual vitality to be the

15. Ava Chamberlain, introduction to *The Works of Jonathan Edwards*, vol. 18, *The
"Miscellanies,"* 501–832, ed. Ava Chamberlain (New Haven: Yale University Press, 2000), 8.

16. Jonathan Edwards, *The Works of Jonathan Edwards*, vol. 13, *The "Miscellanies,"*
a–500, ed. Thomas A. Schafer (New Haven: Yale University Press, 1994), 102, 106, 462–
63, 512–13.

17. David D. Hall, introduction to *Ecclesiastical Writings, Works*, 12:46.

trend toward Arminianism, the elevated view of human ability in the spiritual realm and the consequent devaluation of God's absolute sovereignty. Arminian formalism would cool down the spiritual climate to such a degree that the way of salvation would be lost. Jonathan Edwards invited his people to join him at the very edge of what the genteel Boston clergy considered respectable religion. At the same time, he did so with some care, wary of the chaos Puritans associated with unbridled "enthusiasm." At the conclusion of "A Divine and Supernatural Light," for example, he preached that "this light, and this only"—that is, not natural ability or "notional understanding"—"has its fruit in an universal holiness of life." Pointing in the direction he would go in *Religious Affections* after his disappointment with massive backsliding after the Awakening of 1740–42, Edwards concluded, "This light, as it reaches the bottom of the heart, and changes the nature, so it will effectually dispose to an universal obedience . . . a sincere love to God, which is the only principle of a true, gracious and universal obedience." As Ann Taves has shown, Edwards argued that "the Spirit of God operated *directly* through its indwelling in the new spiritual sense of the saints," but without relying on a subjective "witness of the Spirit" apart from objective, external, biblically grounded, behavioral fruits of the Spirit. Edwards sought to lead his people to the experiential edge, but without plunging into enthusiasm. It was a dangerous place to be, a place where it is easy to be misunderstood by both sides.[18]

Edwards' balancing act became more difficult in the 1740s when he analyzed the impact of the Great Awakening on New England religion. He delivered "The Distinguishing Marks of a Work of the Spirit of God" at the Yale commencement in September 1741, just after James Davenport's hysterical and disruptive evangelistic summer tour of southern Connecticut. It was an effort to salvage the revival through calm diplomacy: "Some of the true friends of the work of God's Spirit have erred in giving too much heed to impulses and strong impressions on their minds, as though they were immediate significations from heaven to them of something that should come to pass, or something that it was the mind and will of God that they should do, which was not signified or revealed anywhere in the Bible without those impulses." Edwards was especially vigilant against the notion that spiritual persons could distinguish between who was saved and who was not. A few years later, in *Religious Affections*, he criticized such "en-

18. *JE Reader*, 124; Ann Taves, *Fits, Trances & Visions: Experiencing Religion and Explaining Experience from Wesley to James* (Princeton: Princeton University Press, 1999), 34–41, 48–50.

thusiastical supposed manifestation[s]," which were "excited in the
imagination" or by "some pleasant bodily sensation" at the natural
level "by the animal spirits, or by the body," concluding that they were
not only mistaken but could be "delusions of Satan." Despite the horror he saw in the "dreadful dance" and "woeful extravagancies" of enthusiasm, though, he refused to back away from the powerful and intimate relationship with God through the indwelling Holy Spirit in the
"new spiritual sense." He even dared to appropriate the epithet "enthusiasm" in a positive way. In *Some Thoughts concerning the Present
Revival of Religion* in 1742, he described his wife Sarah's remarkable
experience (without naming her) as exemplary of true piety. He was
simply in awe of the manner in which she was "perfectly overwhelmed and swallowed up with light and love and a sweet solace . . .
for five or six hours together" with a "sense of the infinite beauty and
amiableness of Christ's person, and the heavenly sweetness of his excellent and transcendent love." He rhapsodized, "Now if such things
are enthusiasm, and the fruits of a distempered brain, let my brain be
evermore possessed of that happy distemper!"[19]

Edwards presented the life of a young friend, an ailing missionary
to Native Americans who died in the Northampton parsonage, as his
final effort to typify true religious experience. *The Life of David
Brainerd*, Edwards' edited version of his diary and journal published
in 1749, reveals Brainerd as a deeply introspective and God-absorbed
believer whose faith expressed itself in sacrificial service, constant
travel on behalf of the gospel, pious behavior, and faithfulness in sick-
ness and death. Despite his chronic, crippling melancholia—toned
down somewhat by Edwards' editing—*The Life of David Brainerd* expressed, in Ann Taves' words, "the devotional ideal embraced by the
moderate Reformed wing of the revival" with its middle way between
formalism and enthusiasm. It was "the popular capstone" to Edwards'
writings on the spiritual life through the decade and a half since the
onset of the revivals. The revivals needed to be vindicated, according
to Edwards, because "experimental religion" and even the experience
of "being 'born again'" had fallen into disrepute on account of "the
bad lives of some professors" who "manifest[ed] no abiding alteration
in their moral disposition and behavior." Brainerd's life would demonstrate that there was "such a thing as true experimental religion, arising from immediate divine influences, supernaturally enlightening
and convincing the mind, and powerfully impressing, quickening,

19. *Great Awakening, Works,* 4:278, 282, 332, 341; Jonathan Edwards, *The Works of Jonathan Edwards,* vol. 2, *Religious Affections,* ed. John E. Smith (New Haven: Yale University Press, 1959), 286, 288; Taves, *Fits, Trances & Visions,* 61–62.

sanctifying, and governing the heart." Recounting the attributes of his friend's spiritual life, Edwards once again challenged, "[I]f all these things are the fruits of enthusiasm, why should not enthusiasm be thought a desirable and excellent thing?" But of course Edwards' point was that Brainerd was no enthusiast. He explained that Brainerd's sense of "the sanctifying and comforting power of God's Spirit did not begin in some bodily sensation, any pleasant warm feeling in his breast that he (as some others) called the feeling the love of Christ in him, and being full of the Spirit." Indeed, "if we look through the whole series of his experiences, from his conversion to his death, we shall find none of this kind." No trances, no extraordinary visions, no personal communications or secret knowledge, not even a special sense of "joy excited from a supposed immediate witness of the Spirit" could be found in the diary according to Edwards. When passages did seem to verge on describing some "immediate witness," Edwards would edit or omit them altogether.[20]

Unhappily, by 1749 it was too late for Edwards to sustain his ministry in a way that effectively charted some middle course. His desire for the church to become a purer community of believers able to testify to the "new spiritual sense" of God's indwelling Holy Spirit drove him into conflict with his people. Finally, the congregation voted to remove Edwards as pastor, forcing him to leave Northampton. What may have taken Edwards by surprise was that the vote to dismiss him came from church members who had experienced conversion and been received into the covenant under his pastorate. After battling his whole career between the extremes of rationalistic Arminian formalism and antinomian, or radically evangelical, enthusiasm, he seems to have been blindsided by a religious alternative he had not adequately discerned or taken seriously. David Hall, in his substantial introduction to the Yale edition of the documents pertaining to the controversy, has identified a strain of "popular religion" in the Connecticut River Valley. For many church members, the priority was neither Enlightenment rationalism nor evangelical experientialism but a family-oriented kind of faith in which the sacraments and other community practices were paramount. For these New Englanders, church membership entailed an "intermingling of the social and the religious." Asking the question of why Edwards changed his mind on the issue of admission to the Lord's Supper, Hall points out that he "was not under pressure from a New Light faction in his congregation or from friends

20. Jonathan Edwards, *The Works of Jonathan Edwards*, vol. 7, *The Life of David Brainerd*, ed. Norman Pettit (New Haven: Yale University Press, 1985), 502–5, 81–83; Taves, *Fits, Trances & Visions*, 49–50.

and colleagues in the ministry to purify the church." Edwards had rejected both the Separates' premises that "the regenerate could recognize who was truly a saint and who was not" and the claim that the inner "witness of the Spirit" was reliable. But he did believe that the new "sense of the heart" would result in godly behavior (sanctification) discernibly different from natural efforts at goodness. Evangelical Calvinism held that nature and grace were of two different realms—hence Edwards' insistence, already noted, that in "the renewing and sanctifying work of the Holy Ghost, those things are wrought in the soul that are above nature, and of which there is nothing of the like kind in the soul by nature." Thus, the kind of social, family-based faith of popular religion was not true religion at all. And Edwards did insist, Hall points out, "that true religion could be differentiated from hypocrisy." He had come to the terrible conclusion that "most of his congregation" were hypocrites. The congregation, meanwhile, recognized that their pastor "wished to abolish what for them was basic, the procedures that linked family structure and religion."[21]

The powerful intimacy of Edwards' relationship with his Creator and Redeemer and his keen sense of human sinfulness provided the tension that brought vibrancy to his preaching and helped spark the Great Awakening. His sincere pastoral desire to lift his community to new spiritual heights ironically led to an irreparable rift between him and the congregation. But Edwards' vision of a people redeemed by God's grace and living in personal communion with Jesus Christ could not be so easily dismissed. Following his departure from Northampton, during his Stockbridge ministry, he concentrated on publishing the massive works of theology that would flesh out his understanding of true religion and establish his legacy for future generations. In the years following his death at Princeton in 1758 and then after the American Revolution and through the first decades of the nineteenth century, Edwardsianism remained influential and even flourished for a time. Edwardsians like Samuel Hopkins, Sarah Osborn, Lemuel Haynes, and scores of other New England pastors attempted to spread his kind of evangelical Calvinism in the new nation in ongoing revivals of religion. Of course, it was the evangelical Arminianism of the Methodist movement, with its appropriation of the camp meeting and its broad appeal to blacks and whites throughout the United States, including in the South and on the frontier, that became the chief en-

21. David D. Hall, "Introduction," in *Ecclesiastical Writings, Works,* 12:51–53, 57, 60, 83–84; *JE Reader,* 108. Hall explores popular lay religion in *Worlds of Wonder, Days of Judgment: Popular Religious Belief in Early New England* (New York: Knopf, 1989), esp. 130–39, 150–62.

gine of experiential religion in the early nineteenth century. John Wesley, more than Edwards, had given the "witness of the Spirit"—and even visions and ecstatic responses—a central place in his theology of religious experience.[22] Later in the nineteenth century, the Holiness movement and then Pentecostalism at the turn of the twentieth century carried revivalism forward in ways that contain echoes of the Connecticut Valley in 1734–35 and 1740–42. The issues with which Jonathan Edwards wrestled in his pastoral career, as he strove to share with others the "inward, sweet sense" of Christ that gave his own life meaning—sometimes with glorious success, sometimes in agonizing failure—remain fundamental issues for believers and for the church in the twenty-first century.

22. Taves, *Fits, Trances & Visions,* 50–58.

PART 2

THEOLOGY

5

✦

CHALLENGING THE PRESUMPTIONS OF THE AGE

The Two Dissertations

George M. Marsden

By the 1750s Edwards was feeling an increasing sense of urgency to respond to the intellectual-theological crisis of his time. By that time, what we call "the Enlightenment" and what Edwards called ironically "this age of light and inquiry" was waxing toward its meridian.[1] Edwards was determined to demonstrate, as only a true philosopher of the age could, that what most of its proponents took to be the sun was only a dim, reflected light.

By the time of his death in 1758, Edwards had completed writing the last of his great contributions to this project, the "two dissertations," *Concerning the End for Which God Created the World* and *The Nature of True Virtue*. He had not, however, transcribed these treatises into his legible public hand, so they were not published until 1765. These companion pieces illustrate Edwards' most direct answer to the broad Enlightenment assumptions of his day. Because those Enlight-

---

This chapter is adapted from George M. Marsden, *Jonathan Edwards: A Life* (New Haven: Yale University Press, 2003) and is used by permission.

1. Jonathan Edwards, *The Works of Jonathan Edwards*, vol. 1, *Freedom of the Will*, ed. Paul Ramsey (New Haven: Yale University Press, 1957), 437.

enment assumptions had such a large impact on subsequent Western thought, Edwards' views are still of interest today.

In February 1757, Edwards described these two treatises to Thomas Foxcroft, his Boston colleague and literary agent, as answering "the modern opinions which prevail concerning these two things, [which] stand very much as foundations of that fashionable scheme of divinity, which seems to have become almost universal."[2] The fashionable answers to these two related questions, he believed, lay at the root of what had gone wrong in modern thought: "What is the purpose for which God created the universe?" and "What is the nature of true virtue?"

Why Would God Create a Universe?

The key to understanding Edwards' thought is that everything is related because everything is related to God. Truth, a dimension of God's love and beauty, is part of that quintessentially bright light that pours forth from the throne of God. Every other pretended light, or source of truth, is as darkness if it keeps God's creatures from seeing the great sun of God's light. The created universe itself is a dynamic expression of that light. Yet sin blinds humans from acknowledging the source of the light that surrounds them. Having turned away from the true light of God's love, they now grope in darkness, inordinately loving themselves and their immediate surroundings or chasing after false lights of their own imaginings. Only the undeserved gift of redemption, bought with Christ's blood, can open their eyes and change their hearts so that they see and love the Triune God and the created universe as wholly an expression of God's creative and redemptive will. Only through the prism of the revelation recorded in Scripture can they discover the nature of God's creative and redemptive purposes. Once sinners experience God's love, they begin to love what he loves.

If we recognize this essentially Augustinian framework that shapes all of Edwards' thought, it becomes apparent that the dissertation *Concerning the End for Which God Created the World* was a sort of prolegomena to all his work. Although he paired it specifically with *The Nature of True Virtue*, the most philosophical of his writings, to which its theology is the necessary premise, *Concerning the End for Which God Created the World* might be seen as the logical starting point for

2. Jonathan Edwards to Thomas Foxcroft, 11 February 1757, in Jonathan Edwards, *The Works of Jonathan Edwards*, vol. 16, *Letters and Personal Writings*, ed. George S. Claghorn (New Haven: Yale University Press, 1998), 696.

all of his thinking.[3] Had he lived to work on his great projected "History of the Work of Redemption," the dissertation would have surely been a point of departure for that "body of divinity in an entire new method."[4]

Concerning the End for Which God Created the World, while often highly acclaimed, is one of the less read (and less easy to read) of Edwards' treatises because it focuses on the narrow starting point for this larger theological vision. Nevertheless, this theological and scriptural prolegomena is essential for understanding how Edwards positioned himself in relation to the prevailing philosophies of the era.

Eighteenth-century moral philosophers and moral popularizers were increasingly speaking of the deity as a benevolent governor whose ultimate interest must be to maximize human happiness. Alexander Pope's *Essay on Man* (1734) is the best-known popular expression:

> All Chance, Direction, which thou canst not see:
> All Discord, Harmony not understood;
> All partial Evil, universal Good:
> And, spite of Pride, in erring Reason's spite,
> One truth is clear, "WHATEVER IS, IS RIGHT."

Edwards himself might have assented to these few lines, justifying the ways of God to man. He and his friends were deeply engaged in a similar enterprise.[5] But in Pope's version the natural order was essentially benevolent.

> God in nature of each being, founds
> Its proper bliss, and sets its proper bounds:
> But as he fram'd the Whole, the Whole to bless,
> On mutual Wants built mutual Happiness:

3. Edwards had developed the basic argument in earlier "Miscellanies," such as nos. 445, 461 (1729–30) in Jonathan Edwards, *The Works of Jonathan Edwards,* vol. 13, *The "Miscellanies," a–500,* ed. Thomas A. Schafer (New Haven: Yale University Press, 1994); and "Miscellanies," 702 (1736–37) in Jonathan Edwards, *The Works of Jonathan Edwards,* vol. 18, *The "Miscellanies," 501–832,* ed. Ava Chamberlain (New Haven: Yale University Press, 2000).

4. Jonathan Edwards to Trustees of the College of New Jersey, 19 October 1757, in *Letters and Personal Writings, Works,* 16:727–28.

5. Bellamy, for instance, published his sermon on "The Wisdom of God in Permission of Sin" in 1758, which Edwards had likely read and approved before he left Stockbridge. See Joseph Bellamy, *Sermons upon the Following Subjects, viz. The Divinity of Christ, The Millenium, The Wisdom of God, in the Permission of Sin* (Boston: Edes and Gill, and S. Kneeland, 1758).

So from the first, eternal ORDER ran,
And creature link'd to creature, man to man.[6]

Voltaire's *Candide* (1759), a bitter satire on the idea of the "best of all possible worlds," written in the aftermath of the Lisbon earthquake of 1755 and at nearly the same time Edwards was finishing his dissertation, represents another well-known pole in this same debate concerning God's purposes. Whether the "best of all possible worlds" was celebrated by a popularizer like Pope or a sophisticate like the German Leibniz (who was in some ways like Edwards without the Calvinism),[7] the French *philosophe* thought it demonstrably nonsense. Yet like other moralists of his day, Voltaire believed that following the light of nature would lead toward human self-improvement.

Edwards' *Concerning the End for Which God Created the World*, in the meantime, sidestepped all secondary questions such as the problem of evil or of eternal punishment and concentrated on a crucial prior issue. If "our modern freethinkers"[8] were determining God's character by gauging what sort of universe would maximize human happiness, they were starting at the wrong end by looking first at humans' interests rather than at God's. In effect, they were setting up principles regarding human happiness as higher than God, since they were insisting God must conform to these principles. Or, to put it in the framework in which Edwards addressed the issue, they were setting up their own perceptions of what constituted the greatest human happiness as the ultimate (or highest) end or reason that God created the universe.

Edwards insisted that any inquiry into the ultimate end for which God created the universe must be derived from knowledge of the revealed character of God. The heart of Edwards' exposition was his analysis of the many scriptural references indicating that the highest end of creation is "the glory of God." As in all of Edwards' thought, his premise was that God is infinitely above all his creatures and is infinitely good. While it would be inappropriate for an inferior being to be ultimately motivated by self-love, preeminent love to self is not in-

6. Alexander Pope, *An Essay on Man*, ed. Maynard Mack (London: Methuen, 1950 [1734]), epistle 1, lines 289–94, 50–51; epistle 3, lines 109–14, 103.

7. For some comparison of Edwards with Gottfried Wilhelm Leibniz (1646–1716), see Paul Ramsey, "Introduction," in *Freedom of the Will, Works*, 1:113–17.

8. Edwards uses this phrase in a reference to the antagonists to whom the dissertation is addressed. Jonathan Edwards, *Concerning the End for Which God Created the World*, in *The Works of Jonathan Edwards*, vol. 8, *Ethical Writings*, ed. Paul Ramsey (New Haven: Yale University Press, 1989), 536.

appropriate to a being who is infinitely good, since self-love in that case is simply to love what is infinitely good.

Yet why would such an infinitely good, perfect, and eternal being create? How could creation of the time-bound and less than perfect be anything other than a diminishment of God? Here Edwards drew on the Christian trinitarian conception of God as essentially interpersonal. While Edwards did not emphasize the trinitarian basis of the argument (as with most topics, he had expounded that subject in another manuscript),[9] he did allude to it to make the point that God's infinite goodness is essentially the goodness of love, expressed first in intertrinitarian love such as between the Father and the Son.

The ultimate reason that God creates, said Edwards, is not to remedy some lack in God but to extend that perfect internal communication of the Triune God's goodness and love. It is an extension of the glory of a perfectly good and loving being to communicate that love to other intelligent beings. God's joy and happiness and delight in divine perfections is expressed externally by communicating that happiness and delight to created beings. God's internal perfections or glory radiates externally like the light that radiates from the sun. The glory of God, according to Edwards,

> is fitly compared to an effulgence or emanation of light from a luminary, by which this glory of God is abundantly represented in Scripture. Light is the external expression, exhibition and manifestation of the excellency of the luminary, of the sun for instance: it is the abundant, extensive emanation and communication of the fullness of the sun to innumerable beings that partake of it.[10]

The happiness of humans, then, when rightly understood, is not an ultimate end of creation in any way apart from God and God's glory. As Edwards observes, "The beams of glory come from God, and are something of God, and are refunded back again to their original. So that the whole is *of* God, and *in* God, and *to* God; and God is the beginning, middle and end in this affair."[11]

This last sentence encapsulates the central premise of his entire thought. It is as though the universe is an explosion of God's glory. Perfect goodness, beauty, and love radiate from God and draw creatures to share ever increasingly in the Godhead's joy and delight.

9. See Jonathan Edwards, *An Unpublished Essay of Edwards on the Trinity*, ed. George P. Fisher (New York: Charles Scribner's Sons, 1903).

10. *Concerning the End, Works*, 8:530, cf. 526–30.

11. Ibid., 531.

"God's respect to the creature's good, and his respect to himself," Edwards explains,

> is not a divided respect; but both are united in one, as the happiness of the creature aimed at is happiness in union with himself. . . . The more happiness the greater union: when the happiness is perfect, the union is perfect. And as the happiness will be increasing to eternity, the union will become more and more strict and perfect; nearer and more like to that between the Father and the Son.

The ultimate end of creation, then, is union in love between God and loving creatures. Since eternity is infinite, this union between God and the saints can be ever increasing, like a line ascending toward an infinite height but never reaching it. So the saints' happiness will continually increase as they are drawn ever closer toward perfect union with the Godhead.[12]

This conception of an exploding, God-centered universe in which God creates in order to share divine happiness ever increasingly with his creatures had countless theological implications that Edwards had long since been working on in his publications and notebooks. He looked forward to his *magnum opus*, "The History of Redemption," where he would treat all of these and many other theological issues in their place. First, however, he was determined to show how a consistent theology that recognized a loving and dynamic creator God would undercut the most influential philosophy of the era.

"True Virtue" in an Age of "Virtue"

Edwards addressed *The Nature of True Virtue* to the eighteenth-century philosophers. Though he paired it with a theological treatise, he had kept the theology of *Concerning the End for Which God Created the World* as broadly Christian as he could in order to establish a wide foundation for his philosophical analysis of virtue. Unlike any of his other works, in *The Nature of True Virtue* Edwards did not quote any Scripture, although he did appeal to its authority for the theistic basis of his ethics. His object was to establish an analysis in which, if one granted merely a few essential principles of Christian theology, one would be forced to reconsider the whole direction of eighteenth-century moral philosophy.

12. Ibid., 533 (quotation), 534.

To feel the force of this challenge, we must view Edwards and *The Nature of True Virtue* in their international context.[13] In broadest terms, the British moralists since the time of John Locke were attempting to establish a new moral philosophy as a science that would be equivalent to the new natural philosophy, or natural science. True to the spirit of the age, modern thinkers were striving to establish firm foundations for knowledge that would be universally valid for all humans. Christendom, ever since the Reformation, had been torn by the absolutist dogmas of warring religious authorities. The grand hope of the modern moral philosophers was that they could discover universally valid moral standards with which they could adjudicate competing absolute claims and in effect stand above them.

In the English-speaking world, the overwhelming consensus was that the foundations for a universal morality must have an empirical as well as a rational base. Just as the natural laws of the physical world could be established on the foundations of universal principles of perception, so the philosophers of the day believed that moral principles could be based on similarly firm foundations that no reasonable person could doubt. John Locke was the best-known progenitor of this project. Not only did he develop an empirical philosophy that explained perceptions of the physical world, but he also established a political philosophy based on "self-evident" first principles of morality, most notably the rights to life, liberty, and property. Since Locke's time, the discussions had advanced on many fronts among a whole school of British moralists. Most were attempting to show that normal human beings were endowed with powers to know and to obey the moral laws that were built into the scheme of things, just like any other natural laws.

The new moral philosophy was part of the modern project that made nature normative for understanding the self and self-understanding normative for morality. The Reformation challenged the mediatorial role of the church but asserted the authority of Scripture as the preeminent source of theology and ethics. It also encouraged, as was notable among Puritans, examination of one's own experience to determine whether one was truly a recipient of God's redeeming

13. Norman Fiering, *Jonathan Edwards's Moral Thought and Its British Context* (Chapel Hill: University of North Carolina Press, 1981), provides by far the most comprehensive account of the context for Edwards' moral thought. Equally important are Paul Ramsey's extensive editorial comments, *Works*, vol. 8, including his introduction, notes on the text, and lengthy appendices, especially appendix 2, "Jonathan Edwards on Moral Sense, and the Sentimentalists," 689–705, in which he takes serious issue with Fiering. My account is informed by these and many other works, although I do not think it follows any one closely, except as indicated.

grace. In England after the Puritan era, the immediate sequel was
Cambridge Platonism, which de-emphasized dogma and asserted human abilities to be attuned to the divine. The next step, suggested especially by the Third Earl of Shaftesbury (1671–1713), was to posit a
natural moral sense that was a reliable guide to the moral principles a
benevolent creator had built into the natural order.[14]

Francis Hutcheson (1694–1746), a Scottish ex-Calvinist, best developed Shaftesbury's views. His *Inquiry concerning Beauty, Order, Harmony, Design* (1725) established him as the most influential moral
philosopher of the era and the one whom Edwards was most eager to
counter. Moralists since Locke were agreed that humans must be endowed by the Creator with a natural faculty with which to make reliable moral judgments. They were divided, however, between those
who insisted that this moral faculty was dependent on the right judgment of intellect and those who, like Shaftesbury and Hutcheson,
viewed it as a "moral sense." All agreed that the moral faculty led people to approve of benevolence and that benevolence could be perceived as a type of beauty, since benevolence promoted harmony versus disharmony. Hutcheson argued that the moral sense, also called
"conscience," was closely analogous to a *sense* of beauty: "What is approved by this sense we count as *right* and *beautiful,* and call it *virtue;*
what is condemned, we count as *base* and *deformed* and vicious."[15]

Edwards' language and categories sounded a lot like Hutcheson's
because the two had worked within the same wider eighteenth-century discourse. Edwards had long since expounded on a spiritual
sense analogous to a sense of beauty and had made that familiar principle the bedrock of his analysis in *Religious Affections.* For Edwards a
truly spiritual sense of beauty was what distinguished the regenerate
from the unregenerate. Hutcheson, by contrast, had been arguing that
all of humankind were endowed by their Creator with a sense of
moral beauty sufficient to lead them, if they followed its dictates, to a
life of virtue for which they were also promised eternal rewards.

Though Hutcheson and Edwards worked in the same universe of
discourse, their views were poles apart because the Scottish philosopher, like most of his contemporaries, was assuming that nature and
human nature provided normative guides to human life. In the view
of Hutcheson and his peers, God must be a benevolent deity who cre-

14. Charles Taylor, *Sources of the Self: The Making of the Modern Identity* (Cambridge, Mass.: Harvard University Press, 1989), 248–50.
15. Francis Hutcheson, *A Short Introduction to Moral Philosophy* (Glasgow, 1747),
16–17.

ated a universe designed for moral harmony. Humans needed only to discover and follow the inbuilt natural laws.

Such assumptions about the sources of morality had immense implications for shaping the modern world. They were crucial for teaching people that they could free themselves from external authorities and at the same time internalize moral principles that would make themselves useful citizens. Attitudes of self-discipline were socially useful in helping to produce free individuals who could compete in the new commercial culture. Another common view of the era was that even private vices, growing out of self-interest, could result in public virtue.[16] A generation later, Hutcheson's countryman Adam Smith (1723–90) most famously applied such assumptions regarding benevolent natural laws explicitly in defense of a free market economy. Hutcheson's own emphasis on sentiment anticipated the romantic views of the self, reliant on the guidance of nature from within, so important to the emergence of the nineteenth-century middle classes.[17]

Much of American thought from the Revolution to the Civil War was shaped by the immensely impressive Scottish Enlightenment. It is illuminating to think of Edwards in that Scottish context. American colonists in the 1750s thought of themselves as British provincials and increasingly looked to Scotland, the preeminent British province, for intellectual guidance.[18] Edwards was no exception. He depended on his Scottish correspondents for the latest intelligence and for a supply of many of the books he needed to participate in the international conversation.

Just at the time Edwards was writing his great treatises in the 1750s, Scotland was emerging as the brightest intellectual center in the Western world. In addition to Hutcheson were Henry Home, Lord

16. Cf. Roy Porter, *The Creation of the Modern World: The Untold Story of the British Enlightenment* (New York: Norton, 2000), 175–76. The idea that "'private vices' beget 'public benefits'" was suggested by Bernard Mandeville and even by Alexander Pope in the first half of the century, well before one finds it in David Hume and Adam Smith.

17. Cf. Taylor, *Sources of the Self*, 248–302.

18. Ned Landsman, *From Colonials to Provincials: American Thought and Culture, 1680–1760* (New York: Twayne, 1997), 3–4. See also Ned Landsman, *Scotland and Its First American Colony, 1683–1765* (Princeton: Princeton University Press, 1985); and Henry May, *The Enlightenment in America* (New York: Oxford University Press, 1976), 342–50. William Small, a Scottish advocate of Hutcheson's thought, came to the College of William and Mary in 1758, where he was Thomas Jefferson's most influential teacher (Garry Wills, *Inventing America: Jefferson's Declaration of Independence* [New York: Doubleday, 1978], 176–80). John Witherspoon, an orthodox Presbyterian Scottish moralist who became president of Princeton in 1766, taught James Madison and was himself an influential signer of the Declaration of Independence.

Kames, to whose views on the will Edwards contrasted his own in 1757, and David Hume, whose *A Treatise on Human Nature* (1739–40) Edwards read with great interest. Edwards did not live quite long enough to learn of the work of two other Scottish philosophers who had the most influence in America: Thomas Reid (1710–96), the most famous articulator of "common sense" philosophy, and Adam Smith, moral philosopher and political economist who authored *The Wealth of Nations* (1776).

Nonetheless, Edwards thought of himself first of all as a British citizen and was especially in touch with the Scottish Enlightenment. Late in 1755, Edwards wrote to John Erskine that he had read Lord Kames' *Essay on the Principles of Morality* (1751) "and also that book of Mr. David Hume's which you speak of. I am glad of an opportunity to read such corrupt books; especially when written by men of considerable genius; that I may have an idea of the notions that prevail in our nation."[19] Edwards' use of "our nation" is one of those inconspicuous clues that reveals how he thought of his national identity. Great Britain was crucial to him because it was a Protestant nation. Now even Presbyterian Scotland, where he found his strongest allies, was in danger of being destroyed by the new corrupt thought.

In 1757, as he was finishing *The Nature of True Virtue*, Edwards could for the first time begin to see some fulfillment of his lifelong ambition to lend his own considerable genius to the great philosophical debates of the day. *Freedom of the Will* had put him on the intellectual map. *The Nature of True Virtue* had the potential to extend the challenge. In the very first sentence, Edwards signaled both that he was entering into this international conversation on moral philosophy and that he was at home with its fundamental terms. "Whatever controversies and variety of opinions there are about the nature of virtue," he began, "yet all (excepting some skeptics who deny any real difference between virtue and vice) mean by it something *beautiful*, or rather some kind of *beauty* or excellency." Further, this same sentence indicates that he was not here particularly concerned to sort out all the "controversies and variety of opinions there are about the nature of virtue." Unlike most of his other treatises, this one did not mount polemics against the statements of particular authors, Hutcheson or anyone else. Rather, he was laying gunpowder at the foundations of the entire project of all the celebrated moral philosophers of the day.

Edwards' basic point was as simple as it was characteristic of all his thought. "Nothing is of the nature of true virtue," he explained, "in

19. Edwards to John Erskine, 11 December 1755, *Letters and Personal Writings*, *Works*, 16:679.

which God is not the *first* and the *last.*" God is love and the source of all love. True love, true benevolence, is love that resonates with God's love and is in harmony with it. This conclusion, Edwards pointed out, is a necessary implication of "the preceding discourse of *God's End in Creating the World.*" God's very being is "love and friendship which subsists eternally and necessarily between the several persons in the Godhead." The ultimate end or purpose of creation is as an expression of that love. Intelligent beings are created with the very purpose of being united in love with the Godhead. And to be united in love with the Godhead means to love what God loves, or all being. God is "the foundation and fountain of all being and all beauty; from whom all is perfectly derived, and on whom all is most absolutely and perfectly dependent; *of whom,* and *through whom,* and *to whom,* is all being and all perfection; and whose being and beauty is as it were the sum and comprehension of all existence and excellence: much more than the sun is the fountain and summary comprehension of all the light and brightness of the day."[20]

Since Edwards was writing primarily for moral philosophers, he subordinated such theological language to more abstract arguments—the sorts of arguments that only philosophers might love. "True virtue," he said in his primary statement of his thesis, "most essentially consists in benevolence to Being in general." "Or perhaps to speak more accurately," he continued, "it is that consent, propensity and union of heart to Being in general, that is immediately exercised in a general good will."[21] These statements become clearer if seen in their theological framework. True virtue, or universal benevolence, is possible only if one's heart is united to God, who is love and beauty and the source of all love and beauty. Any other loves, absent this properly highest love, will be love for much less than all that one ought to be loving and hence contrary to the very purpose for which one was created.

Edwards' central argument to this conclusion was simply an expansion of a distinction, common to the modern moralists, between private interests and benevolence. Hutcheson, for instance, argued "[t]hat we have a *moral sense* or determination of our mind, to *approve* every *kind affection* either in our selves or others and all publicly useful actions which we imagined do flow from such affection without

20. *The Nature of True Virtue,* in *The Works of Jonathan Edwards,* vol. 8, *Ethical Writings,* ed. Paul Ramsey (New Haven: Yale University Press, 1989), 539, 560, 557, 551. Edwards recognized that almost all the contemporary philosophers included some mention of duty to God. Yet he regarded them as simply *adding* that onto theories based "on benevolence to the *created system.*" "If true virtue consists partly in a respect to God," he countered, "then doubtless it consists *chiefly* in it" (ibid., 552–53).

21. Ibid., 540.

our having a view to our *private happiness,* in our appropriation of these actions." So, for instance, all people will instinctively approve when they hear of someone who found a treasure and used it for benevolent purposes. Even people who themselves would use the treasure only for private self-indulgence will share this sentiment of approval of those who use it in the public interest.[22] All Edwards was doing was taking this distinction between private interests and public benevolence and pressing it to its conclusion if one considered the entire universe.

Much of what was lauded as true virtue, Edwards pointed out, was no more than private interests writ large. People universally admired, for instance, familial love. Yet love for one's own family, however admirable in itself, was still quite evidently an expression of private rather than public benevolence. Families often are very selfish with respect to other families. Other wider loves, such as for community or nation, were only larger illustrations of the same principle. Such loves were indeed admirable within their limited contexts but not ultimately virtuous in the sense of promoting universal benevolence. "Hence," wrote Edwards, "among the Romans love to their country was the highest virtue: though this affection of theirs, so much extolled among them, was employed as it were for the destruction of the rest of the world of mankind." The general principle that followed was simple: "The larger the number is that private affection extends to, the more apt men are, through the narrowness of their sight, to mistake it for true virtue; because then the private system appears to have more of the image of the universal system."[23]

Benevolence within such private systems is so widely admired, said Edwards, because it partakes of "secondary beauty." "As a few notes in a tune," he explained, "taken only by themselves, and in their relation to one another, may be harmonious; which, when considered with respect to all the notes in the tune, or the entire series of sounds they are connected with, many be very discordant and disagreeable."[24] Humans naturally admire the harmonies of benevolence on a purely human scale. The more complete the harmonies, the more they admire them. Yet if such benevolences, however attractive in themselves, are out of tune with the great symphony of God's love that animates the universe, they are ultimately discordant, rather than truly beautiful.

22. Francis Hutcheson, *An Essay on the Nature and Conduct of the Passions and Affections* (London, 1728), 210–11, quotation 211.
23. *True Virtue, Works,* 8:611.
24. Ibid., 540.

Like the other moral philosophers, Edwards believed that humans had an inbuilt moral faculty. Yet he saw it not as a reliable subjective sensibility so much as a rational ability to approve of proportion and harmony, as one might appreciate the proportions of a triangle or the harmonies of a melody. For instance, natural conscience most characteristically involves a sense of justice, or an appreciation of the harmony of acts and their appropriate consequences. All normal people have a sense of desert with respect to themselves, and they can develop a sense of justice for others by imagining themselves in others' places. Conscience tells people when they are out of harmony with their own best judgments or acting inconsistently with what they would approve in others.[25]

This natural moral faculty is in fact, said Edwards, of great value for regulating society. Though the ultimately limited expressions of natural benevolence or its approval of acts of justice are not *true* virtue, they have "a true *negative* moral goodness in them." "By 'negative' moral goodness," Edwards explained, "I mean the negation or absence of true moral evil."[26] So Edwards could heartily endorse all acts of benevolence, compassion, justice, and the like, whether by individuals or governments, which limited vice. These were expressions of "common grace," or gifts that God bestowed on all humanity. It was consistent with this view, for instance, that Edwards strongly supported the British military, even though he was appalled by the impiety and lax morals of most of its members. They were being used by God to restrain evil.

At the same time that Edwards granted the value of "true *negative* moral goodness," or of the "virtues" of a limited, purely human system of morality, he also insisted that nothing can be *true* virtue when the benevolence is not first of all benevolence to God or to most of the beings in the universe. "Such a private affection, detached from general benevolence and independent on it, as the case may be, will be *against* general benevolence, or of a contrary tendency; and will set a person *against* general existence, and make him the enemy to it." The reason for this sharp dichotomy is that one's private affections, apart from

25. Ibid., 568–72. On the subtle distinctions between Edwards' and other eighteenth-century formulations, see Fiering, *Jonathan Edwards's Moral Thought*, e.g., 345.

26. *True Virtue, Works,* 8:613–14. Justice is an objective concept having to do with proportion, so anyone might appreciate it as a "secondary beauty," and even evil persons may promote justice. True virtue, on the other hand, has ultimately to do with motive. True benevolence to being in general will entail a hearty approval of all justice and benevolence. The difference is that true virtue is based on the most extensive love for persons, while a love for justice, without true virtue, is more like a love for the proportions of the shapes of nature or of music (ibid., 568–73).

God, no matter how much extended to family, community, or nation, will inevitably be one's *highest* loyalty, *above* loyalty to God or to Being in general: "For he that is influenced by private affection, not subordinate to regard to Being in general, sets up its particular or limited object *above* Being in general; and this most naturally tends to enmity against the latter. . . . Even as the setting up another prince as supreme in any kingdom, distinct from the lawful sovereign, naturally tends to enmity against the lawful sovereign."[27]

True love, Edwards pointed out, is to identify our interest with that of others.[28] What makes others happy makes us happy. In an essentially interpersonal universe, persons are either united to or divided from each other by their affections. One's love can either be confined to some limited set of created persons and things, or it can be first of all love to the Creator, which will entail love to all being. Characteristically, Edwards was insisting that the only important question in life is whether one is united to God or in rebellion against God. If united with God (which for Edwards was always an ongoing process), then one will learn to love all that God loves—which includes benevolence and justice toward others. God's happiness will be our happiness.

True virtue is ultimately distinguished from its imitators by motive or disposition. This crucial point needs to be underscored because it reflects Edwards' overall vision of a personal universe and affective religion. True virtue grows out of a disposition to true love. True love is the widest possible affection for persons and all that is good (being) in the universe. It is doing good for its own sake—for its beauty. Merely natural "virtue," which superficially may look very similar, is ultimately motivated by humans' natural inclinations to love themselves and their own kind.[29]

In *The Nature of True Virtue*—an intellectual gem by any standard— Edwards was challenging the project that dominated Western thought, and eventually much of world thought, for the next two centuries. The grand ideal of that hopeful era was that humans would find it possible to establish on scientific principles a universal system of morality that

27. Ibid., 555–56.

28. Edwards made this point in the context of pointing out that "self-love" is not bad if it simply means to love our own happiness, which is simply to love what we love. The question is whether our happiness, or our disposition, is ultimately defined by private or selfish interests or by God's universal interests (ibid., 576–77).

29. While Hutcheson argued that natural humans had a moral sense, Edwards regarded only truly spiritual persons as having a "truly spiritual sense or virtuous taste" (ibid., 596). Edwards argued, for instance, that a gang of robbers will have a natural sense of gratitude to someone who warns them that the sheriff is about to raid their hideaway. So their natural moral sentiments are not to be relied upon to approve of that which is in the public interest (ibid., 583).

would bring to an end the destructive conflicts that had plagued human history. Only after the first half of the twentieth century, when the clashes of such ideals had led to the bloodiest era in history and threatened to annihilate humanity, did much of the faith in that project collapse, even though there were no clear alternatives to put in its place. Edwards' recognition of the vast importance of the assumptions that lay behind such efforts and his insight into their faults arose, not because he was so far ahead of his time, but because his rigorous Calvinism—and his position in a distant province—put him in a position to scrutinize critically his own era. His theological commitments alerted him to the momentous implications of trends that were already formidable in Britain when he first came on the intellectual scene and that during his lifetime advanced rapidly, even in New England. Edwards was a thoroughly eighteenth-century figure who used many of the categories and assumptions of his era to criticize its trends. Though he may have underestimated the short-term benefits of the emerging culture, he had genuine insight into the emptiness of its highest hopes.

6

OPEN THEISM IN THE HANDS OF AN ANGRY PURITAN

Jonathan Edwards on Divine Foreknowledge

C. Samuel Storms

The contemporary fascination with Jonathan Edwards shows little sign of abatement. If anything, scholarly interest is on the rise. Harry Stout believes "the reasons for this compelling attraction vary widely over time and individual persuasion: some have approached Edwards for religious inspiration, others to exorcise the ghosts of their Puritan forebears; some have come to appreciate true virtue, others to understand the reality of total evil; some have discovered a great anachronism, others a prophet of modernity."[1]

Stephen Stein accounts for Edwards' popularity by suggesting that some scholars are preoccupied with his "eighteenth-century world; he serves for them as a window into that century. Others address perennial philosophical or theological questions by means of engagement

I am grateful to Bruce Ware, Stephen Spencer, and my teaching assistant, Stephen George, for the helpful comments and suggestions they provided in reading an earlier draft of this article. Of course, they should not be held accountable for any errors it may still contain.

1. Harry S. Stout, "Introduction," in *Jonathan Edwards and the American Experience,* ed. Nathan O. Hatch and Harry S. Stout (New York: Oxford University Press, 1988), 3.

with his answers to those questions. Still others are most concerned about Edwards' influence on subsequent generations of American thinkers."[2] And then, notes Stein, "there are the admirers—those who are convinced that he was religiously correct in his formulations of Christian thought and practices or those who simply stand in awe of his intellectual efforts."[3] I am unashamedly an "admirer" of Edwards and am attracted to him for precisely the reason Stein notes: I believe Edwards was, in large measure, "religiously correct" in his formulation of Christian theology and, in particular, in his unqualified endorsement of exhaustive divine foreknowledge (hereafter EDF).

The purpose of this article is not primarily descriptive. Whereas I do hope to provide some insight into the structure and rationale of Edwards' arguments for EDF, my aim is to use Edwards as a catalyst for a biblical and theological examination of contemporary open theism. Were Edwards alive today, I believe his response to open theism would be less one of anger (notwithstanding the title of this article) than of utter incredulity. "One would think," says Edwards, "it should be wholly needless to enter on such an argument [for EDF] with any that profess themselves Christians."[4] However, he concedes that "God's certain foreknowledge of the free acts of moral agents, is denied by some that pretend to believe the Scriptures to be the Word of God."[5]

The Structure of Edwards' Argument for EDF

Edwards' argument for EDF appears within the larger framework of his response to the Arminian notion of free will. The Arminianism to which Edwards addressed himself insisted, among other things, that for the will properly to be free and thus "capable of virtue or vice, and properly the subject of command or counsel, praise or blame,

2. Stephen J. Stein, "Introduction," in *Jonathan Edwards's Writings: Text, Context, Interpretation*, ed. Stephen J. Stein (Bloomington: Indiana University Press, 1996), xi.

3. Ibid. Aside from his reservations regarding Edwards' salvific particularism, Michael Jinkins provides an excellent introduction to his theological perspective in "'The Being of Beings': Jonathan Edwards' Understanding of God as Reflected in His Final Treatises," *Scottish Journal of Theology* 46 (1993): 161–90.

4. Jonathan Edwards, *The Works of Jonathan Edwards*, vol. 1, *Freedom of the Will*, ed. Paul Ramsey (New Haven: Yale University Press, 1957), 239.

5. Ibid. Allen Guelzo addresses how Edwards might have responded to contemporary open theism (which he describes as the "'evangelicalizing' of process pragmatism") in "The Return of the Will: Jonathan Edwards and the Possibilities of Free Will," in *Edwards in Our Time: Jonathan Edwards and the Shaping of American Religion*, ed. Sang Hyun Lee and Allen C. Guelzo (Grand Rapids: Eerdmans, 1999), 87–110.

promises or threatenings, rewards or punishments,"[6] it must be contingent, "as to be without all necessity."[7] But contingency is precluded by EDF. Thus, Edwards set himself to the task of demonstrating two things: first, "that God has a certain foreknowledge of the voluntary acts of moral agents; and secondly . . . how it follows from hence, that the volitions of moral agents are not contingent, so as to be without necessity of connection and consequence."[8]

Unlike the Arminians[9] of Edwards' day, contemporary open theists readily concede Edwards' second point. Classical Arminianism, be it in the eighteenth century or our own, has typically affirmed EDF (or if not "exhaustive," at least extensive) but has insisted, no less strenuously, that such is "no evidence of any necessity of the event foreknown."[10] Much to their credit, open theists have pointed out the inconsistency of this position.

As I read most open theists, it appears their argument rests on two foundational assumptions. First, human choices are morally relevant, indeed *must* be, lest we denude life of meaning and depersonalize the love relationship between God and man (a point, be it noted, with which both Edwards and all compatibilists would heartily agree). But if human choices are necessary, say the open theists, they are unavoidable, and if unavoidable they are worthy of neither reward nor punishment. In other words, necessary events are morally vacuous events. The Bible portrays human choice as morally significant, and both common sense and experience confirm it as such. Therefore, human choice cannot be necessary. A foreknown choice is a necessary choice. Therefore, God does not foreknow human choice. To this is added the second and corollary point, that morally relevant choices are, by definition, contingent, and contingent choices are, by definition, unknowable antecedents to their being chosen. Therefore, God does not, indeed cannot, have EDF of the volitions of free moral agents.

Edwards' case for EDF is thus relevant to contemporary open theism in two respects. First, notwithstanding the latter's insistence

6. *Freedom of the Will, Works*, 1:171.

7. Ibid., 239.

8. Ibid.

9. Edwards directed most of his comments toward three men: Daniel Whitby (1638–1726), an Anglican divine; Thomas Chubb (1679–1747), a Deist; and Isaac Watts (1674–1748), a hymn writer who more closely approached Edwards' general theological perspective than the other two. For more on these men, see Paul Ramsey's introduction to *Freedom of the Will, Works*, 1:65–118; and Conrad Wright, "Edwards and the Arminians on the Freedom of the Will," *Harvard Theological Review* 35 (1942): 241–61.

10. *Freedom of the Will, Works*, 1:257.

that foreknown choices are morally irrelevant choices, Edwards demonstrates that the Bible says otherwise. He compiles an impressive body of exegetical evidence that he believes proves that God infallibly foreknows human volitions for which he holds the individual morally accountable. These choices, says Edwards, being infallibly foreknown, are necessary. As noted, on this point open theists agree. If EDF exists, contingency or libertarian freedom does not.[11] Edwards' second argument is that the necessity logically entailed by EDF is perfectly compatible (hence, "compatibilism") with moral accountability. This latter point is the focus of Edwards' work on free will, a treatise that in my opinion has yet to be successfully refuted, notwithstanding the many efforts to that end.[12] My focus will be on the first of these two points. I want to examine several (but by no means all) of Edwards' biblical arguments for EDF. I will leave it to the philosophers to determine whether the necessity that EDF demands is compatible or incompatible with moral accountability.[13]

11. It is perfectly demonstrable, says Edwards, "that if there be any infallible knowledge of future volitions, the event [i.e., the human volition] is necessary; or, in other words, that it is impossible but the event should come to pass" (ibid., 258). Again, "on the whole, I need not fear to say, that there is no geometrical theorem or proposition whatsoever, more capable of strict demonstration, than that God's certain prescience of the volitions of moral agents is inconsistent with such a contingence of these events, as is without all necessity; and so is inconsistent with the Arminian notion of liberty" (ibid., 268–69). See Edwards' detailed argument for this in ibid., 257–69.

12. The most rigorous response to Edwards' work came from the pen of James Dana of Wallingford, Connecticut. It was published in two parts: An Examination of the Late Reverend Edwards's "Enquiry on Freedom of Will" (Boston: Daniel Kneeland, 1770), and The "Examination of the Late Rev'd President Edwards's Enquiry on Freedom of Will," Continued (New Haven: Thomas and Samuel Green, 1773). See my detailed response to Dana in C. Samuel Storms, Tragedy in Eden: Original Sin in the Theology of Jonathan Edwards (Lanham, Md.: University Press of America, 1985), 199–206; as well as C. Samuel Storms, "Jonathan Edwards on the Freedom of the Will," Trinity Journal, n.s., 3 (1982): 131–69. See also the interaction with Dana in Allen C. Guelzo, Edwards on the Will: A Century of American Theological Debate (Middletown, Conn.: Wesleyan University Press, 1989), 155–64.

13. An especially insightful engagement with Edwards' philosophical arguments for necessity is found in Alvin Plantinga's "On Ockham's Way Out," Faith and Philosophy 3 (1986): 235–69. See the brief response by Linda Trinkaus Zagzebski, The Dilemma of Freedom and Foreknowledge (Oxford: Oxford University Press, 1991), 28–30; as well as the discussion in George I. Mavrodes, "Is the Past Unpreventable?" Faith and Philosophy 1 (1984): 131–46. Although he does not interact directly with Edwards, John M. Frame agrees with him that libertarian freedom, so essential to the incompatibilist and open theistic perspective, is incoherent and actually destructive of moral accountability. See his recent book No Other God: A Response to Open Theism (Phillipsburg, N.J.: P&R, 2001), esp. 119–41.

A Biblical Case for EDF[14]

Edwards' task is to prove "that God has an absolute and certain foreknowledge of the free actions of moral agents."[15] He appeals to five arguments, only one of which concerns us here. Edwards' principal argument is that foreknowledge is proved from the fact of prophetic prediction. In the absence of foreknowledge, prediction is mere conjecture, however well informed it may be. And conjecture, he insisted, is denigrating to the glory of God. What he would have been shocked to discover is that conjecture is precisely what certain open theists today believe divine "prediction" to be. According to John Sanders, "[G]iven the depth and breadth of God's knowledge of the present situation, God forecasts what he thinks will happen. In this regard God is the consummate social scientist predicting what will happen. God's ability to predict the future in this way is far more accurate than any human forecaster's, however, since God has exhaustive access to all past and present knowledge."[16] Such a view of divine prediction opens the door for divine error, something Edwards found abhorrent, yet Sanders readily embraces.[17]

Furthermore, to deny God's foreknowledge of the volition of moral agents is to deny it of those events that are consequent to and dependent upon it. This would serve to increase divine ignorance beyond reason, given the incalculable number of events set in motion by the choices of moral agents.[18] In other words, if God cannot foreknow the future volitions of moral agents, "then neither can he certainly foreknow those events which are consequent and dependent on these volitions."[19] Edwards beckons us to envision, if possible, the seemingly infinite number of events and decisions that are consequent into eternity on but one human choice, the multiplied series of consequent happenings, each of which itself generates multiplied series of complex oc-

14. My focus will be on the argument as it appears in *Freedom of the Will*, although Edwards does address the issue elsewhere, but considerably more briefly. See especially "Miscellanies" nos. u, 16, 19, 29, 63, 74, and 82 in Jonathan Edwards, *The Works of Jonathan Edwards*, vol. 13, *The "Miscellanies," a–500*, ed. Thomas A. Schafer (New Haven: Yale University Press, 1994); and "Miscellanies" nos. 704 and 762 in Jonathan Edwards, *The Works of Jonathan Edwards*, vol. 18, *The "Miscellanies," 501–832*, ed. Ava Chamberlain (New Haven: Yale University Press, 2000).

15. *Freedom of the Will, Works*, 1:239.

16. John Sanders, *The God Who Risks: A Theology of Providence* (Downers Grove, Ill.: InterVarsity, 1998), 131.

17. Ibid., 132.

18. On this point, see the excellent brief article by John Piper, "The Enormous Ignorance of God: When God Doesn't Know the Future Choices of Man," 2 December 1997 (online: www.desiringgod.org/library/topics/foreknowledge/ignorance_god.html).

19. *Freedom of the Will, Works*, 1:239.

currences, ad infinitum. If God does not have EDF, he is not capable of knowing these any more than he can know the first volition from which they issue.

What Edwards has in mind may be illustrated by conceiving of the earth as if it were a giant billiard table. Any single human volition or deed is akin to a cue ball hitting fifteen colored balls and scattering them across the table. In turn, each of the fifteen then becomes another cue ball that strikes yet another fifteen, which in turn become cue balls hitting yet another fifteen, and so on, ad infinitum. This is not to suggest that the universe is an impersonal and mechanistic cause-and-effect world. Rather, the point is that for every thought or emotion or resolution or act or word or choice, there is set in motion a multitude of diverse effects, each of which has the potential to become a cause of yet innumerable other diverse effects, ad infinitum.[20]

If God does not foreknow the first cue ball (or human choice/deed, as the case may be) on which all its subsequent effects depend, he cannot know the latter or the subsequent effects they each cause. If God does not have EDF, not only is his ignorance incalculable, but there is no possibility that God could ever predict or prophesy any volition or event or deed in the vast web of interrelated causes and effects represented by the multitude of interactive billiard balls. Neither could he even foreknow what he himself intends to do, given the fact that *what* he does (not to mention *when* and *how*) is itself dependent on and only possible within the historical framework created by the incalculable web of human decision making, the latter of which open theists insist he cannot know.

For example, how can God know an event, say, in the middle of the third set of fifteen balls set in motion by the eighth ball of the second set, set in motion by the fourth ball of the first set? How can he interpose to do something in their midst, given the potential multiplicity of positions and movements of the balls, as well as factors of changing velocity, resistance, the angle at which they strike each other, and the tightness of the rack, all of which are physical factors that represent

20. The temptation among open theists may be to exploit my analogy to demonstrate that the Calvinist worldview, one element of which is EDF, is fatalistic and relationally lifeless and thus incompatible with the spontaneity of human choice and the joy of a love relationship with God as our Father. But this would be to misunderstand the point of the illustration, which is simply to highlight the complex and multifaceted interconnectedness of what is in fact a highly interactive and dynamic relationship between God and mankind. So again, I'm *not* saying that *people*, in their relationship with God and others, *are* unthinking and unfeeling billiard balls, but that their deeds and decisions are causally interrelated in a way that is analogous to, yet on a far more expansive scale than, the physical impact of countless billiard balls one on the other.

only a tiny fraction of the incalculably vast number of spiritual and emotional and volitional consequences entailed by human decision making and response? What Edwards wants us to see is that no movement of any one ball (i.e., no decision or action of any one person) can be foreknown apart from foreknowledge of every movement of every ball (volition) antecedent to it. But what about that particular "ball" that open theists might identify as the "event" produced by God's sovereign intervention in human affairs? In response, Edwards would quickly point out that

> these [i.e., the things God himself has determined to bring to pass] can't be foreseen, unless it can be foreseen when there shall be occasion for such extraordinary interposition. And that can't be foreseen, unless the state of the moral world can be foreseen. For whenever God thus interposes, it is with regard to the state of the moral world, requiring such divine interposition. Thus God could not certainly foresee the universal deluge, the calling of Abraham, the destruction of Sodom and Gomorrah, the plagues on Egypt, and Israel's redemption out of it, the expelling the seven nations of Canaan, and the bringing [of] Israel into that land; for these all are represented as connected with things belonging to the state of the moral world. Nor can God foreknow the most proper and convenient time of the day of judgment, and general conflagration; for that chiefly depends on the course and state of things in the moral world.[21]

Edwards proceeds to cite numerous biblical examples of God being portrayed as knowing the future moral quality and conduct of people, that is, those decisions for which he holds them accountable and thus either worthy of praise or liable of blame. A few examples include the moral conduct of Ahab (1 Kings 22:20–22), of Hazael (2 Kings 8:12–13), and of Cyrus (Isa. 44:28; 45:13; 2 Chron. 36:22–23; Ezra 1:1–4).[22] One example is deserving of more comment. First Kings 13:1–6 describes,

---

21. *Freedom of the Will, Works*, 1:250–51.

22. Additional examples where God foreknows both the wicked and righteous deeds of moral agents include the future cruelty of the Egyptians against Israel (Gen. 15:13–14), the continuation of iniquity among the Amorites (Gen. 15:16; see Acts 7:6–7), the pride of Babylonian leaders (Isa. 13, 14, 47), and the return of the Jews from Babylon (Jer. 31:35–40; 32:6–15, 41, 44; 33:24–26), as well as the time it would occur (Jer. 25:11–12; 29:10–11; 2 Chron. 36:21; Ezek. 4:5–6). Edwards observes, "And yet the prophecies represent their return as consequent on their repentance. And their repentance itself is very expressly and particularly foretold" (*Freedom of the Will, Works*, 1:243–44). Yet, if libertarian freedom is true, God could not have infallibly foreknown that they would repent, for it must be in their power equally not to repent. Edwards proceeds to cite more than thirty examples where God predicts the malice, cruelty, conspiracy against, and rejection of the Messiah by individual moral agents (ibid., 244–45).

three hundred years in advance, the birth and moral behavior of a man, together with the name by which he would be called: Josiah. Sanders argues that predictions such as this may be accounted for in one of three ways, none of which requires EDF: "God can predict the future as something he intends to do regardless of human response, or God may utter a conditional statement that is dependent on human response, or God may give a forecast of what he thinks will occur based on his exhaustive knowledge of past and present factors."[23] But it would appear that none of these three adequately explains the prediction of Josiah's birth and behavior three hundred years before it came to pass.

How could God foreknow that Josiah would become king, unless he foreknew that his father, Amon, Manasseh's son, would do evil and walk in the ways of his father, as a result of which his servants conspired to kill him? If Amon had chosen, like others, to repent and walk in righteousness (none of which, according to open theism, God could have infallibly foreknown), his life would have been spared. And if he had lived, his son Josiah would not have ascended the throne at the precise time to make possible the fulfillment of the prediction in 1 Kings 13. How could God have predicted the birth of Josiah and his religious beliefs and moral behavior unless God exhaustively foreknew the history of all his ancestors? The possibilities for the disruption of the physical lineage that would result in the birth of Josiah are mind-boggling: the death of any one of hundreds of people, decisions whether and whom to marry, decisions regarding children, decisions by countless individuals in a three-hundred-year span to act or not to act in a way that would terminate the possibility of Amon and Jedidah meeting, falling in love, getting married, having a male child, and deciding to give him the name Josiah.

And how could God predict that Josiah would live long enough and righteously as king if he did not foreknow that none of those who opposed Josiah would succeed in killing him or that Josiah would not fall prey to a fatal illness or that he would not follow the example of others who rebelled against God? God had to know that Josiah would not rebel or fall into unbelief or idolatry as so many before him had. He had to know that his heart would incline toward God. He had to know that Josiah would be so angered by unbelief and idolatry that he would go so far as to burn the bones of the priests. Yet, how could any of this be true, apart from EDF?

Boyd interprets this prediction as illustrative of how God "set strict parameters around the freedom of the parents in naming" Josiah.[24]

23. Sanders, *God Who Risks*, 136.
24. Gregory A. Boyd, *God of the Possible: A Biblical Introduction to the Open View of God* (Grand Rapids: Baker, 2000), 34.

He adds, "It also restricted the scope of freedom these individuals could exercise *as it pertained to particular foreordained activities.*"[25] The examples of Josiah and Cyrus merely "show that Yahweh is the sovereign Lord of history and can predetermine (and thus foreknow) whatever he pleases, but they do not justify the conclusion that he has settled the entire future ahead of time."[26] But this simply will not do. At the heart of open theism is the insistent argument that necessity is incompatible with moral accountability, praise and blame, as well as meaningful relationships governed by love. But if it is now acknowledged that such does not apply in *all* cases, such as those of Josiah and Cyrus, one must ask why it applies in *any* case.

Edwards cites several examples of the moral conduct of nations and peoples and individuals foretold by God, together with those events consequent to and dependent upon them. Chief among these is the prophecy of Jerusalem's destruction and the Babylonian captivity. He points out that Jerusalem's destruction "was foretold in Hezekiah's time, and was abundantly insisted on in the book of the prophet Isaiah, who wrote nothing after Hezekiah's days. It was foretold in Josiah's time, in the beginning of a great reformation (2 Kings 22)," all of which, says Edwards, point to the absolute and unalterable nature of the prediction.[27] He writes,

> And yet this event was connected with, and dependent on two things in men's moral conduct: first, the injurious rapine and violence of the king of Babylon and his people, as the efficient cause; which God often speaks of as what he highly resented, and would severely punish; and secondly, the final obstinacy of the Jews. That great event is often spoken of as suspended on this (Jer. 4:1; 5:1; 7:1–7; 11:1–6; 17:24 to the end; 25:1–7; 26:1–8, 13; and 38:17, 18). Therefore this destruction and captivity could not be foreknown, unless such a moral conduct of the Chaldeans and Jews had been foreknown. And then it was foretold, that the people "should be finally obstinate," to the destruction and utter desolation of the city and land (Is. 6:9–11; Jer. 1:18, 19; 7:27–29; Ezek. 3:7 and 24:13, 14).[28]

Open theists cannot easily dismiss these prophetic predictions as conditional or mere forecasts of the future, given the fact that they are presented by Isaiah as proof that Yahweh alone is God. What demonstrates God to be God is precisely the specificity and certainty with

25. Ibid. (emphasis in the original).

26. Ibid. See also Gregory A. Boyd, *Satan and the Problem of Evil: Constructing a Trinitarian Warfare Theodicy* (Downers Grove, Ill.: InterVarsity, 2001), 121 n. 7.

27. *Freedom of the Will, Works,* 1:242.

28. Ibid., 242–43.

which he predicts the future moral decisions of men and women. God proves his deity, that he and he alone is God, by appealing to his exhaustive foreknowledge of the future and his ability to predict to the smallest of details everything that is coming to pass. He calls on all so-called gods and idols to do the same. In the final analysis, *if God does not have knowledge of the future, he is no better than the stone and wood idols before which misguided men and women bow down in futile allegiance.* Let us take Edwards' suggestion and consider in more detail the contribution to our debate of just a few texts in Isaiah 41–48.[29]

We begin with Isaiah 43:8–13 and the destruction of Babylon, an event that encompassed tens of thousands, perhaps millions, of human decisions and actions and countless consequences to each.[30] In order for the captives to be released by Cyrus, there first had to have been a mother and father who decided to give birth to a child whose life would in turn be filled with thousands of decisions that would culminate in his being at the right place at the right time (all of which must itself be brought to pass by thousands of decisions and actions of perhaps thousands of other people). Furthermore, for the Jews to be released from captivity, they first had to be taken captive. For this to occur, the Babylonians had to decide to invade Jerusalem. Countless military decisions and maneuvers would be involved on both sides of the battle lines. For God to foreknow and predict the fall of Babylon and the release of the people through Cyrus, he must foreknow hundreds of thousands, perhaps millions, of other events and choices on which the "fall" and "release" depended. As we noted earlier, no event occurs in a vacuum or stands in isolation from other events. Any single event in history is itself both the product of and the precursor to a complex web of countless millions of other events. How could one know infallibly the certainty of any one event apart from infallible knowledge of every preceding event that in its own way contributed to that one event coming to pass and apart from which that one event would *not* have come to pass?

29. For a more extensive interaction with Isaiah 40–48, see the excellent treatment in Bruce Ware, *God's Lesser Glory: The Diminished God of Open Theism* (Wheaton: Crossway, 2000), 100–119.

30. John Oswalt offers this observation on verse 9: "Each of the nations and peoples has its god, but *Who among them* (the gods) *can declare* (foretell) a future like *this?* The indefiniteness of *this* has given rise to a number of interpretations. The most common one is that it refers to the destruction of Babylon and the release of the captives by Cyrus (41:2–4, 25–26). While this view seems likely, we should also ask why the author chose the ambiguous demonstrative. Perhaps he had in mind the entire situation of sin and exile and return and reestablishment. In that case, we would do a disservice to the text to limit it too narrowly" (*The Book of Isaiah, Chapters 40–66,* New International Commentary on the Old Testament [Grand Rapids: Eerdmans, 1998], 145).

Second, in Isaiah 44:6–8 we see that the fundamental proof of God's uniqueness, what sets him apart from all "gods" and "idols," is his ability to predict what seems impossible, to declare that it will be, and then to bring it to pass. Verse 7 is explicit: "If you claim to be like Me," says the Lord, "proclaim and declare the future like I do!" Note well the object of God's knowledge: the things that are coming and the events that are going to take place, all of which encompass the lives, decisions, thoughts, reactions, feelings, and destinies of men and women and children, and not simply the actions that God himself, in isolation from others, intends to accomplish.

Finally, we are told in Isaiah 44:24–28 that God foreknows and fore-tells that Jerusalem will be "inhabited" once again. But for this to happen, people would have to make decisions: they must deliberate, they must weigh competing evidence, they must wrestle in their souls and among their families with a variety of options and the countless consequences that come with each, and they must choose to live there. All these voluntary, free choices on the part of the people are entailed in the repopulation of the city. Apart from these voluntary, free choices of the people, there will *not be* a repopulating of the city. Yet God *knows* the city will be inhabited yet again. Therefore, *God foreknows the voluntary, free choices made by the people* and knows them in such a way that they remain *both voluntary and free*, on the one hand, and *absolutely certain to occur*, on the other.

Open theists contend that God cannot foreknow the free choices or feelings or actions of morally responsible individuals. If such events are foreknown, they are certain to occur. And if they are certain to occur, they are not truly free. Isaiah begs to differ. He has made it repeatedly clear that God *does* infallibly foreknow and predict the future choices of people and that such knowledge in no way eliminates or diminishes the voluntary nature of their choices or the moral accountability that such choices demand (hence, the doctrine of compatibilism).

Edwards also points out that unless the volitions of moral agents are foreseen, all prophecies relating to the events and decisions and consequences of the great apostasy that he believed would immediately precede the second advent, all of which are of a moral nature, "are uttered without knowing the things foretold."[31]

The predictions relating to this great apostasy are all of a moral nature, relating to men's virtues and vices, and their exercises, fruits and consequences, and events depending on them; and are very particular; and

31. *Freedom of the Will, Works,* 1:245.

most of them often repeated, with many precise characteristics, descriptions, and limitations of qualities, conduct, influence, effects, extent, duration, periods, circumstances, final issue, etc. which it would be very long to mention particularly. And to suppose, all these are predicted by God without any certain knowledge of the future moral behavior of free agents, would be to the utmost degree absurd.[32]

Biblical prophecies are almost all "either predictions of the actings and behaviors of moral agents, or of events depending on them, or some way connected with them."[33] In addition,

almost all events belonging to the future state of the world of mankind, the changes and revolutions which come to pass in empires, kingdoms, and nations, and all societies, depend innumerable ways on the acts of men's wills; yea, on an innumerable multitude of millions of millions of volitions of mankind. Such is the state and course of things in the world of mankind, that one single event, which appears in itself exceeding inconsiderable, may in the progress and series of things, occasion a succession of the greatest and most important and extensive events; causing the state of mankind to be vastly different from what it would otherwise have been, for all succeeding generations.[34]

The one text that illustrates this point and may prove to be the theological Achilles' heel of open theism is Daniel 11.[35] Edwards' comments on the passage are especially worthy of note:

Their corruption, violence, robbery, treachery, and lies. And particularly, how much is foretold of the horrid wickedness of Antiochus Epiphanes, called there a "vile person," instead of "Epiphanes," or illustrious. In that chapter, and also in 8:9–14, 23, to the end, are foretold his flattery, deceit and lies, his having "his heart set to do mischief," and set "against the holy Covenant," his "destroying and treading under foot the holy people," in a marvelous manner, his "having indignation against the holy Covenant, setting his heart against it," and "conspiring against it," his "polluting the sanctuary of strength, treading it under foot, taking away the daily sacrifice, and placing the abomination that maketh desolate"; his great pride, "magnifying himself against God," and "uttering

32. Ibid., 245–46.
33. Ibid., 248.
34. Ibid.
35. I have looked closely at the works by Sanders, Boyd (including his recent *Satan and the Problem of Evil*), and Pinnock (including his recent *Most Moved Mover: A Theology of God's Openness* [Grand Rapids: Baker, 2001]), as well as most of the periodical literature, and have failed to detect a single substantive response to the implications of Daniel 11 for open theism.

marvelous blasphemies against Him," till God in "indignation should destroy him." Withal the moral conduct of the Jews, on occasion of his persecution, is predicted. 'Tis foretold, that "he should corrupt many by flatteries" (11:32–34). But that others should behave with a glorious constancy and fortitude, in opposition to him (ver. 32). And that some good men should fall, and repent (v. 35).[36]

Most agree that chapter 11 begins with a reference to the Persian kings who followed Cyrus, extends through Alexander the Great and his successors, and then provides a detailed summary of the ongoing conflict between the Seleucid and Ptolemaic dynasties (the primary powers of the Greek empire), with special emphasis on Antiochus IV Epiphanes. Let us consider the implications of open theism on the interpretation of this passage.

If God does not have EDF, how could he have predicted in Daniel 11:2 that "three more kings [Cambyses (530–522 B.C.), Smerdis (pseudo-Smerdis or Gaumata; 522 B.C.), and Darius I Hystaspes (522–486 B.C.)] are going to arise in Persia"? A prediction of this sort would require foreknowledge of countless thousands of human volitions necessary for three such men to be in precisely those circumstances at precisely the appropriate time to make their ascent to power possible, to say nothing of the countless thousands of other events and decisions that would serve to create the necessary historical and political framework. If God does not have EDF, how could he have predicted in Daniel 11:2 that Xerxes I (486 B.C.), a "fourth," would "gain far more riches than all of them" and would "arouse the whole empire against the realm of Greece"? If God does not have EDF, how could he have predicted in Daniel 11:3 that Alexander the Great (336–323 B.C.) would come to power, "rule with great authority and do as he pleases"? And how could he have predicted in Daniel 11:4 that when his kingdom broke up, it would be "parceled out" to people other than his own sons, who, as it turned out, were both murdered (Alexander IV and Herakles)?

If God does not have EDF, how could he have predicted in Daniel 11:5–20 the multitude of intricate details, human emotions, volitional resolve, and strategic decisions that were to transpire in the ongoing conflict between the Ptolemaic (Egyptian), or "southern king," and the Seleucid (Syrian), or "northern king," all of which occurred between the death of Alexander in 323 B.C. and the emergence of Antiochus Epiphanes in 175 B.C.? Apart from EDF, how could God have known and prophesied that the southern king would "grow strong" (Dan. 11:5) rather than "weak"? And apart from EDF, how could God have

36. *Freedom of the Will, Works,* 1:241.

known and prophesied that "one of his princes" (Seleucus I Nicator [312/11–280 B.C.]) would "gain ascendancy over him and obtain dominion"? And apart from EDF, how could God have known and prophesied in Daniel 11:6 that Ptolemy II (285–246 B.C.) would make a treaty of peace in 250 B.C. with the Seleucid ruler, Antiochus II Theos (grandson of Seleucus; 261–246 B.C.)? And how could God have known and prophesied that Berenice, "the daughter of the king of the South" (Dan. 11:6) would "come to the king of the North to carry out a peaceful arrangement," only to lose her power (indeed, she was murdered, along with Antiochus, by the latter's powerful ex-wife, Laodice)? And apart from EDF, how could God have known and prophesied that one of her descendants (Ptolemy III Euergetes [246–221 B.C.]) would decide to attack the king of the North in retaliation for the murder of his sister?

And how could God have known that Ptolemy III would choose to refrain from attacking the king of the north for two years? And apart from EDF, how could God have known and prophesied that the king of the north would have two sons (Seleucus III Ceraunus [226–223 B.C.] and Antiochus III the "Great" [223–187 B.C.]) and would decide to "mobilize and assemble a multitude of great forces" against the king of the south (Dan. 11:10)? And apart from EDF, how could God have known and prophesied that Ptolemy IV Philopator (221–203 B.C.), the king of the South, would be "enraged and go forth and fight with the king of the North" rather than capitulate in cowardice or pursue peaceful negotiations or any number of other reactions (Dan. 11:11)? And how could God have predicted that the armies of the king of the North would be defeated (Dan. 11:11; Ptolemy's victory occurred in 217 B.C. at Raphia, near Palestine)? And apart from EDF, how could he have known and prophesied that Ptolemy's heart would "be lifted up" (Dan. 11:12) in arrogance and pride rather than humbled with gratitude or some other understandable response given the circumstances of the day? And how could God have known that Antiochus III, Philip V of Macedon, and other insurrectionists in Egypt would "rise up against the king of the South" (Dan. 11:14)? Envision for a moment the multitude of decisions and military deliberations and alternative courses of action available to such leaders, any one of which could have derailed the eventual choice that they should attack, none of which, according to open theism, God *could* have known, yet apart from which the ultimate decision, which God *did* foreknow, could not have happened.

Daniel continues to prophesy of Antiochus and his decision to "set his face to come with the power" of his kingdom, yet with a "proposal of peace" (Dan. 11:17), as well as of the decision of his daughter (Cleo-patra) to give her loyalty to her husband Ptolemy rather than to her fa-ther (11:17), as well as of the latter's decision to attempt the capture of several Mediterranean islands (Dan. 11:18–19), as well as of Antiochus' ultimate demise (he was murdered by an angry mob in 187 B.C.). If that were not enough, additional predictions are made of his son, the infa-mous Antiochus Epiphanes. But apart from EDF, how could God have known and prophesied that this man would be "despicable" (Dan. 11:21) rather than kind and that he would "seize the kingdom by in-trigue"? After all, Demetrius I, young son of Seleucus IV, was next in line to receive the crown. On what possible grounds could even the consummate divine "social scientist" know that the man who, given the available data, should have been crowned would in fact be outma-neuvered by another? And apart from EDF, how could God have known and prophesied the strategic "alliance" or the "deception" or the decision to distribute plunder or the "schemes" he was to devise, all of which are described in Daniel 11:23–24? Explicit declarations of yet fu-ture "courage" rather than cowardice or hesitancy (Dan. 11:25), care-fully devised counter "schemes" (Dan. 11:25), the mutual intent of "evil" in the hearts of the kings (Dan. 11:27), their resolve to lie one to another rather than speak the truth (Dan. 11:27), and the choice of An-tiochus in his "heart" to set himself "against the holy covenant" (Dan. 11:28) are inexplicable apart from EDF. And apart from EDF, how could God have known and prophesied of Antiochus' being "disheart-ened" and "enraged," yet showing favor to the unfaithful in Israel (Dan. 11:30)?

Every human decision; every volitional resolve; every state of the hearts of those described in this period of history; and every counter-decision, retaliatory strike, and choice that the former evoked is de-scribed one hundred, two hundred, three hundred years in advance. Each of these human volitions was part of an indescribably complex nexus or interrelated web of cause and effect that entailed yet mil-lions more of other decisions, no less a part of yet more millions of decisions, all of which are portrayed as morally relevant, deserving of either praise or blame, the very thing that open theists insist is not possible, since they avow that EDF and free choice are incompatible with one another. It would appear that only three options are avail-able to the open theist: either acknowledge that the foundational in-compatibilist assumption on which their view rests is unbiblical, or silently ignore Daniel 11 altogether and pray that no one notices, or, what I suspect is likely to occur, eliminate Daniel 11 from the debate by conveniently interpreting this portion of the book as history rather than prophecy (*vaticinium ex eventu*).

The *mere existence* of the many rulers, emperors, kings, and military commanders described in Daniel 11 and elsewhere, notes Edwards,

> undoubtedly depended on many millions of acts of the will, which followed, and were occasioned one by another, in their parents. And perhaps most of these volitions depended on millions of volitions of hundreds and thousands of others, their contemporaries of the same generation; and most of these on millions of millions of volitions of others in preceding generations. As we go back, still the number of volitions, which were some way the occasion of the event, multiply as the branches of a river, till they come at last, as it were, to an infinite number. . . . [The mere conception in the womb of such persons] must depend on things infinitely minute, relating to the time and circumstances of the act of the parents, the state of their bodies, etc. which must depend on innumerable foregoing circumstances and occurrences; which must depend, infinite ways, on foregoing acts of their wills; which are occasioned by innumerable things that happen in the course of their lives, in which their own, and their neighbor's behavior, must have a hand, an infinite number of ways. And as the volitions of others must be so many ways concerned in the conception and birth of such men; so, no less, in their preservation, and circumstances of life, their particular determinations and actions, on which the great revolutions they were the occasions of, depended.[37]

Edwards is led to conclude that "these hints may be sufficient for every discerning considerate person, to convince him, that the whole state of the world of mankind, in all ages, and the very being of every person who has ever lived in it, in every age, since the times of the ancient prophets, has depended on more volitions, or acts of the wills of men, than there are sands on the seashore."[38]

Conclusion

It should come as no surprise to those who have read extensively in Edwards and have come to appreciate the magnitude of his mind that he effectively answered many of the arguments that contemporary open theists are now proposing. Given the evidence and arguments proffered by Edwards and others, one is left wondering what it would take to persuade open theists of the error of their position. What

37. Ibid., 249.
38. Ibid., 250.

would count as sufficient evidence against their view? Or has open theism assumed a posture that is philosophically unfalsifiable? I echo Edwards' incredulity at the denial of EDF. But I strongly suspect that notwithstanding his own substantive response, as well as that of many today, open theism will not soon disappear. Of course, that is not something I can foreknow infallibly. But I am confident and thankful that God can.

7

⭐

JONATHAN EDWARDS ON APOLOGETICS

Reason and the Noetic Effects of Sin

K. Scott Oliphint

This essay, as the title reflects, looks at Edwards' notion of reason and the noetic effects of sin. It does so, however, in order to show that the substance of a Reformed approach to apologetics is found in the thought of Jonathan Edwards. By "a Reformed approach," I mean an approach to apologetics that maintains, at the least, a consistent application of the basic tenets of Reformed theology. More specifically, I want to show that Edwards' view of the pervasiveness of sin in creatures made in God's image, and the concomitant notion of the necessity of revelation for apologetics, serve to locate Edwards within a Reformed approach to a defense of the Christian faith, particularly with respect to the question of the function of reason.

The Faculties

First, we should look at Edwards' anthropology. In order to understand properly Edwards' anthropology, particularly as it relates to apologetics and the noetic effects of sin, we must first make clear his position on the so-called faculty psychology. Since the Middle Ages, it had been assumed that humanity's reason controlled the imagination and will.[1] Likewise, the emotions were, in this scheme, subdued to the will. The primary faculty, therefore, was reason, and it was reason that dictated to the imagination and the will just what should be done or thought. Because of this construct, it was thought that an appeal to the passions alone was immoral. Any appeal that sought to bypass reason was seen as unnatural and therefore illegitimate.[2] This view persisted well into the modern era, and it was with this background in mind and in this context that Edwards wrote what is considered by many to be his greatest work, *A Treatise concerning Religious Affections*. In this work, Edwards sought to show not only that the long-standing medieval scholastic psychology was unwarranted but also that his own position of the organic unity of a person was both biblical and explanatory of the nature of revival.

While the enthusiasts were concentrating on the emotions and the anti-enthusiasts were focusing on the intellect, Edwards was attempting to understand the person as a unity. As Heimert and Miller point out, in *Religious Affections* Edwards not only set for himself the task of setting forth what he believed to be a biblical view of the affections but also was attempting to set forth an anthropology that was completely foreign to his audience.[3] He suffered, therefore, at the outset of this task from a double handicap.

In the introduction to *Religious Affections*, John Smith emphasizes that Edwards neither identified nor separated the head and the heart.[4] This is not only significant in light of the above-mentioned medieval scholasticism,[5] but it will also become significant as we discuss Edwards' anthropology and its relationship to the function of reason.

Edwards explains our human faculties in the following way:

1. See Alan Heimert and Perry Miller, eds., *The Great Awakening* (Indianapolis: Bobbs-Merrill Educational Publishing, 1967), xxxv–xliii.

2. Ibid., xl.

3. Ibid.

4. Jonathan Edwards, *The Works of Jonathan Edwards*, vol. 2, *Religious Affections*, ed. John E. Smith (New Haven: Yale University Press, 1959), 13.

5. The influence of medieval thought on the culture in which Edwards was writing is emphasized again by Allen C. Guelzo in his book *Edwards on the Will: A Century of American Theological Debate* (Middletown, Conn.: Wesleyan University Press, 1989), esp. the introduction. Though his book will be questioned by other experts on New England theology in general and Edwards in particular, I believe his introduction to be, in the main, a sound interpretation of Edwards and his times. On page 3 Guelzo notes, "According to the categories of the Protestant scholastic thought of the seventeenth century, the most critical relationship among the faculties of the mind was considered to be one of intellect and will, both of which were viewed, along with perception and judgement, as subdepartments of the overall phenomenon of mind. Because of the inherent bias of Christian theology toward teleological considerations, the Protestant

God has indued the soul with two faculties: one is that by which it is capable of perception and speculation, or by which it discerns and views
and judges of things; which is called the understanding. The other faculty is that by which the soul does not merely perceive and view things,
but is some way inclined with respect to the things it views or considers;
either is inclined to 'em, or is disinclined, and averse from 'em; or is the
faculty by which the soul does not behold things, as an indifferent unaffected spectator, but either as liking or disliking, pleased or displeased,
approving or rejecting. This faculty is called by various names: it is
sometimes called *inclination*: and, as it had respect to the actions that
are determined and governed by it, is called the *will*: and the *mind*, with
regard to the exercises of this faculty, is often called the *heart*.[6]

One of Edwards' primary concerns in this discussion was the sup-
position by some that the will as a faculty was inherently indifferent.
Edwards was opposed to such a notion of the will, and his opposition
was set in the context of his debate with the Arminians. One of the
primary tenets of an Arminian approach to "free will" was that the
will was inherently unaffected by the fall, a tenet that Edwards takes
up and tears down in his book *Freedom of the Will*. Any indifference of
the will, according to Edwards, would be tantamount to religious neutrality. He does, however, admit that certain exercises of the will are
"but a little beyond a state of perfect indifference," while others are
"more vigorous and sensible exercises."[7]
One of the more important Edwardsian distinctions in this regard is
a distinction with respect to how we understand or define knowledge.
Edwards speaks of a kind of knowledge, for example, of a square or a
triangle, as mere notional knowledge, while sensible knowledge, on the
other hand, "not only beholds, but has inclination."[8] This distinction is
important with respect to our understanding of the use and function of
reason. It seems that Edwards simply wants to distinguish between
what might be called "superficial knowledge" (what he calls "speculation") and what might be called "sensible knowledge." Sensible knowledge would include superficial knowing but is more than mere speculation. One can know in the sense that one perceives, for example,
though with that perception come simply "signs," as Edwards calls

---

scholastics—Turretin, Burgersdyck, Voetius, de Maastricht, all of whom Jonathan Edwards was to read as a Yale undergraduate—structured these subdepartments, or faculties, as a hierarchy, and graded them from the most important to the least." It seems to
me that Edwards was reacting against such a hierarchy.

6. *Religious Affections, Works*, 2:96.
7. Ibid., 96–97.
8. Ibid., 272.

them.[9] Knowledge that goes beyond mere perception is knowledge that is affected, knowledge with strong inclination.

Although it is difficult to categorize adequately notional or speculative knowledge, it might be useful to think of it as a kind of "formal" knowledge; it is the kind of knowledge that discerns the mere "form" of the thing and not its "matter," or substance. Edwards himself refers to Romans 2:20 in his explanation of speculative (or notional) knowledge, wherein the apostle asserts that there is a "form of knowledge, and of the truth in the law" (KJV).[10] Such speculative (or notional or formal) knowledge is merely one way of thinking and understanding—"apprehending," to use Edwards' term.[11] The other type of apprehension is that which includes within it a more significant "sensible" element, that is, a sense of the heart.

Given Edwards' revision of the faculty psychology of his day, we can now see the importance of his distinction with respect to knowledge. Namely, given that one of Edwards' most important tasks in *Religious Affections* was to transcend the assumed opposition, or strict separation, between the head and the heart—the kind of separation seen, for example, in Charles Chauncy—knowledge itself will be contextualized differently as well.[12] If one were to assume the head and heart to be in opposition, one could contend, as did the enthusiasts, that there could indeed be true religious affections without the understanding. If that were the case, then the affections alone, without any rational or reasonable content whatsoever, would be sufficient proof of spiritual conversion or spiritual change. In order to promote what Edwards conceived to be a more biblical approach to an analysis of revival, he opposed this kind of separation. He argued that holy affections, in order to be in fact holy, must always be accompanied by true understanding. There could be no true heat (affections) without true light (understanding).[13] But the converse is true as well. True understanding, if it *is* true, must always be accompanied by holy affections. To put it provocatively, knowledge is not true spiritual knowledge until and unless it is accompanied by holy affections. So, says Edwards with respect to true religion,

> As on the one hand, there must be light in the understanding, as well as an affected fervent heart, where there is heat without light, there can be

9. Perry Miller, "Jonathan Edwards and the Sense of the Heart," *Harvard Theological Review* 41 (1948): 135–36.

10. *Religious Affections, Works,* 2:273.

11. Miller, "Sense of the Heart," 135.

12. *Religious Affections, Works,* 2:33.

13. Ibid., 265.

nothing divine or heavenly in that heart; so on the other hand, where there is a kind of light without heat, a head stored with notions and speculations, with a cold and unaffected heart, there can be nothing divine in that light, that knowledge is no true spiritual knowledge of divine things.[14]

The important thing to note at this point, therefore, is that true spiritual knowledge can exist only when and where there is the combination of understanding and holy affections. True spiritual knowledge does not exist where there is mere notional knowledge. Neither does it exist where there is strong disinclination to such knowledge. There must be sensual knowledge combined with holy affections for there to be true spiritual knowledge of any kind. Without one or the other, there can be no knowledge or affections that amount to anything other than condemnation.

The importance of Edwards' revised faculty psychology for our purposes is to underline the fact that knowledge always and everywhere includes both understanding and will. While the will may be little affected in some cases, it is nevertheless affected, and thus the unity of the faculties plays a significant role in Edwards' understanding of human beings. In addition, since the faculties are united in this way, the effects of sin on us cannot be seen as "faculty specific" so that one faculty is more affected, or more directly affected, than another. That kind of view would be amenable to the very Arminianism that Edwards was seeking to refute.

Given the fact that true spiritual knowledge can exist only when understanding is combined with holy affections, the necessity of revelation for true knowledge must be maintained by Edwards as well. But what of knowledge that is not accompanied by holy affections? Here we should take note of Edwards' notion of the image of God.

The Image of God and Reason

A central and most significant distinction in Edwards' anthropology is that between the natural and the moral image of God in man. Edwards notes,

As there are two kinds of attributes in God, according to our way of conceiving of him, his moral attributes which are summed up in his holiness and his natural attributes of strength, knowledge, etc., that constitute the greatness of God; so there is a two-fold *imago Dei* in man, his moral or spiritual image, which is his holiness . . . and man's natural im-

14. Ibid., 120.

age, consisting in man's reason and understanding, his natural ability and dominion over the creatures, which is the image of God's natural ability.[15]

This distinction between the natural and the moral image of God relates directly to Edwards' view of the use of reason. Edwards contends that, while the moral and natural attributes of God are inseparable in God, in humans the moral image was lost at the fall, though the natural image was retained. Man lost holiness but retained reason and understanding.[16] Man's reason, therefore, is intact, even after the fall.

But what does it mean for reason to be "intact"? Does it mean that reason is meant to function, or able to function properly, after the fall, without need of revelation or regeneration? Does the fact that reason is intact mean that it can acquire true knowledge, more specifically true knowledge of God, without recourse to revelation or regeneration? Is reason virtually unaffected by the fall? If so, then it would be able, quite apart from revelation, to come to the proper and true conclusions about God and this world on its own.

This does not, however, seem to be consistent with Edwards' notion of the natural/moral image of God. There is invariably, according to Edwards, a direct effect of the moral on the natural after the fall. Though reason is still intact in human beings after the fall, it was and is still nevertheless affected, and affected seriously, by the fall into sin. Edwards seeks to describe this in terms of a further distinction between natural and moral ability and inability. Says Edwards,

> We are said to be *naturally* unable to do a thing, when we can't do it if we will, because what is most commonly called nature don't allow of it, or because of some impending defect or obstacle that is extrinsic to the will. . . . *Moral* inability consists not in any of these things; but either in the want of inclination; or the strength of a contrary inclination; or the want of sufficient motives in view, to induce and excite the act of the will, or the strength of apparent motives to the contrary.[17]

Moral inability, then, is present either because of a lack of something or because of the strength of something contrary to the moral. It would, therefore, be the case that the faculty of reason would be morally unable to do certain things, either because of a lack of some-

15. Ibid., 256.
16. I am not sure at this point how reason and understanding differ in Edwards' conception, except to say that reason would be seen as a *part of* understanding, the latter of which would also include perception.
17. Jonathan Edwards, *The Works of Jonathan Edwards*, vol. 1, *Freedom of the Will*, ed. Paul Ramsey (New Haven: Yale University Press, 1985), 159.

thing or the strength of something to the contrary, or perhaps a combination of both. There can be no question that Edwards applies this natural/moral ability/inability to knowledge. Edwards writes, "Natural qualifications are either excellent or otherwise, according as they are joined with moral excellency or not. Strength and knowledge don't render any being lovely, without holiness; but more hateful."[18] That which we have naturally, after the fall, is condemnable unless and until combined with the moral. This is not to say that there is no knowledge or, perhaps better, no *kind* of knowledge apart from the restoration of the moral image. Unbelievers *can* and *do* know some things "after a fashion." It must be said, however, that, even in knowing "after a fashion," those who remain in the natural image of God but without the restoration of the moral image are nevertheless unable to know God truly because they lack that moral image.[19] Or to put it another way, though reason is still intact after the fall, it is, by its fallen nature and apart from the moral image, essentially and wholly disinclined toward true spiritual knowledge of God and of the world.

Though people may have a *kind* of knowledge that is useful and helpful in a limited way, that knowledge, when according to the natural image, will not and cannot produce spiritual light. It is a kind of knowledge that is limited, fleeting, shadowy, superficial, and in the end condemnable. So, says Edwards, speaking of the limitations of reason:

> Ratiocination, without . . . spiritual light, *never will* give one such an advantage to see things in their true relations and respects to other things, and to things in general. . . . A man that sets himself to reason without divine light is like a man that goes in the dark into a garden full of the most beautiful plants, and most artfully ordered, and compares things together by going from one thing to another to feel of them all, to perceive their beauty.[20]

Reasoning according to the natural image, therefore, is like groping in the dark. Clearly, then, the process of reasoning is seriously affected by the fall, according to Edwards.

18. *Religious Affections, Works*, 2:257.
19. Edwards' view of the moral image is consistent with the biblical and Reformed notion that, when converted, the process of restoration unto true knowledge, righteousness, and holiness begins. See Ephesians 4:24 and Colossians 3:10.
20. "Miscellanies" no. 408, in Jonathan Edwards, *The Works of Jonathan Edwards*, vol. 13, *The "Miscellanies," a–500*, ed. Thomas A. Schafer (New Haven: Yale University Press, 1994), 470, emphasis mine.

It is likely that Edwards is echoing the thought of Calvin at this point. In speaking of the knowledge of those who partake only of the natural image, to use Edwards' category, Calvin notes,

> They are like a traveler passing through a field at night who in a momentary lightning flash sees far and wide, but the sight vanishes so swiftly that he is plunged again into the darkness of the night before he can take even a step—let alone be directed on his way by its help.[21]

And elsewhere Calvin notes with respect to the unregenerate, "and man with all his acumen is as stupid in understanding the mysteries of God as an ass is inept at understanding a symphony."[22]

It should be noted here that in each of these examples from Edwards and Calvin, what is deficient is not the external evidence but rather the internal or subjective faculty. One who is surrounded by the beauty of a garden does not fail to see the garden for what it is because of a defect in the garden but rather because one's faculty or faculties have rendered the garden dark and thus virtually unknowable. Likewise, an ass at a symphony is not suffering because of external deficiencies; he is just too dull to understand the beauty that surrounds him. Thus it is with the faculty of reason. While it may be intact, that is, it still remains a reasoning faculty, it is also, nevertheless, affected by the fall.

It should be noticed also, though we cannot develop the point here, that Edwards' example above seems to include all manner of knowing. Without divine light, says Edwards, one cannot see *anything* in its true context. As Edwards says, without spiritual light the reasoning process *never will* give one such an advantage to see things in their true relations and respects to other things and to things in general. Such is the case because any one thing's relationship to other things and to things in general must include, to be known truly, the context of God's creating and sustaining that thing and its relationship to other things. In other words, a thing is what it is by virtue of the plan and activity of God. A thing holds relationships to other things and to all things generally because of, and only because of, that all-sufficient plan. To attempt to know some "thing," therefore, without knowing it as having its being and meaning by virtue of God's plan is, in some impor-

21. John Calvin, *Institutes of the Christian Religion*, ed. J. T. McNeill, trans. F. L. Battles, 2 vols. (London: SCM, 1961), 1:277.

22. The original reads: "A . . . et homo cum toto suo acumine perinde est stupidus ad intelligenda per se Dei mysteria atque asinus ineptus est ad symphoniam" (John Calvin et al., *Ioannis Calvini opera quae supersunt omnia*, *Corpus Reformatorum; v. 29–87* [Brunsvigae: C. A. Schwetschke, 1863], 49:325).

tant sense, not to know it truly at all. Thus, without spiritual light, all knowledge is skewed and twisted by the process of reasoning. What is needed, therefore, for any person to understand properly the world that God has made, as well as who God is and what he has done, is revelation and regeneration.

It may sound strange to ascribe revelational necessity with respect to apologetics generally and to knowledge more specifically to one who himself was committed to writing a "Rational Account" of the Christian religion.[23] Wouldn't a rational account of the Christian religion seek to make that religion understandable, perhaps even palatable, to reason alone? What could such an account include? It seems, at least, that it could *not* include an account that would be suitable to or for reason alone.

In fact, Ava Chamberlain argues that since the "Rational Account" was meant to be a transatlantic assault on Deism, it was never meant to promote or propagate the notion that Christianity was itself simply a rational religion. It was exactly *that* point that the Deists were attempting to set forth. According to Chamberlain, for example, "In *Christianity Not Mysterious* John Toland criticized the view that miracles testify to the truth of revelation, maintaining that both miracle and mystery are affronts to reason." As Christians tried to defend Christianity against Deism on rational grounds, there was, according to Henry F. May, a "tactical mistake" because some doctrines appeared to be self-evidently irrational.[24] To seek to defend Christianity against Deism on rational grounds was like injecting oneself with the enemy's disease in order to prove how healthy one was. The project was doomed at the outset.

Edwards was aware of, and thus sought to avoid, this kind of tactical mistake. For this reason, at least, Edwards saw revelation as essential to the right use of reason. It was unreasonable to think otherwise. At one place Edwards notes that the gospel itself, with all of its mysteries, is reasonable: "[T]his is the truth which the mind first and most

23. For a skeletal outline of the never-completed project "A Rational Account of the Main Doctrines of the Christian Religion Attempted," see Jonathan Edwards, *The Works of Jonathan Edwards*, vol. 6, *Scientific and Philosophical Writings*, ed. Wallace E. Anderson (New Haven: Yale University Press, 1980), 396–97.

24. Ava Chamberlain, "Introduction," in Jonathan Edwards, *The Works of Jonathan Edwards*, vol. 18, *The "Miscellanies," 501–832*, ed. Ava Chamberlain (New Haven: Yale University Press, 2000), 26–27. Although it cannot be elaborated here, it should be noted that the same kind of "tactical mistake" was and still is made by many in the Christian tradition who did and still do attempt to answer the evidential objection to Christianity on evidential grounds alone. As with reason, so with evidence, such grounds carry with them the effects of the fall and cannot simply be presented as in any way religiously neutral.

directly feels under a conviction of, viz., that the way of salvation which the gospel reveals is a proper, suitable and sufficient way, *perfectly agreeable to reason* and the nature of things. . . ."[25] And elsewhere, speaking again of Deism, he says,

> Tindal's arguing, in his *Christianity as old as the Creation*, proceeds on this ground, That since reason is the judge whether there be any revelation, or whether any pretended revelation be really such; therefore reason, *without* revelation, or *undirected* by revelation, must be the judge concerning each doctrine and proposition contained in that pretended revelation. This is an *unreasonable* way of arguing.[26]

Furthermore, according to Chamberlain, Edwards' most common argument in the "Miscellanies" (which were themselves at one point meant to *be* the "rational account") is that revelation is an absolutely essential and necessary component of the Christian religion. So, says Edwards in response to the Deists,

> 'Tis very unreasonable to make it an objection against the Christian revelation, that it contains some things that are very mysterious and difficult to our understandings, and that seem to us impossible. If God will give us a revelation from heaven of the very truth concerning his own nature and acts, counsels and ways, and of the spiritual and invisible world, 'tis unreasonable to expect any other, than that there should be many things in such a revelation that should be utterly beyond our understanding, and seem impossible.
>
> For when was there ever a time when, if there had been a revelation from heaven of the very truth in philosophical matters, and concerning the nature of created things—which are of a vastly lower nature, and must be supposed to be more proportioned to our understandings—and there would not have been many things which would have appeared, not only to the vulgar but to the learned of that age, absurd and impossible? It surely becomes us to receive what God reveals to be truth, and to look upon his Word as proof sufficient, whether what he reveals squares with our notions or not.[27]

25. Quoted in Miller, "Sense of the Heart," 145, emphasis mine.
26. Jonathan Edwards, "Miscellaneous Observations on Important Theological Subjects," in *The Works of Jonathan Edwards*, ed. Edward Hickman, 2 vols. (1834; reprint, Edinburgh: Banner of Truth Trust, 1974), 2:479, emphasis mine. Edwards' specific point in this refutation is that reason can never be a *substitute* for revelation. By implication, that which would be true of the substitution of reason for revelation would also be true for any affirmation of reason's supposed *independence* from revelation. Both positions seek to separate reason from revelation at some apologetically crucial points.
27. "Miscellanies" no. 583 (*Works*, 18:118–19).

It should be noted here that Edwards sees the revelation of God as carrying within it its own authority. Thus, as he says, the Word of God ought to be looked upon as "proof sufficient." He does not think that it is a part of Christian theology to insist that all doctrine meet the constraints of the laws of reason or of our ability to understand.[28] As a matter of fact, given the character of God, it would be most unreasonable to think such a thing.

Is there no room, therefore, given this understanding of reason and revelation, for the so-called theistic proofs? Though Edwards does refer to and even incorporates proofs for God's existence in some of his writings, the question with regard to such proofs is not, in the first place, their *use*, but rather the context in which they are thought to be useful. That context does not seem to be one of an independent reasoning process. Notice what Edwards says about the attempt of human reason to move independently from this world to a god:

> I cannot tell whether any man would have considered the works of creation as effects, if he had never been told they had a cause. We know very well, that, even after the being of such a cause was much talked of in the world, and believed by the generality of mankind; yet many and great philosophers held the world to be eternal; and others ascribed, what we call the works of creation to an eternal series of causes. If the most sagacious of the philosophers were capable of doing this, after hearing so much of a first cause and a creation, what would they have done, and what would the gross of mankind, who are inattentive and ignorant, have thought of the matter, if nothing had been taught concerning God and the origin of things; but every single man left solely to such intimation as his own senses and reason could have given him? We find, the earlier sages of the world did not trouble themselves about the question, whether the being of God could be proved by reason, but either never inquired into the matter, or took their opinions, upon that head, merely from tradition. But, allowing that every man is able to demonstrate to himself, that the world, and all things contained therein, are effects, and had a beginning, which I take to be a most absurd supposition, and look upon it to be almost impossible for unassisted reason to go so far; yet, if effects are to be ascribed to similar causes, and a good and wise effect must suppose a good and wise cause, by the same way of reasoning, all the evil and irregularity in the world must be attributed to an evil and unwise cause. So that either the first cause must be both good and evil, wise and foolish, or else there must be two first causes, an evil and irrational, as well as a good and wise principle. Thus man, left to himself, would be apt to reason, "If the cause and effects are similar

---

28. This would be a helpful lesson to learn for anyone entertaining the notion of so-called open theism.

and conformable, matter must have a material cause; there being nothing more impossible for us to conceive, than how matter should be produced by spirit or any thing else but matter." The best reasoner in the world, endeavouring to find out the causes of things, by the things themselves, might be led into the grossest errors and contradictions, and find himself, at the end, in extreme want of an instructor.[29]

In other words, the reasoning process, due to its own fallenness, and combined with the condition of the fallen world, renders even the best reasoning both erroneous and contradictory. Given the fall into sin, Edwards argues here that even if reason were able, which he holds to be "a most absurd proposition," it could only properly conclude for the existence of a cause that was "both good and evil, wise and foolish, or else there must be two first causes, an evil and irrational, as well as a good and wise principle."

How, then, do we account for Edwards' zeal, at least initially, for writing a "Rational Account" of the Christian faith?[30] Chamberlain accounts for it this way:

Unlike the latitudinarian opponents of the deists, however, Edwards' rational defense did not weaken his adherence to the fundamental doctrines of Reformed orthodoxy. He remains convinced of the rationality of these doctrines at least in part because *he uses a standard of rationality not shared by his opponents*. He accepted the position first articulated by Locke that religious belief must conform to the principles of reason, but tempered it with the belief that divine, not human, reason was the ultimate standard of judgment. Consequently, he frequently presupposes not only the existence of God but the truth of the very doctrine that is the object of demonstration.[31]

It would seem, then, that for Edwards that which is rational is that which, first and foremost, conforms to the mind of God as revealed in Holy Scripture. It should not go without notice that Chamberlain notes that Edwards frequently presupposes the truth of God's existence in order to demonstrate its truth. Edwards is elsewhere insistent that reason *alone* will never grasp the truth. In his "Man's Natural

29. Edwards, "Miscellaneous Observations," in *Works of Jonathan Edwards*, ed. Hickman, 2:476.
30. I say "initially" because, as Chamberlain notes, "A purely rational defense of Christian doctrine would have required Edwards to use, as did the latitudinarians in their anti-Deist polemic, the standard of rationality advocated by his opponents. To avoid this 'tactical mistake' Edwards may have abandoned the 'Rational Account' and adopted a more historical approach to the defense of Christian doctrine" (Chamberlain, "Introduction," in *Works*, 18:29).
31. Ibid., 28, emphasis mine.

Blindness in the Things of Religion," Edwards says that the minds of men are so dark that they are as contrary as possible to reason.[32] This suggests not only that men cannot reason independently to God but also, and this is significant, that what is reasonable is biblical and vice versa. Reason itself is identified, not as independent of revelation, but as consistent with revelation. By that fact, reason itself must always presuppose revelation as its criterion and its content.

Apologetic Implications

What does all of this mean with respect to apologetics? More specifically, what might Edwards' notion of the faculties, combined with his understanding of the necessity of revelation and regeneration, mean with respect to an appeal to the reasoning process in attempting to show Christianity to be true? One of the clearest expositions of Edwards' approach (at least one aspect of it) comes from his *Freedom of the Will*. In speaking of the limitations of our ability (and here he must be speaking of moral ability) to know God, he summarizes his approach:

> [T]he way that mankind come to the knowledge of the being of God, is that which the Apostle speaks of (Rom. 1:20), "The invisible things of Him, from the creation of the world, are clearly seen; being understood by the things that are made; even his eternal power and Godhead." We first ascend, and prove a posteriori, or from effects, that there must be an eternal cause; and then secondly, prove by argumentation, not intuition, that this being must be necessarily existent; and then thirdly, from the proved necessity of his existence, we may descend, and prove many of his perfections a priori.[33]

How are we to understand this assertion, particularly when compared to the notion, cited above, that reason alone can only conclude with a god who is both good and evil, wise and foolish? The obvious answer to that question is that in the citation just quoted, Edwards is *not* thinking that our a posteriori ascent from effects to cause *should* be done by any kind of supposed independent reasoning process. When Edwards says that we first ascend a posteriori and prove that there must be an eternal first cause, he is attempting to explicate Romans 1:20.

---

32. Jonathan Edwards, "Man's Natural Blindness in the Things of Religion," in *Works of Jonathan Edwards*, ed. Hickman, 2:249.
33. *Freedom of the Will, Works*, 1:182.

Because Romans 1:18–25 is such a key passage with respect to apologetics generally, and the condition of unbelief more specifically, it may be helpful to summarize its contents here. The general topic that Paul introduces in Romans 1:18 is the wrath of God that is revealed from heaven against sin. But the sin that Paul specifies against which God's wrath comes is what we might call the "psychological" sin of suppressing, or holding down, the truth in unrighteousness.[34] By truth, the apostle Paul means that there are those things about God, namely his invisible attributes and divine nature, that are both clearly seen and understood. The reason that they are clearly seen and understood is because God has made himself known, clearly and without deficiency, in and through all of his creation. God is known because he reveals himself within us (Rom. 1:19) and without us (Rom. 1:20).

Thus, according to the apostle, a necessary aspect of being made in God's image is knowing the God who made us. When Edwards refers us to Romans 1:20, which notes that our knowledge of God comes *through the things that are made*, and then argues that we must first ascend a posteriori, he is arguing for such an ascent within the context, and on the basis, of God's clear and sufficient revelation to us in creation. He is not arguing for the sufficiency of reason to find what is otherwise hidden in creation. He is arguing that, given the sufficiency of God's clear revelation, we can show that those things that now exist necessitate an eternal cause. In other words, Edwards is maintaining just what Scripture itself maintains—that the a posteriori, as well as the a priori, with respect to the knowledge of God *presuppose that God has revealed himself in creation*.

It is *not*, therefore, the case that our reasoning can, in and of itself, reach an eternal first cause. It can only do so, if it does, by virtue of the fact that God is revealed in creation, through creation, and by creation such that any reasoning process takes into account the fact of God's clear and clearly understood revelation in creation. In other words, it is crucial to see at this point that the context in which Edwards affirms both a posteriori and a priori reasoning is the context of God's revelation to us in nature. Such revelation presupposes, even as one is reasoning a posteriori, that God in fact exists and reveals himself. In ascending a posteriori, then, it is safe to say that Edwards himself is presupposing, not some kind of rational neutrality, but both the existence of God and the fact that he has revealed himself through the things that are made.

34. "Psychological" is meant here, not in its more modern usage, but in its etymological sense of a knowledge of the soul.

We should also note, as Elwood comments, that while it is true that Edwards affirms a posteriori reasoning, this does not mean that Edwards affirms *that way* to be the best. Elwood observes, "Edwards himself arrived at the knowledge of the being of God by the reverse order."[35] As a matter of fact, Edwards argues, "The being of God may be argued from the desirableness and need of it thus: we see in all nature everywhere that great necessities are supplied."[36] It seems one can start anywhere and everywhere in arguing for the existence of God *just because God is revealed anywhere and everywhere.*

Of course, for Edwards, reason can be convinced of the truth of rational (biblical) argumentation only if the Spirit of God infuses faith into the hearts of those with whom we reason. According to Edwards,

> [W]hen a person has discovered to him the divine excellency of doctrines, this destroys the enmity, removes those prejudices, *sanctifies the reason and causes it to lie open to the force of arguments for their truth. . . . It not only removes the hindrances of reason but positively helps reason.*[37]

Thus, Elwood is right to assert that it is Edwards' view of faith, involving the whole person, that confirms him in the Augustinian dictum, *credo ut intelligam,* against the contemporary rationalists of his own day.[38]

This construct does not, however, provide easy answers to the question of knowledge. There can be no question that since the entrance of sin and the continuation of the image of God in human beings, the problem of knowledge has become most complex and can sound even paradoxical at points. Edwards attempts to explain the paradox somewhat by his teaching of speculative and sensitive knowledge. We may "know" speculatively that which we do not "know" sensibly. We could say that there is in Edwards something like two "levels" of knowing. Thus, the paradox is that in our natural, unregenerate state, we may know and not know the same thing at the same time. In both of these "knowings," reason, it seems, is necessarily involved. Hence the seeming contradiction.

Yet even in the face of this paradox, Edwards wants to be careful in his insistence that the unbeliever can indeed know something, though

35. Douglas J. Elwood, *The Philosophical Theology of Jonathan Edwards* (New York: Columbia University Press, 1960), 14.

36. "Miscellanies" no. 274 (*Works,* 13:375).

37. Jonathan Edwards, "A Divine and Supernatural Light," in *The Works of Jonathan Edwards,* vol. 17, *Sermons and Discourses, 1730–1733,* ed. Mark Valeri (New Haven: Yale University Press, 1999), 414–15, emphasis mine.

38. Elwood, *Philosophical Theology of Jonathan Edwards,* 127.

not adequately. Edwards says that we can endeavor to discover "what the voice of reason is, *so far as it can go*."[39] The "can" in the phrase emphasized is referring to our natural ability but also implies our moral inability. Reason can only take us so far. How far, according to Edwards, can it take us? Remember that in Edwards' distinction between moral and natural, he is willing to say that reason is capable of reasoning rightly, that reason has the natural ability to discern the force of those arguments that prove God's existence. The unbeliever *can* reason, *can* think, and *can* understand. Yet what the unbeliever reasons, thinks, and understands is both clouded by sin and in shadows. Edwards, as was seen above, sees speculative or notional knowledge of spiritual things to be knowledge according to our natural ability, a knowledge shrouded in shadows.

When, however, this notional knowledge, which may be true as far as it goes, is combined with strong affections so that it becomes sensible knowledge, this knowledge, for those outside of Christ, is condemnable. While affirming that human beings are all made in God's image, Edwards also affirms that due to the corruption of that image, knowledge itself is, after the fall, corrupted. Although the fall did not obliterate our humanity, that which we know while unregenerate, we suppress, twist, distort, and reject. With respect to knowledge, the fact of the matter seems to be that since the fall, all knowledge of the unregenerate is a confused mixture of both (notional) truth and (sensible) error. Any apologetic appeal to those outside of Christ, therefore, must be an appeal that presupposes the (sensible) truth of the Christian position and that seeks to show the despair of attempting to maintain any (notional) truth apart from that position.

Thus, Edwards sought to give full weight to our logical and noetic capacities without destroying the depth of sin's effects on our abilities. In the final analysis, he wants to maintain the absolute necessity of God's revealing himself as the backdrop for any true, sensible reasoning, thinking, rejecting, or accepting.

39. Jonathan Edwards, *Concerning the End for Which God Created the World*, in *The Works of Jonathan Edwards*, vol. 8, *Ethical Writings*, ed. Paul Ramsey (New Haven: Yale University Press, 1989), 463, emphasis mine.

8

★

JONATHAN EDWARDS
AND THE NATIONAL COVENANT

Was He Right?

Gerald R. McDermott

In July 1736, when Northampton, Massachusetts, was suffering the effects of drought, Jonathan Edwards informed the anxious farmers that rain had not come because "God is displeased," for he had seen the "corruption in our hearts." Repentance and reformation were therefore in order. Seven years later, when worms devoured the crops, Edwards again knew why: God was judging Northampton's stinginess to its poor. "If a people would but run the venture of giving their temporal good things" to God through the poor, Edwards said, "it would be a sure way to . . . [have] those Judgments Removed that would destroy them & to have a plenty of them bestowed."[1]

Edwards' claim to understand the ways of God surprised no one, for this was standard fare in New England's Reformed orthodoxy. In a tradition stretching back to the Reformation and before, God was conceived as entering into covenant with a people or nation and blessing or punishing that people in proportion to their fidelity to the terms of the covenant. As John Winthrop had told the New England founders,

1. Edwards, MS sermon on Deuteronomy 28:12 (July 1736), Beinecke Library, Yale University; and MS sermon on Malachi 3:10–11 (July 1743), 2. All sermons cited in this paper are MS sermons from the Beinecke collection unless otherwise noted.

the Lord would "expect a strict performance of the articles contained in" his covenant with them. He warned, "If we shall neglect the observation of these articles . . . the Lord will surely break out in wrath against us, be revenged of such a perjured people, and make us know the price of the breach of such a covenant."[2]

New England's religious leaders found the national covenant useful for interpreting the colonies' troubles. This covenant had no salvific value or reference to life beyond the grave, but it could help interpret what happened in this life. Hence, Indian attacks as well as crop failures and a diversity of other natural disasters were attributed to failure to keep the national covenant with God. Nearly all seem to have believed that "in all Ages since their [the Jews'] national Rejection, God has had, in some Country or other, a peculiar people owning his revelation and their Covenant Engagement to him." Since New England was the latest peculiar people, its calamities were "Signs of his Displeasure." Evangelicals and liberals alike preached that God will "favor a righteous nation" and punish nations "for every act of unrighteousness."[3] The eighteenth century brought little abatement of covenantal rhetoric.[4]

2. John Winthrop, "A Model of Christian Charity," in *The Puritans in America: A Narrative Anthology*, ed. Alan Heimert and Andrew Delbanco (Cambridge, Mass.: Harvard University Press, 1985), 90–91. For other examples of use of the national covenant among the first generation, see Thomas Hooker, "The Danger of Desertion," in *Thomas Hooker: Writings in England and Holland, 1626–1633*, ed. George H. Williams et al. (Cambridge, Mass.: Harvard University Press, 1975), esp. 230–32; George William Hooke, *New Englands Teares for Old Englands Feares* (London, 1641), 15, 18–19; John Norton, *Sion the Outcast Healed of Her Wounds* (Cambridge, 1664), 3–5, 11–12; John Higginson, *The Cause of God* (Cambridge, 1663), 8; and Edward Johnson, *History of New England* [Johnson's preferred title was *The Wonder-Working Providence of Sion's Saviour in New England*] (London, 1654; reprint, New York: Scribner, 1910), 60–121, 238.

3. See, for example, Solomon Stoddard, *An Appeal to the Learned* (Boston, 1709), 55; Thomas Prince, *The Salvation of God in 1746* (Boston, 1704), 8; Thomas Prince, *The Natural and Moral Government* (Boston, 1749), 34; John Barnard, *The Throne Established by Righteousness* (Boston, 1734), in *The Wall and the Garden: Selected Massachusetts Election Sermons 1670–1775*, ed. A. W. Plumstead (Minneapolis: University of Minnesota Press, 1978), 273, 275, 288; Joseph Sewall, *Repentance* (Boston, 1727); and Nathanael Eels, *Religion Is the Life of God's People* (Boston, 1743), 38–43.

4. Until somewhat recently, scholars had assumed that the national covenant disappeared with the rise of "secularism" at the end of the seventeenth century. Perry Miller, *The New England Mind: From Colony to Province* (Cambridge, Mass.: Harvard University Press, 1953), 447–63; Timothy Breen, *The Character of a Good Ruler: A Study of Puritan Political Ideas in New England, 1630–1730* (New Haven: Yale University Press, 1970), 150ff., 204ff. Sacvan Bercovitch and Harry S. Stout, however, have refuted this claim (Bercovitch, *The American Jeremiad* [Cambridge, Mass.: Harvard University Press, 1978], 93–154; Stout, *The New England Soul: Preaching and Religious Culture in Colonial New England* [New York: Oxford University Press, 1986], 166–79). Stout argues that scholars have focused exclusively on the sections of eighteenth-century election

Edwards, of course, believed that most of Northampton's and New England's fortunes, both good and bad, could be explained by reference to God's covenant with those societies. In this he was no different from generations of New England theologians before him. Successes were unmerited blessings, results of God's mercy, perhaps even warnings to repent. (Blessings as rewards for good behavior were so rare as to hardly be worth mentioning.) Defeats and disasters were visitations of God's anger and, once again, invitations to repent. Both good and bad fortune were directed by a sovereign God in order to motivate people to keep the terms of the covenant. Consequently, no major event in a nation's history was without meaning. Citizens might chafe under what they considered to be the severity of God's discipline, but they were spared the despair that comes from the belief that history is meaningless.

In most quarters today, the notion of national chosenness seems, at best, presumptuous or even arrogant. Historians and theologians remember the triumphalism of nineteenth-century Manifest Destiny, which enabled generations of Americans to think that God endorsed their depredations of Indian lands. The twentieth-century renewal of interest in eschatology has also tended to minimize any notion of God's work in the course of ordinary events, and the Vietnam War has proven for many that the notion of national chosenness (which was often invoked to ratify that contest) is narcissistic at best and self-deceptively jingoist and murderous at worst.

Yet to a large number of fundamentalist and evangelical Christians in America, the idea appears to be perfectly defensible. The Bible, they argue, often portrays God dealing with whole societies and using particular nations for his purposes on the basis of a covenant. Biblical writers, it is claimed, address promises and threats to large groups of people, not just individuals. Theologically, the concept of national covenant seems to follow from the doctrines of God's sovereignty and providence. Some conservative pastors and writers have used the idea to help interpret America's history and particularly its church history.[5]

---

sermons that are addressed to royal audiences and have overlooked the "sacred portions" that use the national covenant (Stout, *New England Soul*, 140–41).

5. See, for instance, Jerry Falwell, *Listen, America!* (Garden City, N.Y.: Doubleday, 1980); Peter Marshall and David Manuel, *The Light and the Glory* (Old Tappan, N.J.: Revell, 1977); Marshall Foster and Mary Elaine Swanson, *The American Covenant: The Untold Story* (Thousand Oaks, Calif.: Foundation for Christian Self-Government, 1981); James Robison with Jim Cox, *Save America to Save the World: A Christian's Practical Guide for Stopping the Tidal Wave of Moral, Political, and Economic Destruction in America* (Wheaton: Tyndale House, 1980); and Rosalie Slater, *Teaching and Learning America's Christian History: The Principle Approach* (San Francisco: Foundation for American Self-Education, 1965).

It is not only the religious right, however, that uses the concept of national chosenness. A small number of recent and current thinkers interested in public theology and public philosophy—none of them fundamentalist or evangelical—has also entertained the concept (or something like it). For instance, in an early response to his critics, Robert Bellah asked, "What Christians call the Old Testament is precisely the religious interpretation of the history of Israel. Is it so clear that American analogizing from the Old (or New) Testament is necessarily religiously illegitimate? Why should the history of a people living two or three thousand years ago be religiously meaningful but the history of a people living in the last two or three hundred years be religiously meaningless?"[6]

Philosopher Leroy Rouner argues, similarly, that America has historical significance and suggests that this "fact is largely lost at present because the left has fallen out of love with its homeland, and the right has celebrated it for mostly wrong reasons."[7] German theologian Wolfhart Pannenberg thinks that the notion of national covenant has often accurately described the fortunes of a people relative to other peoples: "It would be unfair to belittle the obvious element of truth in this sense of historical destiny. The English revolution did indeed pioneer the political emancipation in the Western world." Pannenberg adds that the notion of covenant is useful because of its explanatory power. The destruction of Germany in World War II, for instance, "may have been" a judgment on Germany's persecution and attempted annihilation of the Jewish people.[8]

H. Richard Niebuhr interpreted historical contingencies from a similar perspective. He suggested that the rise of Marxism was a judgment of the injustices and class interests of "Christian" communities and interpreted dust storms on the American prairies as "signs of man's sinful exploitation of the soil."[9] Niebuhr's explanation of these interpretations by his doctrine of responsibility was remarkably analogous to Edwards' doctrines of divine sovereignty and national covenant. In all actions impinging upon the self, Niebuhr contended, God is acting. The responsible self must therefore respond to all actions so

6. Robert Bellah, in *The Religious Situation in 1968*, ed. Donald R. Cutler (Boston: Beacon, 1968), 391.

7. Leroy S. Rouner, "To Be at Home: Civil Religion as Common Bond," in *Civil Religion and Political Theology*, ed. Leroy S. Rouner (Notre Dame: University of Notre Dame Press, 1986), 137.

8. Wolfhart Pannenberg, *Human Nature, Election, and History* (Philadelphia: Westminster, 1977), 79, 104.

9. James Gustafson, introduction to *The Responsible Self: An Essay in Christian Moral Philosophy*, by H. Richard Niebuhr (New York: Harper, 1963), 34–35.

as to respond to God's action. The same interpretation must be given to the events happening to a community.

> At the critical junctures in the history of Israel and of the early Christian community the decisive question men raised was not "What is the goal?" nor yet "What is the Law?" but "What is happening?" and then "What is the fitting response to what is happening?" When an Isaiah counsels his people, he does not remind them of the law they are required to obey nor yet of the goal toward which they are directed but calls to their attention the intentions of God present in hiddenness in the actions of Israel's enemies. The question he and his peers raise in every critical moment is about the interpretation of what is going on, whether what is happening be, immediately considered, a drought or the invasion of a foreign army, or the fall of a great empire.[10]

It is unlikely that today's public theologians will want to use the concept of the national covenant as extensively as did Edwards, who seemed to claim to know the reason for every event of significance in Northampton's history. Some might even reject the concept entirely as a temptation to hubris. They might say that the only thing we can know about God's purposes in history is that we *cannot* know God's purposes in history.

If some find the concept of national chosenness presumptuous and arrogant, others think it borders on the idolatrous.[11] Pannenberg, however, responds by saying that while some uses of the national covenant certainly have been idolatrous, the idea itself does not necessarily involve idolatry. This is because the concept, he argues, places a nation under the judgment of universal moral standards: "Christian theology should consider such a pledge [to a national covenant] to be of positive value, because it renders the policies of a nation accountable to the will of God as expressed in the Bible and places the nation under the judgment of God . . . it [the nation] makes itself accountable to the terms of God's covenant."[12]

As I have shown elsewhere, Edwards was not free from presumption and pride concerning Northampton's and his own role in the history of redemption. Quite regularly he accused his congregation of all

10. Niebuhr, *Responsible Self*, 67.
11. George Marsden, "The American Revolution: Partisanship, Just Wars and Crusades," in *Wars of America: Christian Views*, ed. Ronald A. Wells (Grand Rapids: Eerdmans, 1981), 24; see also Mark A. Noll, *One Nation under God? Christian Faith and Political Action in America* (San Francisco: Harper and Row, 1988), 8.
12. Wolfhart Pannenberg, *Human Nature*, 81, 97. Interestingly, two contemporary American Lutheran ethicists also interpret national crises as visitations of divine "wrath" (Robert Benne and Philip Hefner, *Defining America: A Christian Critique of the American Dream* [Philadelphia: Fortress, 1974], 125–35).

manner of sin, both individual and corporate—indeed, this helps explain why Northampton ejected its famous pastor from the largest pulpit outside Boston. Edwards also considered himself to be something of a world historical figure called by God to provide critical leadership at a fulcrum point in history.[13]

Yet it is also clear that Edwards often used the covenant in the manner that Pannenberg outlines, as a way to point his audiences to their failure to conform to its moral standards. He explained both natural disasters and moral corruption as divine judgments upon a covenant-forsaking society. The first he attributed to the direct action of God chastising a sinful people (as when worms, he charged, were sent to blight crops because of Northampton's failure to help the poor). The second was explained as the result of God's abandonment of a covenant people to their own devices. Pannenberg, interestingly, offers a comparable interpretation of spiritual declension: "When God seems absent not only from the world but from the hearts of human beings, this does not indicate, as a superficial evaluation would suggest, that perhaps he died. Rather, it foretells impending judgment over a world that alienated itself from the source of life."[14]

Edwards used the covenant to invoke fear even in times of spiritual prosperity. Times of religious vitality, he warned, should not necessarily be interpreted as signs of divine favor. They might instead be signals of coming judgment and destruction. God's goodness is meant to lead to repentance, so revival should cause citizens to search their hearts and fear for their future, both temporal and eternal.

Hence, judgment was a prominent theme in Edwards' sermons on public days.[15] He repeatedly excoriated New England's impiety and social contention, the venality of corrupt politicians and their cynical use of religion, and sins of the flesh, such as excessive drinking and fornication.[16] But these and all other sins were subsumed by the fun-

13. Gerald R. McDermott, *One Holy and Happy Society: The Public Theology of Jonathan Edwards* (University Park: Pennsylvania State University Press, 1992), chaps. 1 and 2.

14. Pannenberg, *Human Nature*, 93.

15. McDermott, *One Holy and Happy Society*, chap. 1.

16. MS sermon on Proverbs 14:34, pp. 10, 27; MS sermon on Jeremiah 51:5, p. 28; see also MS sermon on Matthew 18:7, pp. 47–48; MS sermon on Jeremiah 2:5, p. 32; MS sermon on Acts 19:19, p. 21; MS sermon on Proverbs 14:34, p. 25. Outside of the context of the national covenant, Edwards said that the greatest sins were the sins of the spirit, not the sins of the flesh. Of all the sins of the spirit, pride was the worst. Of all the kinds of pride, spiritual pride was the most dangerous (Jonathan Edwards, *The Works of Jonathan Edwards*, vol. 2, *Religious Affections*, ed. John E. Smith [New Haven: Yale University Press, 1959], 181; Jonathan Edwards, *Some Thoughts concerning the Revival*, in *The Works of Jonathan Edwards*, vol. 4, *The Great Awakening*, ed. C. C. Goen [New Haven: Yale University Press, 1972], 415–16, 467).

damental sin of ingratitude. That is, sins of impiety, contention, injustice, venality, and sensuality were simply various manifestations of an underlying attitude—ungratefulness to God for the unparalleled covenant mercies showered upon New England. Ultimately, it was this attitude that caused God's anger toward New England. New England had been given the greatest of civil and religious privileges, yet its people had arrogantly abused them. They were more guilty than Sodom and Gomorrah, for if those towns had received the same blessings, they certainly would have "awakened . . . and reformed." Indeed, because of its unprecedented blessings, New England was more guilty than any other people in history. Those blessings made the colony more nearly parallel to Israel than any other people on earth, but this was cause for alarm, not congratulation. For Israel was a "whore" and a "witch," and her children were "bastards." In 1747 Edwards told his Northampton parishioners—three years before they ejected him—that New England was on the verge of committing "the unpardonable sin against the Holy Ghost." Two years later he declared that New England was worse than Pharaoh, who responded in part to some of God's judgments despite having fewer means of grace. Since New England's means were greater, its guilt would be greater. And, as with Pharaoh, New England's obstinacy would result in "utter destruction."[17] This meant that God might even entirely forsake his covenant with her. In fact, considering the enormity of her sins, it was a wonder that New England had not been exterminated already.

Edwards' doctrine of the national covenant, therefore, was neither tribalist nor provincial. The Massachusetts pastor was a prophet in the tradition of the New England jeremiad, who never consistently embraced the optimistic nationalism often attributed to him. God's judgment on a sinful people was the predominant message of his sermons on public and civil concerns. As his career progressed, he became more convinced that since New England was the most blessed of all peoples, it was also the most guilty. Hence, the two early-eighteenth-century awakenings were signs, not of God's pleasure, but of his anger and perhaps omens of coming destruction. For neither awakening had brought reformation. If New England was to be a redeemer nation, it would be by default. Its unfaithfulness might cause God to transfer his covenant blessings to another

17. MS sermon on Jonah 3:10, p. 20; MS sermon on Exodus 8:15 (15 June 1749), p. 11; MS sermon on Jeremiah 51:5, p. 10; Jonathan Edwards, *Misrepresentations Corrected, and Truth Vindicated in a Reply to the Rev. Mr. Solomon Williams's Book, Entitled, The True State of the Question concerning the Qualifications Necessary to Lawful Communion in the Christian Sacraments*, in *The Works of President Edwards*, ed. Sereno E. Dwight (New York: Carvill, 1830), 4:568; letter to McCullough, 21 January 1747, in ibid., 1:231–32; MS sermon on Exodus 8:15, pp. 11–12.

people. If Northampton was a light on a hill, the light it radiated to the world only exposed its own corruption, thus inviting contempt.

That Edwards could retain a sense of national guilt while still maintaining a sense of singular national blessedness may seem puzzling. It may reduce one's bewilderment, however, to recall that Edwards was neither the first nor the last American to balance the notion of national chosenness with a sense of national judgment. Not all seventeenth-century jeremiads were able to keep these two concepts in balance. Many emphasized judgment nearly as much as Edwards.[18] Nineteenth-century evangelist Charles Finney (1792–1875) preached that God had entered into covenant with America but that America was under his judgment. Although he stopped supporting abolition after the Tappan brothers' home was attacked in 1834 and told Timothy Weld that the answer to the slavery problem was evangelism rather than abolition, Finney proclaimed that the union was hypocritical for its treatment of blacks.[19]

Abraham Lincoln referred to America as "the almost chosen people" and "the last, best hope of earth." In terms not unlike Edwards' invocation of the national covenant, Lincoln proclaimed in an 1863 proclamation of a general fast,

> We have been the recipients of the choicest bounties of Heaven. We have been preserved, these many years, in peace and prosperity. We have grown in numbers, wealth and power, as no other nation has ever grown. But we have forgotten God.
>
> We have forgotten the gracious hand which preserved us in peace, and multiplied, enriched and strengthened us; and we have vainly imagined, in the deceitfulness of our hearts, that all these blessings were produced by some superior wisdom and virtue of our own. Intoxicated with unbroken success, we have become too self-sufficient to feel the necessity of redeeming and preserving grace, too proud to pray to the God that made us! It behooves us then, to humble ourselves before the offended Power, to confess our national sins, and to pray for clemency and forgiveness.[20]

18. Stout, *New England Soul*. Nevertheless, Edwards exceeded nearly all in severity of denunciation and pessimism. See McDermott, *One Holy and Happy Society*, chap. 1.

19. Charles Finney, *Lectures on Revivals of Religion* (New York, 1835), 274–75, 283–84; William G. McLoughlin, "Charles Finney," in *Ante-Bellum Reform*, ed. David Brion Davis (New York: Harper and Row, 1967), 104; Charles G. Finney, *Lectures on Systematic Theology* (1878; reprint, Grand Rapids: Eerdmans, 1951); see also Charles G. Finney, *Memoirs* (New York, 1876), 324.

20. "Proclamation of a National Fast, March 30, 1863," in *Voices from the Heart: Four Centuries of American Piety*, ed. Roger Lundin and Mark A. Noll (Grand Rapids: Eerdmans, 1987), 172.

Like Edwards, Lincoln believed that God punishes a people corporately for its corporate sins. Lincoln applied this paradigm to the Civil War and concluded that it was just such a punishment. "And, insomuch as we know that, by His divine law, nations like individuals are subjected to punishments and chastisements in this world, may we not justly fear that the awful calamity of civil war, which now desolates the land, may be but a punishment, inflicted upon us, for our presumptuous sins, to the needful end of our national reformation as a whole People?"[21] Two years later, in his often-quoted Second Inaugural Address, Lincoln again referred to the war as a judgment of God.

> If God will that it [the Civil War] continue, until all the wealth piled by the bond-man's two hundred and fifty years of unrequited toil shall be sunk, and until every drop of blood drawn with the lash, shall be paid by another drawn with the sword, as was said three thousand years ago, so still it must be said "the judgments of the Lord, are true and righteous altogether."[22]

If Edwards, Finney, and Lincoln are any indication, Pannenberg may be right when he asserts that use of the national covenant motif need not be necessarily idolatrous. Certainly, the possibility—perhaps probability—exists of presumptuous and disastrous identification of one's nation with divine ideals. History is full of examples of this self-deception, as when New Testament scholar Gerhard Kittel lectured in Cambridge in the 1930s wearing Nazi armbands, and American Christians fought integration in their churches. But if any of today's public theologians want to see how the covenant can be used without lapsing into idolatry of the nation, they would do well to look at Edwards.

So perhaps Christian thinkers should not dismiss the concept of national covenant so quickly. Of course, there are enormous differences between twenty-first-century America and eighteenth-century New England: our country today is far less religiously homogeneous, and, despite the fact that pollsters tell us a large majority of Americans call themselves Christians, few of us would call this a Christian nation.

But neither did Edwards. Both his occasional sermons and formal treatises reveal that Edwards' denial of Northampton's (and, by implication, New England's) righteousness was fundamental. No polity, he indicated, can be righteous in the sense that the majority of its citizens are Christian or relatively free from sin. There never has existed a whole nation outwardly moral or even with a majority of its people in the visible Christian church. Edwards referred to "Christian coun-

21. Ibid.
22. Lincoln, *Second Inaugural Address* (1865), quoted in Noll, *One Nation under God*, 101.

tries," of which New England was one, but by that designation he meant no more than polities whose formal adherence was to Christianity. The majority of people in all "Christian" lands were not regenerate, he believed, and even the "godly" had an abundance of sin in their hearts. Therefore, New England was a Christian land only in the sense that Christianity was the established religion. There were some virtuous Christians in New England, of course; in his occasional sermons Edwards praised New England's founding fathers, and in revival treatises he lauded the piety of his wife Sarah, a four-year-old girl, and a dying woman.[23] But most New Englanders were not true Christians.

By suggesting that we should consider seriously the concept of national covenant, I do not recommend a "providential history" that presumes that any historian, secular or believing, could study history and simply read off God's purposes from it. No, this is a tool for God's people to help them understand at critical junctures the meaning of what is happening. It is a way of thinking about God and history, for those who believe that God is active in history, that suggests that God deals not only with individuals but also with nations. If God can sometimes make his purposes known to individuals about what he is doing in their lives, then perhaps he can also make known to his church at certain times what he is doing to a whole people. In other words, Robert Bellah's question is apropos: If Israel's history had meaning, why not America's? Or Russia's? Or Afghanistan's?

Of course, this raises a number of important questions: What precisely are the differences between *explanation* in general history that all can read and the historical *interpretations* made by Christians for the use of the church? How can we protect such interpretation from being merely arbitrary conjecture—or ideological rather than prophetic? What is the role of Scripture in this interpretation? This is not the place to answer all these questions, but it is the place to say that some of us should begin work on a sensitive and responsible theology of discernment of historical meaning and that we should at least engage the long tradition of reflection on this discipline, which did not start with the Puritans or Edwards. For us to conclude that it is illegitimate for Christian thinkers to reflect on this possibility is to revert to the Enlightenment dogma that history must be hermetically sealed off from the fullest ranges of faith. If Jesus rebuked his contemporaries for failing to "interpret the present time" (Luke 12:56 RSV), it cannot be impossible or theologically illegitimate for his disciples to continue that task of discerning the signs of the times.

23. MS sermon on Deuteronomy 28:12 (July 1736); MS sermon on Malachi 3:10–11 (July 1743), p. 2.

In that task there are some important qualifications—more than I can list here. But at least one is the humility to recognize that it is one thing for God to have purposes for a nation's history and quite another for the church to be able to discern those purposes. Edwards was far too sanguine about his own ability to discern the meaning of every historical contingency that befell Northampton and New England (and this may suggest he was more indebted to the Enlightenment than some have imagined). N. T. Wright points out the critical word "perhaps" in Philemon 15: "Perhaps this is why Onesimus was parted from me for a while, so that you could have him back not just as a slave but as a brother." Wright opines that it is not wrong for Christians at times to claim meaning for a course of events, but these claims "need to be made with a 'perhaps'; which is always inviting God to come in and say, 'Well, actually, no.'"[24]

Second, and not unrelated, we should recall both from Scripture and the historical record that because of self-interest, we are inordinately inclined to self-deception. Hence, we are probably less prone to misjudgment when we claim that God is judging us rather than congratulating us or judging others (such as when Jerry Falwell blamed the terrorist attacks on gays and liberals).

Third, investigating the meaning of historical events can help the church resist jingoism and the church's co-option by nationalism or partisan politics. For example, some Americans interpreted the sudden profusion of the G-word in the public square and increased church attendance after September 11, 2001, as signs of God's blessing on America. Edwards' public theology can remind us, however, that religious revival is sometimes a prelude to judgment. Edwards' reflections might also suggest that this war on terrorism might be not only our judgment of "evildoers" but also God's judgment of America—for its complicity in 35 million abortions since 1973 and egregious materialism, among other things. In other words, Edwards' use of the national covenant can suggest to us that the church is to continue to participate in the prophetic ministry of Jesus Christ.

Finally, it can also suggest to us the need for the priestly ministry of Christ, which would mean recognizing God's blessings and ministering God's comfort in times of both prosperity and peril. Although this chapter focuses on Edwards' prophetic ministry of judgment, he also served a priestly role, particularly in times of war. Here too is material from which theologians can draw to help them construct a theology of public discernment.

24. Cited in Tim Stafford, "Whatever Happened to Christian History?" *Christianity Today*, April 2, 2001.

PART 3

★ ★ ★

LEGACY

9

※

JONATHAN EDWARDS AND THE ORIGINS OF EXPERIMENTAL CALVINISM

D. G. Hart

In an introductory essay to the book *Reformed Theology in America,* George Marsden provides what still is a remarkably useful map of the Reformed tradition in the United States. According to Marsden, who experienced firsthand the different constituencies of American Reformed life, there exist three distinct and yet overlapping ways of answering the question, "What does it mean to be Reformed?" In one group, which he identifies with the church of his upbringing, the Orthodox Presbyterian Church (OPC), the answer comes with careful attention to precise doctrinal formulation. Here only Christians who take subscription to the Reformed creeds seriously are "fully within the pale." For another group, being Reformed means cultural transformation, a pose most noticeable to Marsden during his years in the Christian Reformed Church. According to this outlook, Reformed Christianity is characterized by a "world-and-life view" that applies Christian principles to all walks of life. The last answer to the question of what it means to be Reformed comes from those who regard themselves as both Reformed and evangelical. For them being Reformed is best embodied in such evangelical forms of piety as evangelistic fervor, "personal devotion, Methodist mores, and openness in expressing one's

evangelical commitment." In sum, Marsden identifies three schools of
Reformed thought and spirituality, namely, the doctrinalist, the culturalist, and the pietist.[1]

This map of twentieth-century North American Reformed life raises
an interesting question regarding Jonathan Edwards: If he were alive
today, with which school would he identify? To give the question bite,
let me raise the stakes by asking whether Edwards would be teaching
at Westminster Seminary, Calvin Seminary, or Trinity Evangelical Divinity School. No fair avoiding an answer by responding that Edwards
would not be teaching but instead would be the pastor of Bethlehem
Baptist Church in Minneapolis, Minnesota. Marsden provides a helpful
preliminary answer by arguing that the Puritan tradition in which Edwards stood embodied all three schools since the Puritans highly es-
teemed theological rigor, established a culture modeled on Christian
teaching, and were ever on guard for the dangers of head knowledge
without heart religion.[2]

As helpful as this partial answer may be, Edwards does not easily fit
in any of the schools that Marsden identifies. For instance, it is not altogether clear that Edwards would pass a licensure or ordination exam in
the OPC, and neither is it certain that the Kuyperians in Annapolis, Tor-
onto, and Grand Rapids would make him a poster boy for their efforts
to press the lordship of Christ in the arenas of faith-based initiatives, labor unions, and office furniture. The one school where Edwards fits
best is that of Reformed pietism, though if Trinity Evangelical Divinity
School is its best manifestation, it is not certain that Edwards would be
a natural fit with that school's Scandinavian free-church tradition. Perhaps the best way to characterize Edwards is as an experimental Calvinist, which would make his modern-day soul mates the folks who
write for and edit the books and literature produced by the Banner of
Truth Trust in Edinburgh. In fact, the one correction that Marsden's
otherwise helpful guide to the Reformed tradition could use is to suggest that the pietist school is best represented by the sorts of themes
that the Banner folks have developed over the last forty years or so.
They are earnestly Calvinistic in their soteriology and very friendly toward revivals as an ongoing means of saving souls and edifying the
faithful. What could be a better way of describing Jonathan Edwards?

If the Banner of Truth Trust is the modern-day embodiment of Edwards' theology and piety, then a plausible argument can be made that

1. George M. Marsden, "Reformed and American," in *Reformed Theology in America: A History of Its Modern Development*, ed. David F. Wells (Grand Rapids: Eerdmans,
1985), 2–3.
2. Ibid., 3–5.

in the Northampton pastor's ministry and writings we see the origins of the pietist school of Reformed Christianity. While this line of reasoning is not inherently startling—after all, the Banner's recently retired executive has written a glowing biography of Edwards—it does raise questions to which experimental Calvinists may need to give greater heed. For instance, if experimental Calvinism is a combination of the Reformed doctrines of grace and pietistic forms of devotion, and if Edwards was one of the first exponents of this outlook, are there aspects of Edwards' thought and ministry that raise doubts about such a mix of theology and piety? Here, specifically, the nature of conversion about which Edwards wrote so extensively in *Religious Affections* comes to mind. Did his laudable effort to detect signs of regeneration actually betray Reformed teaching on conversion and therefore compromise Calvinism's doctrine of salvation? What follows is an exploration of Edwards' teaching on conversion and its manifestation in holy affections in the context of historic Reformed teaching on regeneration and the Christian life. The point of this endeavor is not to detract from Edwards' greatness but to generate a better understanding of Reformed teaching about conversion and how the great theologian and pastor of eighteenth-century Massachusetts may have unintentionally undermined the Calvinism that he intended to defend.

Conversion Subjectively Considered

Jonathan Edwards' views on religious experience were not entirely original, but they did establish a significant beachhead for Reformed pietism in the New World. Edwards grew up in the pious parsonage of Timothy and Esther Edwards in East Windsor, Connecticut. Although the surroundings were primitive, Jonathan's upbringing was conventional. In addition to receiving an education that would prepare him for college, he also learned the elements of the Christian faith, both at home and in church.[3] Yet by the time he went away to Yale College in nearby New Haven, he had not experienced a "new sense of things," that is, a lasting commitment to earnest Christian devotion. Then, sometime in the spring of 1721, Edwards encountered God and the truth of the gospel in a powerful way. He described this experience as his response to reading 1 Timothy 1:17, "Now unto the King eternal, immortal, invisible, the only wise God, be honour and glory for ever and ever, Amen" (KJV). This was "the first instance" when he remem-

3. On Edwards' life, see Ola Elizabeth Winslow, *Jonathan Edwards, 1703–1758: A Biography* (1940; reprint, New York: Octagon Books, 1973).

bered "that sort of inward, sweet delight in God and divine things."
Edwards continued,

> As I read the words, there came into my soul, and was as it were dif-
> fused through it, a sense of the glory of the Divine Being; a new sense,
> quite different from any thing I ever experienced before. Never any
> words of scripture seemed to me as these words did. I thought with my-
> self, how excellent a Being that was, and how happy I should be, if I
> might enjoy that God, and be rapt up in him in heaven, and be as it
> were swallowed up in him for ever! . . . From about that time, I began to
> have a new kind of apprehensions and ideas of Christ, and the work of
> redemption, and the glorious way of salvation by him. An inward, sweet
> sense of these things, at times, came into my heart; and my soul was led
> away in pleasant views and contemplations of them.[4]

It is interesting to note in passing how much Edwards' description
of his conversion sounds like that of Henry Alline, another evangelist
but of a very different theological orientation. Compared to Edwards,
Alline—who lived from 1748 to 1784, was a Free Will Baptist who
preached to the poor and illiterate in Canada's Maritime provinces,
and gained a reputation as Canada's George Whitefield—was like a
shooting star, aflame with a radical message and charismatic demeanor. Yet, for all of their cultural and personal differences, Edwards and Alline had each experienced the work of divine grace. Alline did not enjoy the benefits of a Yale education. Nor had he been
steeped in the doctrinal precision of Puritanism. But at the age of
twenty-seven, he underwent an experience very similar to Edwards'.
Alline feared for his life and plummeted to the depths of morbid introspection, only to be lifted to the certainty of God's favor. According to
Alline:

> O the infinite condescension of God to a worm of the dust! for though
> my whole soul was filled with love, and ravished with divine ecstasy be-
> yond any doubts or fears, or thoughts of being deceived, for I enjoyed a
> heaven on earth, and it seemed as if I were wrapped up in God.[5]

For Edwards and Alline, the experience of divine grace that transformed tortured and sorrow-ridden souls into ones assured of God's

---

4. Jonathan Edwards, "Personal Narrative," in *The Works of Jonathan Edwards*, vol.
16, *Letters and Personal Writings*, ed. George S. Claghorn (New Haven: Yale University
Press, 1998), 792–93.

5. Henry Alline, *The Life and Journal* (Boston, 1806), 27, quoted in G. A. Rawlyk,
Ravished by the Spirit: Religious Revivals, Baptists, and Henry Alline (Kingston and Mon-
treal: McGill-Queen's University Press, 1984), 5.

love, thanks to a direct tasting and touching of divine beauty and majesty, was the centerpiece of true Christianity. In turn, the conversion experience became the defining mark of genuine faith. And it led to an earnest form of Christian devotion that gave the spiritually shy the strength to get up and glorify God in what needs to be done. Just listen to several of the resolutions prompted by Edwards' new sense.

1. Resolved, that I will do whatsoever I think to be most to God's glory, and my own good, profit and pleasure, in the whole of my duration, without any consideration of the time, whether now, or never so many myriads of ages hence. Resolved to do whatever I think to be my duty, and most for the good and advantage of mankind in general. Resolved to do this, whatever difficulties I meet with, how many and how great soever.
2. Resolved, to be continually endeavoring to find out some new invention and contrivance to promote the forementioned things.
3. Resolved, if I ever shall fall and grow dull, so as to neglect to keep any part of these Resolutions, to repent of all I can remember, when I come to myself again.
4. Resolved, never to do any manner of thing, whether in soul or body, less or more, but what tends to the glory of God; nor be, nor suffer it, if I can avoid it.[6]

Edwards' own experience of the new sense was just one important factor in the way his understanding of conversion developed. Another was Edwards' own observation of the sorts of changes that took place in church members under his care. As he described the dramatic transformation of Christians in a letter to Benjamin Colman,

There are many that have lately been converted, who have been accounted very knowing persons, especially in the things of religion, and could talk with more than common understanding of conversion, that declare that all their former wisdom is brought to nought, and that they appear to themselves to have been mere babes. . . . The converting influences of God's Spirit very commonly bring an extraordinary conviction of the reality and certainty of the great things of religion. They have that sight and taste of the divinity and divine excellency of the things of the Gospel, that is more to convince them than the readings of hundreds of volumes of arguments without it.[7]

6. Jonathan Edwards, "Resolutions," in *Letters and Personal Writings, Works,* 16:753.
7. Jonathan Edwards, *The Works of Jonathan Edwards,* vol. 4, *The Great Awakening,* ed. C. C. Goen (New Haven: Yale University Press, 1972), 125.

    This description written in 1736 was obviously of a generic nature. When Edwards turned to specific persons who had experienced the white-hot heat of God's searing Spirit, he described their encounter with the divine in terms that echoed his own experience as a young man. One woman in particular drew Edwards' attention in a letter from 1735. This woman was "modest," "bashful," and "pious," not necessarily the sort of attributes we would ascribe to an unregenerate person. And yet, having witnessed the effects of conversion on others and requested from God a "more clear manifestation of himself," she received that for which she asked and experienced "a sense of [God's] glory and love" that lasted intermittently for days until one afternoon she began to sink under this sense. When neighbors discovered her, they feared she would die because of the intensity of her experience. Edwards himself visited her and heard her speak "in a manner that can't be described" of "the sense she had of the glory of God, and particularly of such and such perfections, and her own unworthiness, her longing to lie in the dust, sometimes here longing to be with Christ, and crying out of the excellency of Christ, and the wonderfulness of his dying love."[8] Over time, of course, as counterfeit experiences began to be evident in the revivals of other towns and ministers, Edwards developed criteria for determining which conversions were authentic and which ones were not. Still, the intensity of these experiences did not scare Edwards off, and the reason has to be in part his own conversion and the new sense it yielded.

    Describing the effects of conversion, however, is not the same enterprise as defining conversion itself. The occasional nature of Edwards' writings makes it hard to find a systematic or precise definition of conversion. One place where he does go into some detail on the topic is at the end of *Religious Affections* under the heading of the seventh of the distinguishing signs of truly authentic or gracious affections. There Edwards writes,

> The Scripture representations of conversion do strongly imply and signify a change of nature: such as being born again; becoming new creatures; rising from the dead. . . . Therefore if there be no great and remarkable, abiding change in persons, that think they have experienced a work of conversion, vain are all their imaginations and pretenses, however they have been affected. Conversion . . . is a great and universal change of the man, turning him from sin to God. A man may be restrained from sin, before he is converted; but when he is converted, he is not only restrained from sin, his very heart and nature is turned from

8. Ibid., 105–6.

it, unto holiness: so that thenceforward he becomes a holy person, and an enemy to sin.[9]

This definition did not mean that conversion was always easy to spot or that it followed the same lines of development in the experiences of redeemed souls. As he also cautioned in *Religious Affections*, "[N]o order or method of operations and experiences is any certain sign of their divinity."[10] Yet even if the morphology of conversion was not set or predictable, what was certain was that conversion rested on the mysterious movement of the Spirit, imparting a new and spiritual sense to the convert, and that the change was dramatic, taking the believer from the depths of despair to the ecstasy of faith and love.

Of course, Jonathan Edwards was not unique in his understanding of conversion as a seismic shift in the life of the believer. Indeed, in the words of Alan Simpson, who wrote the classic little book *Puritanism in Old and New England* (1955), the essence of the religious tradition in which Edwards stood is "an experience of conversion which separates the Puritan from the mass of mankind and endows him with the privileges and duties of the elect." Simpson adds that "the root of the matter is always a new birth, which brings with it a conviction of salvation and a dedication to warfare against sin."[11] Certainly, this is an accurate rendering of the sort of transformations Edwards documented and promoted. More recently, Charles Cohen, whose book *God's Caress* (1986) is one of the best treatments of the Puritan psychology, reinforces the point that Simpson made some three decades earlier. Cohen asserts that "to friends [the Puritans] seemed militant soldiers in the army of the Lord; to foes, officious busybodies disrupting village camaraderie, but on at least one point all observers could agree: to be a Puritan meant living a life distinctively ardent." Cohen explains that Puritans were "a hotter sort of Protestant," and that what kept them "bubbling was a religious sensibility intimately bound up with conversion." This experience, he concludes, is an "emotional confrontation with grace borne by the Holy Spirit in the Word."[12] Jonathan Edwards' writings about religious experience and

9. Jonathan Edwards, *The Works of Jonathan Edwards*, vol. 2, *Religious Affections*, ed. John E. Smith (New Haven: Yale University Press, 1959), 340–41.

10. Ibid., 159.

11. Alan Simpson, *Puritanism in Old and New England* (Chicago: University of Chicago Press, 1955), 2.

12. Charles Lloyd Cohen, *God's Caress: The Psychology of Puritan Religious Experience* (New York: Oxford University Press, 1986), 4. For a more recent study that locates Puritan psychology in a larger movement in the West toward the subject of self-awareness, see James Hoopes, *Consciousness in New England: From Puritanism and Ideas to Psychoanalysis and Semiotic* (Baltimore: Johns Hopkins University Press, 1989).

his understanding of conversion are steeped in this essential component of Puritanism.

Where the Northampton minister may have been original was in his ability, some would say genius, to combine the Puritan zeal for holiness with Enlightenment insights into human psychology. Here Edwards brilliantly turned the tables on the Great Awakening's critics who decried the enthusiasm and strange excitements that the revivals appeared to nurture. Instead of regarding enthusiasm as an epithet, Edwards tapped the aesthetics of the Third Earl of Shaftesbury to portray "true enthusiasm" in a good light, that is, as a form of affection for things divine or for the very nature of existence itself. For instance, Shaftesbury compared moments of aesthetic appreciation to religious experience when he asked, "Shall I be ashamed of this diviner love and of an object of love so far excelling all those [other] objects in dignity, majesty, grace, beauty, and amiableness?" If this were enthusiasm, he concluded, then "so may I ever be an enthusiast."[13] Edwards used this line of argument to depict conversion as a form of this good kind of enthusiasm. But for Edwards, as Harry Stout writes, this religious version of good enthusiasm "came from the supernatural activity of the Holy Spirit transforming the heart from love of self to a disinterested love of 'divine excellency,' or 'Being in general.'"[14]

Nowhere was Edwards' masterful transformation of enthusiasm from a burden into an asset more apparent than in his 1746 work *Religious Affections*. Here he defended the new sense of religious experience in an eminently moderate fashion. Edwards was attempting to walk a fine line between the revival's critics and abusers. As such, the question was one of genuine conversion with the most obvious answers being either a reasonable and moral faith as articulated by the likes of Charles Chauncy or a passionate and zealous awakening as promoted by such figures as James Davenport. Edwards attempted to cut through the Gordian knot by overturning the old Puritan psychology that simply carved up the reason and passions and placed them in separate compartments. Instead, he conceived of the relation between head and heart, in today's parlance, as an organic one in which the mind and will always act together, with the will having priority but never independent of understanding or intellect. As John Smith points out helpfully in his introduction to the Yale edition of *Religious Affections*, Edwards *"was trying to transcend [the] opposition"* involved in a

    13. Anthony Ashley Cooper Shaftesbury, *Characteristics of Men, Manners, Opinions, Times etc.*, ed. John M. Robertson, 2 vols. (London, 1900), 2:223, quoted in Harry S. Stout, *The New England Soul: Preaching and Religious Culture in Colonial New England* (New York: Oxford University Press, 1986), 206.
    14. Stout, *New England Soul*, 206.

simple contrast of head and heart.[15] He did so with the notion of
"spiritual understanding," which contained within itself "the new
sense or new creation which has a 'taste' for the beauty and excellence
of divine things." As such, the heart in Edwards' scheme "stands not
for emotion or feeling" but "for an apprehension which already has
inclination or judgment in it." In other words, Edwards' purpose in
Religious Affections (his "chief" one according to Smith) "was to retain
understanding in religion as furnishing a rational criterion, but also to
redefine it as *sensible* light involving direct sensible perception and the
inclination of the heart."[16]

Edwards also had to walk another fine line in *Religious Affections*,
this one again between the revival's critics and abusers but on a different question, namely, the relation between faith and morality, or between moralism and antinomianism. The critics of the Great Awakening were understandably concerned for order and morality in the light
of claims by some converts to have experienced the liberty that comes
with the work of the Spirit. On the other side were the revival's advocates who so emphasized the assurance of forgiveness in conversion
that they downplayed the necessity of good works. Again, Edwards
tried to walk a tightrope by rising above it and merging these neat di-
chotomies into a higher synthesis. Here his understanding of the primacy of the will or inclinations in conversion was again key. The work
of the Holy Spirit in regeneration gives the convert a new sense or
taste for the excellency of divine things, which is the only foundation,
according to Edwards, for holy actions or good works. The reason this
is the only legitimate basis for righteous deeds is that this new disposition removes all sense of self-interest from salvation, whether as a
reward for good works or simply as a means of escaping eternal punishment. For Edwards, in genuine conversion the saint loses all sense
of self and is caught up in the wonder of God. But this wonder is not
so wonderful as to foster a form of mysticism that removes the saint
from reality. Instead, this wonder imparts a relish for spiritual enter-
prise that automatically results in holy actions, thus establishing the
connection that holy affections lead to holy lives, not fits of religious
ecstasy.[17]

In so construing the relationship between conversion and good
works as the Holy Spirit's instilling a new or spiritual sense, Edwards
avoided the Arminian and rationalist error of making true religion

15. *Religious Affections, Works,* 2:33.
16. Ibid., 32, 33.
17. Here I am following William Breitenbach, "Piety and Moralism: Edwards and
the New Divinity," in *Jonathan Edwards and the American Experience,* ed. Nathan O.
Hatch and Harry S. Stout (New York: Oxford University Press, 1988), 182–84.

simply an extension of religious and moral insights already available to men and women in their natural state. Instead, he was insisting that conversion and the holy life are essentially supernatural and require something new, not the refinement of something old. Edwards' teaching on conversion was also developed to avoid the antinomian excesses of the revival's advocates. He did so by emphasizing that genuine conversion is not evident simply by a sense of forgiveness of sin or belief in God's promise to save in Christ. Instead, the selfless character of true religion not only requires a holy disposition to love the things of God but also results in a life devoted to holy actions.[18]

Edwards' probing of the heart in writings such as *Religious Affections* has rightfully earned him the title "theologian of the heart." According to Harold Simonson,

> It was not Edwards' intrepid defense of Calvinism *per se* that made his leadership during the Awakening most notable; it was rather his profound conviction that Calvinist theology was experientially true. . . . Edwards insisted that unless theology was rooted in experience, it could not be anything more than intellectual speculation. . . . Religion, he asserted, consists not merely in speculative understanding but in will, inclination, affection. Religion is a matter of true affections that incline the heart away from self-love towards God. What this means in terms of experience was Edwards' life-long theme.[19]

To be sure, Edwards was not alone in understanding Christianity in this way. He stood in the line of Puritan divines for whom exploring the recesses of the human heart was a full-time job. Yet, because Edwards wrote at the time of revivalism's origins and because he emerged as the most thoughtful and learned defender of awakenings and the heart religion they produced, he deserves special recognition for establishing experiential religion as one of the true marks not only of genuine religion but also of authentic Calvinism. In this sense, Edwards stands at the font of modern-day experimental Calvinism; he became the organizing principle for Calvinistic thinking in the nineteenth and twentieth centuries on the relationships among "personal piety, individual conversion, mass revivalism *and* theology."[20] As such, although Edwards followed well-worn paths of Puritan divinity, his

18. Ibid.
19. Harold P. Simonson, *Jonathan Edwards: Theologian of the Heart* (Grand Rapids: Eerdmans, 1974), 13.
20. Joseph A. Conforti, *Jonathan Edwards, Religious Tradition, and American Culture* (Chapel Hill: University of North Carolina Press, 1995), 5.

celebrity made him into a trailblazer for one of the most powerful versions of contemporary Calvinism.

A Calvinist Alternative?

One reason for referring to Edwards' theology of the heart as only one version of Calvinism is that not all Calvinists have thought about conversion and regeneration in the same way he did. If Edwards represents a perspective on conversion subjectively considered, another strand of Reformed theology emphasizes the objective aspects of the Christian life in such a way that these two forms of Calvinism appear to be at odds. Here the experience of John Williamson Nevin is particularly arresting, not only because his own autobiographical reflections reveal an alternative to the intensity of Edwards' own conversion, but also because Nevin identified the Puritan tradition as a departure from older Reformed understandings of regeneration and the Christian life. Because of his association with the Mercersberg Theology, a tradition that dabbled more in German philosophy than the Princeton theologians believed wise, Nevin has not been a steady partner in the conversation of American Reformed theology of which Westminster Seminary, the Presbyterian Church in America, and the Orthodox Presbyterian Church are part. Yet, Nevin's critique of Charles Grandison Finney in his little pamphlet *The Anxious Bench* (1843), as well as the way he bettered Charles Hodge in debates about Reformed teaching on the Lord's Supper, should earn him enough points for further inspection.[21]

Although Nevin earned his reputation in the German Reformed circles that sponsored such institutions as Mercersberg Seminary and Franklin and Marshall College, his roots were firmly in Scots-Irish Presbyterianism. He was reared in a devout Presbyterian family in Carlisle (south central), Pennsylvania, and later attended college at Union in Schenectady, New York, before enrolling in 1823 at Princeton Seminary. Initially, Nevin labored in Presbyterian vineyards, first teaching at Princeton Seminary to fill in for Charles Hodge, who was studying in Germany, and then in 1829 joining the faculty at Western Seminary, a new Presbyterian seminary on the Pittsburgh frontier. But changes and disputes in the Presbyterian Church, along with his own reflections on what was happening to Protestantism in the United States, prompted Nevin in 1840 to accept a call to Mercersburg, a seminary that was geographically close to his boyhood home but, as

21. The following paragraphs on Nevin are based on material from D. G. Hart, *The Lost Soul of American Protestantism* (Lanham, Md.: Rowman and Littlefield, 2002).

an agency of the German Reformed Church, was religiously and ethnically distant from Scots-Irish Presbyterianism. Eventually, Nevin would hit his stride among the German Reformed, presiding over Franklin and Marshall College, founding and editing the *Mercersburg Review*, and overseeing the revision of the German Reformed Church's liturgy.[22]

One of the events in Nevin's life that may have moved him out of Presbyterian circles and into German Calvinism was his encounter with the sort of Puritan introspection that Edwards embodied and championed. At the age of sixty-seven, Nevin penned some autobiographical reflections in which he recalled the difficulties of his time at Union College. He explained that "being of what is called Scotch-Irish extraction," he was reared in the Presbyterian faith, especially since both his parents were "conscientious and exemplary professors of religion." The senior Nevins' Presbyterianism was of the old style, however. It was, as he described it,

> based throughout on the idea of the covenant family religion, church membership by God's holy act in baptism, and following this a regular catechetical training of the young, with direct reference to their coming to the Lord's table. In one word, all proceeded on the theory of sacramental, educational religion, as it had belonged properly to all the national branches of the *Reformed* Church in Europe from the beginning.[23]

Nevin's claim to have been reared according to the historic Reformed tradition was clearly important in his own conception of Christianity and its organic development. But he was also trying to make the point that conversion was something different from what had become the norm in the post–Civil War United States. It also enabled him to stand apart from the contemporary religious scene. For Nevin, no image better captured this other conception of the Christian life and entrance into it than Calvin's idea of the church as mother. Here he quoted the Geneva Reformer, who wrote that "there is no other entrance into life, save as [the church] may conceive us in her womb, give us birth, nourish us from her breasts, and embrace us in her loving care to the end."[24]

22. On Nevin, see Theodore Appel, *The Life and Work of John Williamson Nevin* (1889; reprint, New York: Arno, 1969); and Sam Hamstra Jr. and Arie J. Griffioen, eds., *Reformed Confessionalism in Nineteenth-Century America: Essays on the Thought of John Williamson Nevin* (Metuchen, N.J.: Scarecrow, 1995).

23. John W. Nevin, *My Own Life: The Earlier Years* (Lancaster, Pa.: Historical Society of the Evangelical and Reformed Church, 1964), 2.

24. Ibid., 3; quotation from John Calvin, *Institutes of the Christian Religion*, 4.1.4.

The turning point for Nevin occurred when he went off to college and encountered Puritan devotion. In Nevin's own words, the New England Puritan faith that informed Union College undermined the faith in which he had been reared:

> I had come to college, a boy of strongly pious dispositions and exemplary religious habits, never doubting but that I was in some way a Christian, though it had not come with me yet (unfortunately) to what is called a public profession of religion. But now one of the first lessons inculcated on me indirectly by this unchurchly system, was that all this must pass for nothing, and that I must learn to look upon myself as an outcast from the family and kingdom of God.[25]

Nevin remembered having no power to "withstand the shock." And when a "'revival of religion,' as it was called," took place at Union, he submitted to the "anxious meetings, and underwent the torture of their mechanical counsel and talk," finally converting, though the change was weak, at the age of seventeen.[26]

However much Nevin's memory may have played tricks on him, his reflections as an older man on the differences between Puritanism and older conceptions of the Reformed faith are useful for gaining a perspective on Edwards and his theology of the heart that is not reverential or hagiographical. As Nevin understood it, the piety of the Puritans featured an "intense subjectivity" that stood in marked contrast to the "grand and glorious *objectivities* of the Christian life."[27] This way of stating the problem may not have been the best, and it may not have been fair in its application to the Puritan tradition in which Edwards stood. But Nevin's critique does make an important point, at least in the sense that the sort of intense introspection of a believer's interior life represents a departure from older Protestant conceptions of piety and the operations of the Spirit upon the soul of the Christian. Nevin himself thought that he was standing on the shoulders of Calvin, a notion that might have struck Edwards' defenders as ironic since Calvin himself has earned the reputation of being a not-too-shabby theologian of the heart. Yet, again Nevin may be on to something when he looks to Geneva rather than Massachusetts not just for inspiration but also, more importantly, for sustenance.

If Jonathan Edwards' reflections on the mysterious workings of the Spirit on the hidden recesses of the human heart were an extension of John Calvin's insights into conversion, then it is at least ironic that the

25. Nevin, *My Own Life*, 9.
26. Ibid., 9–10.
27. Ibid., 11, 14.

French Reformer had no experience that rivaled Edwards' own encounter with grace. According to historian William Bouwsma, the notion of conversion, when applied to the likes of Calvin, "is a more problematic conception than is ordinarily recognized." As a "cultural artifact" or an "individual experience," it is an event that marks a "sharp break with the past." Accordingly, "life before conversion . . . is irrelevant except as preparation for this break or as a stimulus to repentance; life afterward is made new." Bouwsma argues that evidence for a conversion of this type in Calvin's life is "negligible."[28] Most biographers cite a single passage from Calvin's commentary on the Psalms, written in 1557, which reads:

> God drew me from obscure and lowly beginnings and conferred on me that most honorable office of herald and minister of the Gospel. . . . What happened first was that by an unexpected conversion he tamed to teachableness a mind too stubborn for its years—for I was so strongly devoted to the superstitions of the papacy that nothing less could draw me from such depths of mire. And so this mere taste of true godliness that I received set me on fire with such a desire to progress that I pursued the rest of my studies more coolly, although I did not give them up altogether. Before a year had slipped by anybody who longed for a purer doctrine kept on coming to learn from me, still a beginner, a raw recruit.[29]

In Bouwsma's estimate, this passage reflects little more than "a shift and quickening of [Calvin's] interests," certainly nothing incompatible with the evangelical humanism that enraptured university students in Paris. It was simply an expression of willingness to be more teachable, not a decisive break with Calvin's former life. In other words, Calvin's conversion was gradual and progressive. This may explain why, according to Bouwsma, Calvin was not enthusiastic about conversion as a precise event in his discussions of the Christian life. Calvin himself wrote that "we are converted little by little to God, and by stages,"[30] and he was even reluctant to call Paul's encounter with Christ on the road to Damascus a "conversion," explaining that "we now have Paul tamed but not yet a disciple of Christ."[31]

Calvin's reluctance to talk about conversion in the way that most post-Edwardsian Calvinists do is borne out in the Reformed creeds and confessions of the sixteenth and seventeenth centuries. Interest-

28. William J. Bouwsma, *John Calvin: A Sixteenth-Century Portrait* (New York: Oxford University Press, 1988), 10.
29. Quoted in ibid., 10.
30. From Calvin's Commentary on Jeremiah 31:18, quoted in ibid., 11.
31. From Calvin's Commentary on Acts 9:5, quoted in ibid., 239 n. 5.

ingly enough, the Westminster Standards do not address conversion at all, using the word only in connection with "edification" and "salvation" as part of the effects of preaching (Westminster Larger Catechism 159). The Heidelberg Catechism does speak of conversion, but its authors do so in the older Reformed sense of a lifelong process that is best understood as sanctification. Question-and-answer 88 takes up the issue of "genuine repentance or conversion" and describes it as "two things: the dying away of the old self, and coming-to-life of the new." In other words, the sort of conversion in view here is what Reformed divines commonly referred to as mortification and vivification, which is the saint's lifelong struggle with sin and growth in grace. Another confessional guide for understanding conversion is the Canons of Dort, which use the word "conversion" more frequently than other Reformed creeds but do so again with a process in view, not a moment of crisis and illumination. Heads of Doctrine III/IV, article 10, speaks of conversion as involving faith and repentance, while article 11 describes conversion as more or less synonymous with regeneration. As such, true conversion, according to Dort, is the occasion when the Holy Spirit "pervades the inmost recesses of the man; . . . opens the closed, and softens the hardened heart, and circumcises that which was uncircumcised, infuses new qualities into the will, which though heretofore dead, He quickens."

Aside from discussing conversion either as a lifelong process or as regeneration, what also stands out in the sixteenth- and seventeenth-century Reformed confessions is an emphasis on what Nevin called the "objectivities" of Christianity, as opposed to Edwards' apparent preoccupation with the subjective and interior side of faith. Even though Dort, for instance, describes conversion in a series of phrases that all concern the heart, a little later it offers advice that seems foreign to Edwards. The counsel is that "we are to think and to speak in the most favorable way about those who outwardly profess their faith and better their lives" because—and this is key—"the inner chambers of the heart are unknown to us" (III/IV, art. 15). To be sure, Edwards also admitted that conversion does not follow a precise order and that the state of another soul can never be known. At the same time, he was not content with external professions of faith or with people who were outwardly pious. In fact, his descriptions of those most in need of conversion are people who might easily fit into the class described in this article of the Canons of Dort.[32]

32. The woman cited above, in note 7, Edwards described as "pious," "bashful," and "modest," not normally considered the traits of someone in need of conversion. See *Great Awakening, Works,* 4:105. Even the changes in the young people who converted in

In this case, Edwards and the Puritan piety that he labored to propagate stand on one side of a discernible divide in the Calvinistic world,
a side opposite Calvin and Nevin, where the externalities of religion
matter less than an energized and zealous interior life. Of course,
making this divide a deep and wide chasm would be inadvisable, since
Edwards would insist upon the importance of Word and sacrament
while Calvin and Nevin would not deny the importance of the human
heart. Nevertheless, this divide is important for understanding that on
each side is a different understanding of how a Christian gets religion.
For Edwards, Christians come to faith through a dramatic encounter
of soul-wrenching proportions, and his writings give the impression
that the more wrenching, the better the chances of authenticity. We
could call this the "Road to Damascus" model. But for Nevin and
Calvin, the ideal of coming to faith is one of transforming bit by bit
over a lifetime of attending the means of grace and personal devotion.
It is the Isaac model, since its ideal is that of the covenant child who
never knows anything other than that he or she is a child of God.

Perhaps this way of describing the division among Calvinists, that
is, as the experimentalists versus the formalists, is not the best. But
the literature on Puritanism attests that a divide is there in the Reformed tradition. Charles Cohen traces the difference to Theodore
Beza, whom the Puritans followed, who broke with Calvin when he
severed "assurance from faith and open[ed] up the possibility for a
more extensive analysis of religious experience than Calvin thought either necessary or desirable." Cohen also asserts that the "path of assurance, which for Calvin ascends from the believer to the Redeemer
at God's right hand, for Beza descends back into the self, a change of
direction fraught with implications for thinking about conversion."[33]
So too Jerald Brauer believes that Puritans redirected the stress of sixteenth-century Protestantism, though in this case by following the
lead of William Perkins and William Ames. "Because of their focus on
the personal experience of conversion and 'experimental divinity,'"
Brauer contends, "Puritans emphasized the personal appropriation of

---

Northampton, the firstfruits in Edwards' remarkable awakening, seem to say more
about Edwards' own conception of worldliness than about the effects of genuine conversion. Edwards writes that "they were many of them very much addicted to night-
walking, and frequenting the tavern, and lewd practices, wherein some, by their example exceedingly corrupted others" (Great Awakening, Works, 4:146). To be sure, some of
this carousing was a nuisance and may have exhibited godlessness. But someone with
less of a pietistic sensibility may not have prescribed "religious affections" as the cure
for these immature souls.

33. Cohen, God's Caress, 10, 11.

justification more than its givenness." He adds that "under the on-slaught of doubt, Luther could say, I have been baptized, and Calvin could rest in the mystery of God's mercy through eternal election, but the Puritan rehearsed the personal experience of conversion."[34] These analyses may account for C. C. Goen's articulation of the difference as one between the Puritans, who were "evangelical," in contrast to other Protestants, whom he calls "sacramentalists." In his introduction to the Yale *Works of Jonathan Edwards* volume on the Great Awakening, Goen explains that "evangelicalism may be defined as the perspective from which the Christian life is viewed as beginning with an experi-ence of personal conversion and issuing in a pursuit of personal pi-ety," as opposed to sacramentalism, "which regards the Christian life as beginning with the bestowal of grace at baptism."[35]

However this difference is described, it is one that is significant for understanding both Edwards and his relationship to the Reformed tradition. If this division is ignored, so may Edwards' true genius as one who plumbed the depths of Puritan psychology using the latest tools of European philosophy. In other words, if everything Edwards wrote had already been said by Calvin and the Westminster divines, why bother with the length and expense of the Yale series? At the same time, if Edwards is different from what went before in the teach-ings of the Reformed churches, examining this difference is crucial to understanding better the nature and meaning of the Reformed tradi-tion. It may not answer the question of which side is right, but by even raising the point that there may in fact be sides to be taken, the enter-prise of exploring the divide between Edwards' heart religion and Nevin's and Calvin's churchly piety is valuable. Indeed, it may yield theologies, ministries, and lives that are more self-conscious about the truth of the gospel and how it is applied through the sovereign work of the Holy Spirit.

Three Parties or Two?

Part of the reason for highlighting this difference between Edwards and the Puritans, on the one side, and such exponents of the Re-formed faith as Nevin, on the other, is to raise questions about the di-verse schools of the Reformed tradition alluded to at the outset of this chapter. As useful as Marsden's map of the Reformed world is, it virtu-ally ignores the division between Edwards' experimental Calvinism

34. Jerald C. Brauer, "Conversion: From Puritanism to Revivalism," *Journal of Reli-gion* 58 (1978): 234.
35. C. C. Goen, "Introduction," in *Great Awakening*, Works, 4:2.

and Calvin's own churchly piety. Of course, one of Marsden's groups is the family of Calvinists who huddle under the umbrella of experientialism. But the contrast among pietist, culturalist, and doctrinalist Calvinists does not recognize the degree of discord between Calvinistic forms of piety. It is as if the doctrinalist, culturalist, and pietist perspectives each represent an important element of truth in the Reformed faith and so complement each other in healthy ways. But if the experience of Nevin is any indication, the encounter between churchly and experimental Calvinism can be particularly unpleasant.

One way to illustrate this point is to look at the upbringing and experience of Charles Hodge, who clearly fits in the doctrinalist category but also manifested a strain of piety that warms the heart of experimental Calvinists. What is more, Hodge could be said to have a culturalist perspective with his application of Reformed teaching to any number of social and political issues. The point to notice about Hodge, however, is how he came to faith and how few questions have been raised about his conversion. Hodge recalled that as a boy he had the habit of thanking God for everything, avoiding curse words, and praying regularly.[36] Even discounting what may have been an overbearing self-righteousness shaping his memory, his boyhood suggests that his mother, pastor, and elders were raising young Charles as a child of the covenant. But it was not until he went off to the College of New Jersey and sat under Archibald Alexander's preaching that Hodge could finally make a profession of faith, and the occasion for that decision was the revival Alexander led in the winter of 1814–15. One of Hodge's peers who discovered the conversion told a professor excitedly of the news in the following words: "[Hodge] has enlisted under the banner of King Jesus!"[37] This comment suggests that until this decision, the young Hodge, who had been baptized, prayed, tried to live a godly life, and knew that all his life depended upon his heavenly Father, was actually an enemy of Christ. Just as Nevin had discovered, the churchly and covenantal pattern of inheriting the faith of one's parents and church counted for nothing, according to the Edwardsian scheme, until the believer had *the* experience. No other model existed for coming to faith in American Presbyterian circles. And so the sort of instruction that Nevin's communion, the German Reformed Church, offered to catechumens was nonexistent by the early decades of the nineteenth century among American Presbyterians. Yet, this in-

36. David B. Calhoun, *Princeton Seminary: Faith and Learning, 1812–1868* (Carlisle: Banner of Truth Trust, 1994), 106.
37. Ibid., 108.

struction would have been precisely what the young Hodge needed. This advice, published in 1902, reads:

> We require a high degree of fitness for confirmation, namely, an intelligent, sincere and unreserved taking of three most searching and far-reaching vows in the name of the holy Trinity.
>
> Then, too, this fitness for confirmation may be called a "change of heart," though this is only another name for conversion. This change is not sudden, but runs through years. You have not had any wonderful religious experiences, such as you hear about in others; but the Holy Ghost has done much in you in a very quiet way.
>
> Nor need you doubt your conversion, your change of heart, because you cannot tell the day when it took place, as many profess to do. It did not take place in a day, or you might tell it. It is the growth of years (Mark 4:26–28), and therefore all the more reliable. You cannot tell when you learned to walk, talk, think and work. You do not know when you learned to love your earthly father, much less the heavenly.
>
> This is the Reformed doctrine of "getting religion." We get religion, not in bulk but little by little. Just as we get natural life and strength, so spiritual life and strength, day by day.[38]

This way of getting religion was unavailable to Hodge in part, but no small one, because Edwards made such a successful case for a very different way.

If the tension between churchly and experimental Calvinism is as forceful as these examples suggest, then perhaps Marsden's map of the Reformed world needs to be redone in a way that highlights two different territories, not three. Instead of divvying up the land among the culturalists, doctrinalists, and experimentalists, the boundary should be drawn between the *confessionalists*, who can be found in clusters around the churches, and the *pietists*, who are busying teaching doctrine in schools or praying in their closets at home or actively pursuing justice in the public square. If this is the proper rendering of the Reformed land, then it follows Nevin's own ideas about the fundamental divide that was occurring in American Protestantism during the Second Great Awakening when in *Anxious Bench* he wrote that the competing parties were the *bench* and the *catechism*. The former stood for the revivalist system of acquiring faith through personal decisions, while the latter stood for the churchly way of passing on the faith through Word and sacrament. For that reason, Nevin concluded that "the systems are antagonistic." It might be the case that some,

38. Reformed Church in the United States, "Confirmation Explained," in *Heidelberg Catechism of the R.C.U.S.: Twentieth-Century Edition* (Philadelphia: Publication and Sunday School Board of the R.C.U.S., 1902), 183–84.

"standing under one standard, may be to some extent entangled in views and practices properly belonging to the other." But this was simply a form of inconsistency: "Each system . . . has its own life and soul, in virtue of which it cannot truly coalesce with the other."[39]

But if not a new map, then at least we need a new grid for understanding the Reformed faith, one that includes four parties: the doctrinalists, the culturalists, the pietists, and the liturgicals. For without that last party, the Reformed tradition is missing an element that was clearly important to its founders, even if by Edwards' day it appeared to be a barrier to vital religion. Indeed, Edwards and the form of piety he promoted may be responsible for the neglect of a churchly Reformed faith because he and his Puritan forebears thought it ineffective in promoting genuine piety. Yet, if Ronald Knox has any wisdom in his classic assessment of enthusiasm—a dangerous proposition for Protestants because of his loyalty to the Bishop of Rome—then some grounds may exist for raising questions about the wholesomeness of experimental Calvinism's displacement of a churchly piety. Knox concludes his book by asserting that through evangelicalism:

> Religion became identified in the popular mind with a series of moods, in which the worshipper, disposed thereto by all the arts of the revivalist, relished the flavours of spiritual peace. You needed neither a theology nor a liturgy. . . . You floated, safely enough, on the little raft of your own faith, eagerly throwing out the lifeline to such drowning neighbors as were ready to catch it; meanwhile the ship was foundering. It was this by-passing of an historic tradition in favour of a personal experience that has created the modern religious situation in . . . the English-speaking world.[40]

Of course, the tradition Knox had in mind was his own Roman Catholic faith. Still, his point is one that contemporary Calvinists might well consider since experimental Calvinism was so influential in constructing a bypass around Reformed Christianity's historic tradition of a church-centered and catechetical faith. At the end of the day, it might very well be that the triumph of Edwards and experimental Calvinism has involved the elevation of the solitary soul's subjective agonies and struggles above the grand and glorious objectives of the Reformed faith.

39. J. W. Nevin, *The Anxious Bench* (Chambersburg, Pa.: Weekly Messenger, 1843), 56.

40. Ronald Arbuthnott Knox, *Enthusiasm* (New York: Oxford University Press, 1950), 589.

10

❖

TAYLORITES, TYLERITES, AND THE DISSOLUTION OF THE NEW ENGLAND THEOLOGY

Douglas A. Sweeney

Yale's Nathaniel William Taylor and the so-called Taylorite-Tylerite controversy have long stood as benchmarks in the field of American religious history. Planted firmly in historical memory by classic textbooks in American religion, they have been used by scholars to measure all manner of historical developments—from the diminution of what Perry Miller depicted as America's "Augustinian strain of piety" to the spread of what Nathan Hatch has called "the democratization of American Christianity." But nowhere have the Taylorites and the Tylerites loomed as large as in discussions of what Joseph Haroutunian decried as "the passing of the New England Theology," that rich tradition of religious reflection that stemmed from the thought of Jonathan Edwards and later foliated in the work of his Edwardsian followers. Indeed, despite their claims to Edwardsian paternity, for over a century and a half New Haven's Taylorites, especially, have symbolized declension in New England religion away from Edwards' bold theocentric vision. Though unfavorable, this symbolism has

This essay appears in a revised version as chapter 7 of *Nathaniel Taylor, New Haven Theology, and the Legacy of Jonathan Edwards,* by Douglas Sweeney (Oxford and New York: Oxford University Press, 2002). Copyright by Oxford University Press, Inc., and used by permission of Oxford University Press, Inc.

granted them a historical stature that is larger than life and has guaranteed them a lasting, though awkward, place in the American historical canon.[1]

While the Taylorites and the Tylerites have become legends of American religion, few of us know very much about them. That which we "know," moreover, we have usually learned second or third hand, and the significance of their dispute has proved all too easy to misconstrue. Even when theological controversies constituted the most important episodes in many histories of American religion, leading neoorthodox church historians (with the support of their secular sympathizers) dismissed the Taylorites out of hand as important but lamentable Protestant moralists, un-Edwardsian theological pragmatists, and anthropocentric accommodaters to the modern spirit of liberal democracy. Most others have classified the Taylorites as part of a nearly comatose "Old Calvinism," as latter-day leaders of a coalition formed originally to oppose the (Edwardsian) "New Divinity" but kept on life support in the nineteenth century by the mere force of cultural inertia. The Tylerites, named after their best-known theologian, Bennet Tyler, for their part, have been portrayed rather perfunctorily as antagonists, archrivals of the Taylorites typecast as crotchety obscurantists. In recent years, as WASP elites have proved uninteresting to most scholars, historians have bypassed both groups on the superhighway of social history.[2]

1. Perry Miller, *The New England Mind: The Seventeenth Century* (Cambridge: Harvard University Press, 1954), 1–5; Nathan O. Hatch, *The Democratization of American Christianity* (New Haven: Yale University Press, 1989); and Joseph Haroutunian, *Piety versus Moralism: The Passing of the New England Theology* (New York: Henry Holt, 1932). On the historiography of the New England Theology, see Douglas A. Sweeney, "Edwards and His Mantle: The Historiography of the New England Theology," *New England Quarterly* 71 (1998): 97–119.

2. On the interpretations of Haroutunian and his followers, see Sweeney, "Edwards and His Mantle," 108–12. The literature depicting the Taylorites as "Old Calvinists" (or moderate-to-liberal Congregationalists most interested in maintaining what they deemed the religious status quo, in shoring up the clerical establishment, and thus in opposing the theological innovations and religious zeal of the "New Divinity") includes Sidney Mead, *Nathaniel William Taylor, 1786–1858: A Connecticut Liberal* (Chicago: University of Chicago Press, 1942), 12–23, 95–127; Mark A. Noll, "Moses Mather (Old Calvinist) and the Evolution of Edwardseanism," *Church History* 49 (September 1980): passim; Allen C. Guelzo, *Edwards on the Will: A Century of American Theological Debate* (Middletown, Conn.: Wesleyan University Press, 1989), 218–71; David W. Kling, *A Field of Divine Wonders: The New Divinity and Village Revivals in Northwestern Connecticut, 1792–1822* (University Park: Pennsylvania State University Press, 1993), 91–93, 232–43; and William R. Sutton, "Benevolent Calvinism and the Moral Government of God: The Influence of Nathaniel W. Taylor on Revivalism in the Second Great Awakening," *Religion and American Culture* 2 (1992): 28–29, 40.

Significantly, however, the American scholarly community has witnessed a minor renaissance of interest in "Edwardsian culture" during the past two decades, a renaissance located primarily among social and cultural historians of religion. Working in the train of Joseph Conforti, a cadre of specialists has begun to unearth the remains of an Edwardsian civilization that appears to have dominated New England Calvinism during and after the Second Great Awakening, co-opting virtually all its trinitarian Congregationalist institutions—from local churches and their policies to most of the region's best colleges, from the "schools of the prophets" to the fledgling seminaries, and even the parachurch societies of New England's emergent benevolent empire. On the basis of this "discovery," these specialists have called for a revision of traditional arguments for the alleged demise of Edwardsian culture in the late eighteenth century. Rather than continue to suggest, à la Haroutunian and others, that the New England theology declined, devolved, or passed from the cultural scene during and after the difficult years of the American Revolution, these scholars point to the continued vitality of the Edwardsian religious tradition throughout much of the first half of the nineteenth century.[3]

Unfortunately, this new literature on Edwardsian culture in the nineteenth century includes little useful analysis of theological developments and almost nothing on the dispute between the Taylorites and the Tylerites. I have begun to address this problem elsewhere with an analysis of Taylorite theology and its connection to the Edwardsian culture and modifications of Edwardsian language.[4] In what follows, then, I will focus on the consequences of the Taylorite controversy for the subsequent history of the Edwardsian religious tradition. After summarizing the institutional history of the Taylorite-Tylerite split, I will reassess its significance for the later history of the New England theology. Building on my earlier work that explains how both the Taylorites and the Tylerites proved central figures in what was by their day an immensely influential Edwardsian movement, I will argue that their dispute is best interpreted in a new way—not as an *inter*mural battle between increasingly liberal accommodationists and retrograde

3. See especially Joseph Conforti, *Jonathan Edwards, Religious Tradition, and American Culture* (Chapel Hill: University of North Carolina Press, 1995); Kling, *A Field of Divine Wonders;* and Douglas A. Sweeney, "Nathaniel William Taylor and the Edwardsian Tradition: A Reassessment," in *Jonathan Edwards's Writings: Text, Context, Interpretation,* ed. Stephen J. Stein (Bloomington: Indiana University Press, 1996).

4. Douglas A. Sweeney, *Nathaniel Taylor, New Haven Theology, and the Legacy of Jonathan Edwards* (Oxford and New York: Oxford University Press, 2002). An abbreviated version of this analysis can be found in Sweeney, "Nathaniel William Taylor and the Edwardsian Tradition."

hyper-Calvinists, all of whom ministered after the wane of the New England theology, but as an *intra*mural struggle waged in the thick of this tradition, though one that contributed in an ironic and neglected way to its ultimate dissolution.

Edwardsianism in New England on the Eve of the Taylorite-Tylerite Controversy

After a period of slow growth in the second half of the eighteenth century, Edwardsianism exploded during the first third of the nineteenth century. In fact, Edwardsian preaching, polity, institutions, and theology infiltrated New England to such an extent that it would not be inappropriate to speak of an Edwardsian enculturation of the region in this period. Contemporary accounts from many observers all across the religious spectrum suggest that friends and foes alike recognized the strength of the Edwardsian tradition. The liberal William Bentley admitted with regret in 1813 that Samuel Hopkins' theology (i.e., the Edwardsian theology made famous by Edwards' most polemical early disciple) stood as "the basis of the popular theology of New England." Berkshire clergyman Sylvester Burt agreed in 1829 that the main contours of Hopkinsianism, "waiving a few points," had become standards for "the orthodox and evangelical clergy of N. England at the present day." Princetonian Archibald Alexander testified in 1831 that "Edwards has done more to give complexion to the theological system of Calvinists in America, than all other persons together." His colleague Samuel Miller affirmed in 1837 that "for the last half century, it may be safely affirmed, that no other American writer on the subject of theology has been so frequently quoted, or had anything like such deference manifested to his opinions, as President Edwards." Bennet Tyler claimed in 1844 that the Edwardsians comprised the "standard theological writers of New England." Samuel Worcester echoed in 1852 that "within fifty years past," Edwardsianism had "pervaded the orthodoxy of New England." By 1853 the Edwardsian Mortimer Blake could boast that Edwardsianism had "modified the current theology of all New England, and given to it its harmony, consistency, and beauty, as it now appears in the creeds of the churches and the teaching of the ministry."[5]

5. *The Diary of William Bentley, D.D., Pastor of the East Church, Salem, Massachusetts,* 4 vols. (1905; reprint, Gloucester, Mass.: Peter Smith, 1962), 4:302 (for further supercilious testimony from Bentley concerning the prevalence of Edwardsianism, see 1:160, 196–97, and 3:113, 364–65, 412); David D. Field, ed., *A History of the County of Berkshire, Massachusetts; In Two parts: The First Being a General View of the County; The*

Despite their controversial insistence that original sin was "in the sinning," that penitent sinners played an important role in their own regeneration, and that God's grace was never coercive but worked in conjunction with human free will, Nathaniel Taylor and Yale Divinity School participated fully in the Edwardsian culture, defending its boundaries against Unitarians, Old Calvinists, and even Arminians. And though this comes as a surprise to those of us reared on the regnant historiography and repulses of those like the Tylerites who detest Taylor's alterations of Edwardsian doctrine, Taylor and his companions always deemed the New Haven Theology fundamentally Edwardsian. Taylor's daughter Rebecca Taylor Hatch, for example, identified her father as a proponent of what she called the "New Divinity" and distanced him quite clearly from "Old Calvinism." His son-in-law and colleague, Noah Porter, noted that "the works of all the New England divines were the familiar hand-books of his reading." Taylor's succes-

---

Second, an Account of the Several Towns (Pittsfield, 1829), 229; [Archibald Alexander], "An Inquiry into That Inability under Which the Sinner Labours, and Whether It Furnishes Any Excuse for His Neglect of Duty," *Biblical Repertory and Theological Review,* n.s., 3 (July 1831): 362; Samuel Miller, *Life of Jonathan Edwards* (Boston, 1837), 215; Bennet Tyler, *Memoir of the Life and Character of Rev. Asahel Nettleton, D.D.,* 2d ed. (Hartford: Robbins and Smith, 1845; 1st ed., 1844), 274; Samuel M. Worcester, *The Life and Labors of Rev. Samuel Worcester, D.D.,* 2 vols. (Boston, 1852), 1:211; and Mortimer Blake, *A Centurial History of the Mendon Association of Congregational Ministers, with the Centennial Address, Delivered at Franklin, Mass., Nov. 19, 1851, and Biographical Sketches of the Members and Licentiates* (Boston, 1853), 31. For other testimonials to the powerful influence of the Edwardsian theological culture throughout the first two-thirds of the nineteenth century, see the anonymous author of the *Essays on Hopkinsianism* [Boston?, c. 1820], 42, who contended that "many of the students of the theological seminary, at Auburn, . . . one half of the students of the theological seminary at Princeton, . . . [and a] large proportion, some think almost half of the Presbyterian ministers in the United States, adopt the leading sentiments of the Hopkinsian system"; Ebenezer Porter, "Dr. Porter's Letters on Revivals of Religion," *Spirit of the Pilgrims* 5 (June 1832): 318; [Joseph Harvey], *Letters on the Present State and Probable Results of Theological Speculations in Connecticut* (n.p., 1832), 41–42; Lyman Beecher, "Letter from Dr. Beecher to Dr. Woods," *Spirit of the Pilgrims* 5 (July 1832): 394; Eliza Buckminster Lee, *Memoirs of Rev. Joseph Buckminster, D.D., and of His Son, Rev. Joseph Stevens Buckminster* (Boston, 1849), 330; [Harriet Beecher Stowe], "New England Ministers," *The Atlantic Monthly* 1 (February 1858): 487; Leonard Bacon, "Historical Discourse," in *Contributions to the Ecclesiastical History of Connecticut; Prepared under the Direction of the General Association, to Commemorate the Completion of One Hundred and Fifty Years Since Its First Annual Assembly* (New Haven, 1861), 61; Frederick Denison Maurice, *Modern Philosophy; or, A Treatise of Moral and Metaphysical Philosophy from the Fourteenth Century to the French Revolution, with a Glimpse into the Nineteenth Century* (London, 1862); Leonard Woods, *History of the Andover Theological Seminary* (Boston, 1885), 28–41; and Theodore S. Woolsey, "Theodore Dwight Woolsey—A Biographical Sketch," *Yale Review,* n.s., 1 (January 1912): 246.

sor at New Haven's Center Church, the Reverend Leonard Bacon, called him "the last, as the elder Edwards was the first, of the great masters of the distinctive theology of New England. . . . The names in that succession . . . are few,—Hopkins, the younger Edwards, Smalley, Emmons, Taylor,—and the last, not least in the illustrious dynasty." Taylor's student and colleague, George Fisher, referred to Taylor as "the last of our New England schoolmen, . . . the compeer of Emmons and Hopkins, of Smalley and the Edwardses," noting that "probably none of his contemporaries was so well acquainted with the great divines of the New England school of theology, beginning with the elder Edwards. The principal works of President Edwards, Dr. Taylor knew almost by heart." Taylor's best friend, Lyman Beecher, defended his own and Taylor's fidelity to the Edwardsian tradition on many occasions. He spoke glowingly of Edwards. His children pointed to Edwards as their father's "favorite author" or, as Beecher's biographer Stuart Henry phrased it, his "Protestant surrogate for a patron saint."[6] And Taylor himself, though less concerned with theological labels than most of his peers, did not fail to confess his own allegiance to the Edwardsian tradition, working almost exclusively with Edwards and the Edwardsians as his authorities at hand, suffusing his writings and his lectures with Edwardsian themes, and defending Edwardsianism constantly from the criticisms of Unitarians, Methodists, and other Arminians.[7]

6. As Taylor's former student B. N. Martin once said, "Probably no one ever equalled him in the familiarity of his acquaintance with the great works of this eminent divine [Edwards]" ("Dr. Taylor on Moral Government," *New Englander* 17 [November 1869]: 910). See Rebecca Taylor Hatch, *Personal Reminiscences and Memorials* (New York, 1905), 11, 28, 34; Noah Porter, introduction to *Lectures on the Moral Government of God*, by Nathaniel W. Taylor, 2 vols. (New York, 1859), 1:vi; Noah Porter, "Dr. Taylor and His Theology," in *The Semi-Centennial Anniversary of the Divinity School of Yale College, May 15th and 16th, 1872* (New Haven, 1872), 92–97; Noah Porter, "Philosophy in Great Britain and America: A Supplementary Sketch," appendix I in *History of Philosophy from Thales to the Present Time*, vol. 2 of *History of Modern Philosophy*, by Friedrich Ueberweg, trans. George S. Morris (New York, 1874), 452; Leonard Bacon, "A Sermon at the Funeral of Nathaniel W. Taylor, D.D., in the Center Church, March 12, 1858," in *Memorial of Nathaniel W. Taylor, D.D.: Three Sermons* (New Haven, 1858), 8; George P. Fisher, "A Sermon Preached in the Chapel of Yale College, March 14, 1858, the First Sunday after the Death of Rev. Nathaniel W. Taylor, D.D., Dwight Professor of Didactic Theology," in ibid., 32, 35; George P. Fisher, "Historical Address," in *Semi-Centennial Anniversary of the Divinity School of Yale College*, 20, 27–28; George Park Fisher, *History of Christian Doctrine* (1896; reprint, Edinburgh: Clark, 1949), 414–17; Lyman Beecher, *The Autobiography of Lyman Beecher*, ed. Barbara M. Cross, 2 vols. (Cambridge: Harvard University Press, 1961), 2:348, 177; and Stuart C. Henry, *Unvanquished Puritan: A Portrait of Lyman Beecher* (Grand Rapids: Eerdmans, 1973; reprint, Westport: Greenwood, 1986), 254.

7. Taylor's writings bear the ubiquitous presence of Edwards and the Edwardsians. They, rather than the Old Calvinists, were his theological ancestors, those from whose

Tellingly, while the New Haven theology had been developing publicly throughout the 1820s, it was not until the end of that fateful decade that Taylorite views received much criticism. Indeed, before the

---

thought his own thinking began and those to whom he referred when in need of an authoritative pronouncement. To cite all the examples of this would require far too much space, but see [Nathaniel W. Taylor], "Review of Spring on the Means of Regeneration," *Quarterly Christian Spectator* 1 (June 1829): 225; (September 1829): 497–98, 505; (December 1829): 695, 702–3; and [Nathaniel W. Taylor], "Review of Dr. Tyler's Strictures on the Christian Spectator," *Quarterly Christian Spectator* 2 (March 1830): 154–58, 162, 169, 184. For the way in which Edwardsian figures and themes pervaded Taylor's lectures at Yale, see the several extant copies of student lecture notes held at Yale's Sterling and Divinity libraries. One example is Alexander MacWhorter, "Notes on a Course of Lectures in Revealed Theology by Nathaniel W. Taylor, D.D.," 1844, folder 147A, box 30, Yale Lectures, Sterling Memorial Library, Yale University, 147, 151, 152, 403, 404, and passim. For evidence of Taylor's opposition to Arminianism and Old Calvinism, see "On Heaven," in Nathaniel W. Taylor, *Practical Sermons* (New York, 1858), 190; Nathaniel W. Taylor, *Man, A Free Agent without the Aid of Divine Grace*, Tracts, Designed to Illustrate and Enforce the Most Important Doctrines of the Gospel, No. 2 (New Haven, 1818); and Nathaniel W. Taylor, "Letter from Rev. Dr. Taylor," *Spirit of the Pilgrims* 5 (March 1832): 175–76. For the work of Taylor's colleagues against Arminianism, see [Ralph? Emerson], "Review of Adam Clarke's Discourses," *Quarterly Christian Spectator* 1 (December 1829): 575–80; "Review of the Doctrine and Discipline of the Methodist Episcopal Church," *Quarterly Christian Spectator* 2 (September 1830): 483–504; [Chauncey Goodrich], "Review of High Church and Arminian Principles," *Quarterly Christian Spectator* 2 (December 1830): 730–31; and [Eleazar T. Fitch], "Fisk on Predestination and Election," *Quarterly Christian Spectator* 3 (December 1831): 597–640.

    Like other Edwardsians, the Taylorites opposed not only the Arminian soteriology of the Methodists but also their rapid growth through unorthodox and often uncontrolled revivalistic methods. See [Emerson], "Review of Adam Clarke's Discourses," 553–55, and [Ebenezer Porter], "Review of the Doctrine and Discipline of the Methodist Episcopal Church," *Quarterly Christian Spectator* 2 (September 1830): 496–504. Methodist growth in Connecticut in this period was significant but should not be exaggerated. While Francis Asbury visited New Haven as early as 1790, the town did not have a Methodist church until the 1790s, and this church did not have enough support to raise its own building until 1820. See Rollin G. Osterweis, *Three Centuries of New Haven, 1638–1938* (New Haven: Yale University Press, 1953), 214–15. On the rise of Methodism in New England generally, see James Mudge, *History of the New England Conference of the Methodist Episcopal Church* (Boston, 1910); George Claude Baker Jr., *An Introduction to the History of Early New England Methodism, 1789–1839* (Durham: Duke University Press, 1941); William Thomas Umbel, "The Making of an American Denomination: Methodism in New England Religious Culture, 1790–1860" (Ph.D. diss., Johns Hopkins University, 1992), who discusses the interaction between New England's Methodists and Edwardsians/Taylorites on pp. 61–115; and Rennetts C. Miller, ed., *Souvenir History of the New England Southern Conference*, 3 vols. (Nantasket, Mass., 1897). See also Stanford E. Demars, "The Camp Meeting Vacation Resort in New England," *Henceforth* 21 (spring 1994): 8–18, who notes that while Methodists did begin holding camp meetings in New England in the 1830s and 1840s, the camp meeting movement did not flourish in New England until the 1870s, when about one-third of New England's roughly one hundred camp meetings were established. And note the statistical tables in

publication in 1828 of Taylor's *Concio ad Clerum*,[8] a controversial sermon on original sin that some thought supported Charles Finney's "new measures," New England's Congregationalists stood largely united on rather conservative Edwardsian principles. As noted in Beecher's *Autobiography*, "Time was when Taylor, and Stuart, and Beecher, and Nettleton, and Tyler, and Porter, and Hewitt, and Harvey were all together, not only in local proximity, but in the warmest unity of belief and feeling." This claim was not unfounded. In the middle years of the 1820s, these future rivals banded together to battle both Unitarianism back east and Finneyite methods in the west. For example, when Unitarians attempted to divide New England's trinitarian standing order by separating Beecher and New Haven from the region's historic Calvinism, none other than Asahel Nettleton, the fiery conservative soon to serve as the Tylerite party's leading activist, supported Beecher and affirmed the unity of the Edwardsian ranks within Connecticut. "I believe it to be a matter of fact," he claimed, "that you and I are really a different kind of Calvinists from what Unitarians have imagined or been accustomed to manage. Probably [your Unitarian critic] thinks that you are in sentiment at war with the orthodox at the present day, but he is grandly mistaken so far as Connecticut is concerned. . . . We feel no concern for old Calvinism. Let them dispute it as much as they please; we feel bound to make no defense." When the Finneyites in upstate New York threatened to encroach upon their region, moreover, these men joined hands again to keep the new measures out of New England. Beecher and Nettleton led the charge against Finneyite progressives in New Lebanon, New York, when the two sides met there in 1827 to discuss their differences. And while it was

---

John H. Wigger, *Taking Heaven by Storm: Methodism and the Popularization of American Christianity* (New York: Oxford University Press, 1998), 197–200, as well as the estimate in Roger Finke and Rodney Stark, *The Churching of America, 1776–1990: Winners and Losers in Our Religious Economy* (New Brunswick: Rutgers University Press, 1992), 282–83, that by 1850 devout Methodists still constituted only 6 percent of New England's population. On the relatively conservative nature of Taylorite revivalism, see "Review on the Employment of Evangelists in Our Older Settlements," *Quarterly Christian Spectator* 1 (September 1829): 425–38. A major Methodist response to Taylorite criticisms may be found in Wilbur Fisk, *Calvinistic Controversy: Embracing a Sermon on Predestination and Election; and Several Numbers on the Same Subject, Originally Published in the Christian Advocate and Journal* (New York, 1837). On the rise of Methodism in post-Revolutionary America, see especially Russell E. Richey, *Early American Methodism* (Bloomington: Indiana University Press, 1991); Wigger, *Taking Heaven by Storm*; and Dee E. Andrews, *The Methodists and Revolutionary America, 1760–1800: The Shaping of an Evangelical Culture* (Princeton: Princeton University Press, 2000).

8. Nathaniel W. Taylor, *Concio ad Clerum: A Sermon Delivered in the Chapel of Yale College, September 10, 1828* (New Haven, 1828).

Nettleton who left this meeting to become Finney's worst New England nightmare (his zealous revivalistic itinerancy and public relations work for the Tylerites would make him the closest thing to Finney's archrival in New England), it was Beecher who promised to fight him every inch of the way to Boston.[9]

The Institutionalization of the Taylorite-Tylerite Split

Before long, however, things changed along New England's united front, and it proved only a matter of time before the Edwardsian culture was mortally wounded. Nettleton's doctors urged him to move south soon after the end of the New Lebanon conference. His health had never been good, and Finney had worked him into a frenzy.[10] Nettleton obliged them the following winter, staying with Presbyterian colleagues in Virginia and remaining in the South until the spring of 1829. While there, one of his friends, the Presbyterian minister John H. Rice, received copies of Taylor's *Concio ad Clerum* as well as his views on regeneration recently published in New Haven's *Quarterly Christian Spectator*. These items were covered in the mail by a letter from Yale's Chauncey Goodrich attributing Nettleton's own success as a gospel preacher to Taylorite views. Unfortunately, as it turned out,

9. Beecher, *Autobiography*, 2:117, 1:410. For more on this common opposition to Finney, see especially the representative letter from Beecher to Nettleton, 30 January 1827, folder 63, box 2, Beecher-Scoville Family Papers, Sterling Memorial Library, Yale University; Lyman Beecher, *To the Congregational Ministers and Churches of Connecticut. Copy of a Letter from the Rev. Dr. Beecher, to the Editor of the Christian Spectator, Boston, December 18th, 1827* (Boston, 1827); and the published *Letters of the Rev. Dr. Beecher and Rev. Mr. Nettleton on the "New Measures" in Conducting Revivals of Religion. With a Review of a Sermon, by Novanglus* (New York, 1828). On the new Lebanon Conference of July 1827, see Beecher, *Autobiography*, 2:89–108; Garth M. Rosell and Richard A. G. Dupuis, eds., *The Memoirs of Charles G. Finney: The Complete Restored Text* (Grand Rapids: Zondervan, 1989), 216–25; Mead, *Nathaniel William Taylor*, 200–210; Charles E. Hambrick-Stowe, *Charles G. Finney and the Spirit of American Evangelicalism* (Grand Rapids: Eerdmans, 1996), 46–73; George Hugh Birney Jr., "The Life and Letters of Asahel Nettleton 1783–1844" (Ph.D. diss., Hartford Theological Seminary, 1943), 114–54; and the published minutes of the conference in the Unitarian *Christian Examiner and Theological Review* 4 (July and August 1827): 357–70. Significantly, even the Princetonians proved friendly to the Taylorites before the end of the 1820s, as evidenced in Samuel Miller's urgent plea to Beecher to settle in a recently vacated Philadelphia pulpit. See Miller to Beecher, 2 April 1828, The Stowe-Day Foundation, Hartford.

10. The best evidence of Nettleton's now-frenzied opposition to Finney is found in his own correspondence. See especially the letters collected in Birney Jr., "The Life and Letters of Asahel Nettleton," 269–78, 279–95, 307–20, 408–15. See also Hambrick-Stowe, *Charles G. Finney*, 67, who states that, in going after Finney, "Nettleton aimed to kill."

Nettleton's friends found Taylor heretical. Terribly embarrassed, Nettleton labored now to distance himself from New Haven.[11]

Upon his return to New England, Nettleton tried to quiet the Taylorites, hoping to avert any future embarrassments with Presbyterian friends to the south. Failing this, he took up his pen and launched a letter-writing campaign, casting aspersions about Taylor's theology throughout the region.[12] He proved somewhat persuasive at Andover Seminary, whose president, Ebenezer Porter, and leading theologian Leonard Woods soon joined the ranks of those who opposed the New Haven theology. During Andover's anniversary celebration in September 1829, President Porter called a meeting of New England's minds in his study at home. All the region's luminaries were there—Taylor, Beecher, Goodrich, Nettleton, Woods, Stuart, and several others—and they engaged in a charitable airing of their differences. But after the meeting, Woods published a series of captious *Letters to Rev. Nathaniel W. Taylor* (1830), and the battle for control of New England's Calvinist institutions had been joined.[13]

Before this meeting, Beecher had promised to remain a theological peacemaker, telling Porter, "With me it is a fundamental maxim not to expend my strength in contending with the friends of Christ, when so much effort is needed to turn back his enemies." But after the meeting, he spun around nearly 180 degrees, encouraging Taylor to respond to Woods with decisive force. "Attack," he wrote to his friend, so that Woods would "never . . . peep again or mutter. . . . I would have him exposed and pushed with great directness and power, and unsparingly, leaving of his temple not one stone upon another." Always more aggressive than the academicians in New Haven, Beecher now was

11. Sherry Pierpont May, "Asahel Nettleton: Nineteenth Century American Revivalist" (Ph.D. diss., Drew University, 1969), 323. On the general contours of the Taylorite-Tylerite split, see also Mead, *Nathaniel William Taylor,* 211–32, who interprets them much differently than I do.

12. Examples may be found in Birney Jr., "The Life and Letters of Asahel Nettleton," 330–46, 353–55, 366–69; and in Bennet Tyler, *Memoir of the Life and Character of Rev. Asahel Nettleton,* 291–94, 297–301.

13. See Leonard Woods, *Letters to Rev. Nathaniel W. Taylor,* in *The Works of Leonard Woods, D.D.,* 5 vols. (Andover, 1850), 4:343–459. On the meeting in Porter's study, see Bennet Tyler, *Letters on the Origin and Progress of the New Haven Theology* (New York, 1837), 24ff.; and Birney Jr., "The Life and Letters of Asahel Nettleton," 155–94. See also Asahel Nettleton to Charles Hodge, 7 December 1837, folder 2, box 18, ser. 14, Charles Hodge Papers, Princeton University Library. Nettleton notes that Beecher "was the great apologist [and] advocate of Dr. Taylor" at this meeting, "as will be recollected by all present." On Porter's opposition to Taylor, see his letter to Beecher, 22 May 1829, printed in *The Presbyterian* (Philadelphia) 6 (24 December 1836): 202; Lyman Matthews, *Memoir of the Life and Character of Ebenezer Porter, D.D.* (Boston, 1837), 219–25; and Tyler, *Letters on the Origin and Progress of the New Haven Theology,* 33–34.

playing the part of New Haven's battlefield commander. "We are not to be browbeaten," he exclaimed, "and driven off the ground of New England divinity—Bible divinity—by a feeble and ignorant philosophy."[14]

Making matters worse, by this time Beecher had already ruined his friendship with Nettleton, having tried to intimidate him during a conversation held, quite literally, in Beecher's woodshed. Though, as might have been expected, these men interpreted the encounter differently, both allowed that it took place in October 1829 after a meeting of Boston-area clergy held in Beecher's own home at which Nettleton publicized his opposition to Taylor's theology. After the meeting, Beecher and Nettleton spent time alone in Beecher's woodshed, with Beecher chopping wood while the younger Nettleton looked on. At a memorable point in their conversation, Beecher shook his axe at Nettleton and said, "Taylor and I have made you what you are, and if you do not behave yourself we will hew you down." Beecher always remembered this as "a mere playful act of humor," claiming that Nettleton had understood it as such himself. But when word of it spread southward down the seaboard, Nettleton fumed in humiliation, and the story of their encounter generated discomfort wherever it went.[15]

Meanwhile, Taylor's views were stirring up strife in the religious periodicals and theological quarterlies, in which he was gaining a notoriety that would soon catch up with him back home. In 1832 he engaged in a highly publicized exchange on his creedal commitments with friend and colleague Joel Hawes of Hartford's First Church. Published originally in the *Connecticut Observer*, this exchange was reprinted numerous times. Hawes intended it as an opportunity for Taylor to clarify his orthodoxy. But it wound up provoking further dissension—not over the eleven articles Taylor laid out in a basic statement of his beliefs (which he had phrased in fairly traditional Edwardsian terms), but over his annotations to the articles, which struck many as suspiciously elaborate and ambiguous.[16] Beecher took steps

14. Beecher to Porter, June 1829, and Beecher to Taylor, 6 September 1830, both in Beecher, *Autobiography*, 2:128, 171–72.

15. See Beecher, *Autobiography*, 2:287–88; and Nettleton to Charles Hodge, 7 December 1837, folder 2, box 18, ser. 14, Charles Hodge Papers, Princeton University Library.

16. The exchange (including Taylor's eleven-point creed) was published in Hartford's *Connecticut Observer* (20 February 1832): 1–8; New Haven's *Religious Intelligencer* 16 (25 February 1832): 614–16; Boston's *Spirit of the Pilgrims* 5 (March 1832): 173–79; and New Haven's *Quarterly Christian Spectator* 4 (March 1832): 171–76. This exchange led to a major paper war over Taylor's annotations waged between Taylor and Bennet Tyler in *Spirit of the Pilgrims* 5–6 (1832–33), after which an anonymous Taylorite, exhausted, wrote in New Haven's *Religious Intelligencer* 18 (16 November 1833): 392, "There are no doubt wolves in sheep's clothing, but we have seen with pain, a growing

immediately to reclaim New Haven's reputation, soliciting Woods' "cordial" consent to a common statement of New England doctrine.[17] But by 1834, Taylor faced heresy charges at home, as the Reverend Daniel Dow, a ten-year veteran of the Yale Corporation, complained of his failure to adhere literally to Connecticut's historic Saybrook Platform (1708). After an internal investigation, Yale's trustees acquitted Taylor, concluding that throughout the college's history, "excepting the period from 1753 to 1778, it has been an established principle, that the assent to the Confession of faith in question, is to be understood, as only an assent to 'the substance of doctrine therein contained.'" But Dow departed Yale determined to thwart its innovations, and New Haven acquired a reputation for theological legerdemain.[18]

The Taylorites disowned this reputation whenever they had the chance, contesting the Tylerites' frequent claim to be New England's true Edwardsians. They contended that the spirit of the New England Theology had always been one of investigation, of creative advancement of the gospel, not a spirit of fearful clinging to the past. Though the Tylerites seemed to think "that the Congregational ministers of New England should never dream of making a single advance upon the views of Bellamy and Edwards,—that nothing shall be deemed not heretical, except the exact phraseology adopted by these divines," this

disposition among Christians of the present day, to dress every sheep that they can catch out of their own fold, in wolves' clothing, and set the dogs upon them."

17. He did this in an exchange composed of three pairs of letters published in *Spirit of the Pilgrims* 5–6 (1832–33). Of Beecher's Edwardsian-Calvinist creed, Woods wrote, "I cordially agree. . . . The cordial belief of these doctrines is, I think, a solid basis of ministerial fellowship and cooperation, though there may be a variety of opinions on other subjects, and on some subjects which are by no means unimportant" (*Spirit of the Pilgrims* 5 [September 1832]: 505).

18. See Noah Porter et al., "Report on Articles of Faith," 1 August 1834, folder 38, box 7, Divinity School Papers, Sterling Memorial Library, Yale University; as well as Nathaniel W. Taylor, "Dr. Taylor's Statement" and "Dr. Taylor's Explanation," 21 August 1834, in the same folder at Yale (Taylor's formal response to Dow's complaints submitted to the Yale Corporation). Cf. Taylor's original "Declaration of Assent to Saybrook," 31 December 1822, folder 38, box 7, Divinity School Papers, Sterling Memorial Library, Yale University, which includes a creed submitted by Taylor verifying that he did subscribe originally to the Saybrook Platform only "for substance of doctrine." Illuminating early assessments of this controversy at Yale may be found all over the contemporary periodical literature but also in Daniel Dow (who left the Yale Corporation and eventually became a board member at the Tylerites' Theological Institute of Connecticut), *New Haven Theology, Alias Taylorism, Alias Neology; In Its Own Language* (Thompson, Conn., 1834), 52–56 and passim; Tyler, *Letters on the Origin and Progress of the New Haven Theology*, 78–85; and Zebulon Crocker, *The Catastrophe of the Presbyterian Church, in 1837, Including a Full View of the Recent Theological Controversies in New England* (New Haven, 1838), 244–50.

"was not the spirit of Edwards," they insisted—"Not at all." The Taylorites also felt that they had been largely misunderstood and that New England's theologians held more in common than they knew. They pleaded for unity both in print and in their private correspondence "between those who agree in the cardinal points of Calvinism—decrees, election, total depravity by nature, regeneration by the special and direct influence of the spirit, and final perseverance of saints." They viewed the Tylerites as their friends, as Taylor made unmistakably clear early in 1843 when he visited Nettleton on what everyone thought would be his deathbed. As remembered by Leonard Bacon, "There were no dry eyes in that chamber of suffering when Taylor fell weeping on the neck of Nettleton and kissed him." And Taylor repeated on many occasions what all of his friends knew to be true, that "nothing could have been farther from my wishes than to be drawn into a theological controversy with the Rev. Dr. Tyler of Portland; a man for whom an intimate friendship, in early life, has made it impossible for me to entertain any sentiments but those of respect and affection."[19]

But the Tylerites refused to accept the olive branch their friends extended. Taylor had simply gone too far in his dilution of Edwardsian Calvinism, and the future of New England's churches was at stake. While the Taylorites remained the most popular religious party in the region,[20] the Tylerites now laid plans for an ecclesiastical separation

19. "Who Are the True Conservatives?" *Quarterly Christian Spectator* 10 (November 1838): 616; Chauncey A. Goodrich to Charles Hodge, 9 March 1831, folder 9, box 16, Charles Hodge Papers, Princeton University Library; Bacon, "A Sermon at the Funeral of Nathaniel W. Taylor," 8; and Nathaniel W. Taylor, "Letter to the Editor from the Rev. Dr. Taylor," *Quarterly Christian Spectator* 5 (September 1833): 448. Nettleton, who had suffered from poor health throughout his life, did not actually die until May 16, 1844. On the Taylorites' Edwardsian ecumenism, see also Chauncey A. Goodrich to Bennet Tyler, 1 October 1832, MS Vault File, Beinecke Rare Book and Manuscript Library, Yale University, in which Goodrich laments that "no opportunities have been afforded us of comparing our views in *conversation*, where misapprehensions can be removed and objections obviated in a moment"; Nathaniel W. Taylor to Asahel Nettleton, 4 June 1834, folder 2851, box 180, Nettleton Papers, Case Memorial Library, Hartford Seminary; "On Christian Union," *Quarterly Christian Spectator* 9 (March 1837): 65–93, and (June 1837): 289–313; and "On Dissensions among Christian Brethren," *Quarterly Christian Spectator* 9 (December 1837): 554–69.

20. There are various indicators of Taylorite success. Throughout the Taylorite controversy, for example, enrollments increased at Yale Divinity School and always outnumbered those at the Tylerite's Theological Institute of Connecticut. By 1840 there were 72 students at Yale, making it the second-largest divinity school in New England (behind the older and more established Andover Seminary). As Yale's George Park Fisher would note, "The more that young men in other colleges and schools of theology were warned against Dr. Taylor, the more they flocked to his lecture-room." Taylor also remained a very popular churchman throughout the controversy, serving as both moderator and preacher at the annual meeting of the General Association of Connecticut in

and began to associate much more frequently with the emergent Old School Presbyterians than with their neighbors and former colleagues in New England.[21] They disagreed among themselves over the extent to which they should separate, but they all believed that they should "separate as soon as possible." As one anonymous Tylerite wrote, "By continued contact the evil [of Taylorism] will secretly spread, until the whole mass be corrupt. . . . Until we have a separate organization, and are united in our exertions to exclude false teachers from our churches, there will be no effectual barrier to their influx."[22]

After a secret meeting in Norwich in October 1831, at which they formed their own Doctrinal Tract Society, planned their own *Evangeli-*

1830 (in Wethersfield) and as moderator of the annual meetings of 1838 (in Norwalk) and 1841 (in New Haven). Tyler, by comparison, served as preacher only in 1837 and never served as moderator. Nettleton never served in either capacity. Well after Taylor's death, an anonymous reviewer for *The New Englander* would characterize Taylor's resilience by noting that "the attempt to proscribe men for sympathizing with Dr. Taylor's theology is [now] almost as obsolete in New England as the custom of hanging witches." See Fisher, "Historical Address," 21; John T. Wayland, *The Theological Department in Yale College 1822–1858* (1933; reprint, New York: Garland, 1987), 123 and passim; Glenn T. Miller, *Piety and Intellect: The Aims and Purposes of Ante-Bellum Theological Education* (Atlanta: Scholars, 1990), 201–2; *Contributions to the Ecclesiastical History of Connecticut*, 145–46; and "The Princeton Review for January," *The New Englander* 28 (April 1869): 408.

21. The strengthening of ties between the Tylerites and Old School Presbyterians is most evident in the fraternal correspondence that developed among clergymen such as Leonard Woods and Asahel Nettleton of New England and Ashbel Green, Charles Hodge, and Samuel Miller to the south. A good number of their letters remain and are housed primarily in collections such as the Simon Gratz Autograph Collection of the Historical Society of Pennsylvania and the Ashbel Green and Charles Hodge Papers at the Princeton University Library. In one such letter, Samuel Miller wrote to Nettleton speaking for himself and Princeton's patriarch, Archibald Alexander: "Our views [and] feelings with respect to the 'Pastoral Union of Con.' are not only amicable, but cordial [and] fraternal. We view it as a most desirable [and] important association, embarked in a great [and] good cause, [and] likely to accomplish a very important object. True, indeed, in looking over their published Confession of Faith, we do not find every word exactly as we could have wished; but we find quite enough in it that we approve, to be a basis of affectionate confidence, [and] unfeigned good will" (Miller to Nettleton, 14 March 1834, folder 6, box 3, ser. 2, Samuel Miller Papers, Princeton University Library). As demonstrated by May ("Asahel Nettleton," 390–97), the Tylerites sought a formal alliance with moderate Old School Presbyterians that would not only fortify their efforts in New England but might also help to avert a Presbyterian schism. And after the Presbyterians did divide in 1837–38, Connecticut's Congregationalists disagreed strenuously on how to relate to the Old and New School bodies. See Leonard Bacon, *Seven Letters to the Rev. George A. Calhoun, concerning the Pastoral Union of Connecticut, and Its Charges against the Ministers and Churches* (New Haven, 1840), 9–42.

22. *An Address, to the Congregational Churches in Connecticut, on the Present State of Their Religious Concerns* (Hartford, 1833), 54, 58.

cal Magazine, and developed a constitution that would govern the proceedings of their group, the Tylerites met in Hartford in January 1833
to work on a list of doctrinal articles of agreement. This process culminated in a larger meeting in September 1833, held quite symboli-
cally in East Windsor, Jonathan Edwards' hometown. It was there that
the Tylerites formally launched their separate Pastoral Union, electing
the Reverend George Calhoun as their founding president. About forty
clergymen attended from all across the state of Connecticut, adopting
the Tylerite constitution and Articles of Agreement developed earlier
and stipulating that future members of their union would have to be
nominated from within and then approved by a two-thirds vote at the
annual meeting. Most importantly, the new Tylerite Union planned the
establishment of a seminary, naming it the Theological Institute of
Connecticut. They appointed a board of trustees and determined to
build it in East Windsor, literally right down the street from Edwards'
birthplace. On May 13 of the following year, they took the Edwards
family doorstep and laid it ceremoniously as the cornerstone of their
seminary building. By October 1834 the Theological Institute was
open for business, and Bennet Tyler was hard at work as the founding
president and professor of theology.[23]

The Dissolution of the New England Theology

For all intents and purposes, the Taylorites and the Tylerites now
moved in different clerical networks—the most acrimonious days of
their dispute lay in the past. Leonard Bacon and George Calhoun
would wage a paper war at decade's end,[24] and by mid-century the

23. On these institutional developments, see especially Crocker, The Catastrophe of
the Presbyterian Church, 234–68; George A. Calhoun, Letters to the Rev. Leonard Bacon,
in Reply to His Attack on the Pastoral Union and Theological Institute of Connecticut
(Hartford, 1840), 72–79; Charles Hyde, "Theological Institute of Connecticut," in Contributions to the Ecclesiastical History of Connecticut, 185–89; Curtis Manning Geer, The
Hartford Theological Seminary, 1834–1934 (Hartford, 1934), 26–67; and May, "Asahel
Nettleton," 368ff.

24. This skirmish began with a letter to the editor of the New Haven Record (31 August 1839), in which Calhoun opposed the Record's recent coverage of the annual meeting of Connecticut's General Association. It culminated in a lengthy exchange concerning a wide range of ecclesiastical developments that had to be published in pamphlet
form after the Record was criticized for encouraging controversy. See Bacon, Seven Letters to the Rev. George A. Calhoun; Calhoun, Letters to the Rev. Leonard Bacon; and Leonard Bacon, An Appeal to the Congregational Ministers of Connecticut against a Division.
With an Appendix, Containing Short Notes on Mr. Calhoun's Letters (New Haven, 1840).
On Bacon's role in the Taylorite controversy, see also the recent book by Hugh Davis,
Leonard Bacon: New England Reformer and Antislavery Moderate (Baton Rouge: Louisiana State University Press, 1998), 102–6.

Tylerites would begin to squabble among themselves.[25] But by and large the smoke was clearing and the most perceptive members of both groups began to feel as though their differences were no longer as important as they had been. During the 1840s and 1850s, enrollments at both of their schools were low. In fact, by 1855 there was talk of a merger underway. Many regretted that the Taylorite controversy had sapped the region's theological resources, and this in a period of tremendous challenge to New England's churches.[26]

Indeed, as urbanization and industrialization altered the region's religious landscape, and German idealism, biblical criticism, and Darwinian science revolutionized theology, the Edwardsian culture proved as weak as it had been since the eighteenth century, and its leaders, now tired and aging, lacked the resources with which to respond. The coming generation of churchmen began to look elsewhere for intellectual guidance, seeking new and creative solutions to problems the Edwardsians had not addressed. And by the eve of the Civil War, even their teachers began to respond by paying homage to Edwardsian ancestors while offering a much more expansive theological curriculum.

25. In 1854–55, Bennet Tyler and Joseph Harvey debated the now-classic Edwardsian question concerning the ability of the unregenerate to turn to God in faith. Tyler argued in typical Edwardsian terms for the sinner's "natural" (though not moral) ability to repent and believe the gospel, while Harvey concluded in more traditional Calvinist language that "the *entire* impotence and hopelessness of man in himself is a vital truth in the economy of redemption" (emphasis mine). See Bennet Tyler, *Discourse on Human Ability and Inability* (Hartford, 1854); Joseph Harvey, *A Letter to the Rev. Dr. Tyler in Reply to His Discourse on Human Ability and Inability* (Springfield, Mass., 1855); Bennet Tyler, *A Letter to the Rev. Joseph Harvey, D.D., in Reply to His Strictures on a Sermon of the Author, Entitled "A Discourse on Human Ability and Ability [sic]"* (Hartford, 1855); and [Joseph Harvey], *A Review of Recent Publications on Human Ability and Inability* (Hartford, 1855), quotation from p. 29.

26. On these developments, see especially Leonard Bacon to Noah Porter, 15 January 1856, and Noah Porter to unidentified, 1 March 1856, both in folder 29, box 5, Divinity School Papers, Sterling Memorial Library, Yale University; "Meeting of Alumni of Yale Theological Seminary," *The Independent* (7 August 1856): 256; Hyde, "Theological Institute of Connecticut," 188; Fisher, "Historical Address," 21–22; Gerald Everett Knoff, "The Yale Divinity School, 1858–1899" (Ph.D. diss., Yale University, 1936), 8, 14–26, 45–57; Wayland, *The Theological Department in Yale College*, 120–24, 160–70, 409, 414–16; Geer, *The Hartford Theological Seminary*, 99–100; Roland H. Bainton, *Yale and the Ministry: A History of Education for the Christian Ministry at Yale from the Founding in 1701* (San Francisco: Harper, 1957), 161; Theodore Davenport Bacon, *Leonard Bacon: A Statesman in the Church*, ed. Benjamin W. Bacon (New Haven, 1931), 515–16; and Davis, *Leonard Bacon*, 227–28. As Donald M. Scott has shown in *From Office to Profession: The New England Ministry, 1750–1850* (Philadelphia: University of Pennsylvania Press, 1978), the period after the height of the Taylorite controversy was one of socioeconomic decline for New England clergy generally. Many poor and rural students entering the ministry could not afford to attend schools like Yale and consequently often did most of their preparation at smaller, regional colleges.

At Andover, Edwards A. Park would try to drag the movement forward, writing histories of the New England theology that papered over its cracks and fissures. But "progressive orthodoxy" would soon win the hearts and minds of most at Park's own seminary, and its proponents viewed Park and his passions as curious remnants from the past.[27] At Yale, men such as Bacon, Porter, Fisher, and Samuel Harris continued to appropriate Edwardsian themes as well. But they did so more forthrightly in selective acts of historical retrieval. In their increasingly secular, cosmopolitan world, none tried to revive the tradition in whole, ill-adapted as it always remained to the problems of modern, urban America.[28] Perhaps Porter put it best. When asked of his father-in-law's death in March 1858, he replied, "It was not too soon." Taylor "belonged to another world than that now coming on, and he would not have been happy in it."[29]

The New England theology did decline, then, but not at the end of

27. Examples of Park's historical reclamation efforts include Edwards A. Park, "The New England Theology; With Comments on a Third Article in the Biblical Repertory and Princeton Review, Relating to a Convention Sermon," *Bibliotheca Sacra* 9 (January 1852): 170–220; Park's memoir of Samuel Hopkins in *The Works of Samuel Hopkins, D.D.*, ed. Sewall Harding, 3 vols. (Boston: Doctrinal Tract and Book Society, 1852); Edwards A. Park, ed., *The Atonement: Discourses and Treatises by Edwards, Smalley, Maxcy, Emmons, Griffin, Burge, and Weeks* (Boston, 1859); Edwards A. Park, *Memoir of Nathanael Emmons: With Sketches of His Friends and Pupils* (Boston, 1861); and Edwards A. Park, *The Life and Character of Leonard Woods, D.D., LL.D.* (Andover, 1880). On Park's attempt to paper over the internal dissensions within the Edwardsian tradition, see also Joseph Conforti, "Edwards A. Park and the Creation of the New England Theology, 1840–1870," in *Jonathan Edwards's Writings*, ed. Stein, 193–207; and Anthony C. Cecil Jr., *The Theological Development of Edwards Amasa Park: Last of the "Consistent Calvinists"* (Missoula, Mont.: Scholars, 1974). On the rise of "progressive orthodoxy," consult Daniel Day Williams, *The Andover Liberals: A Study in American Theology* (Morningside Heights, N.Y.: King's Crown, 1941); Frank Hugh Foster, *The Modern Movement in American Theology: Sketches in the History of American Protestant Thought from the Civil War to the World War* (New York: Revell, 1939); William R. Hutchison, *The Modernist Impulse in American Protestantism* (Cambridge: Harvard University Press, 1976); and Gary Dorrien, *The Making of American Liberal Theology: Imagining Progressive Religion, 1805–1900* (Louisville: Westminster John Knox, 2001).

28. On this period of transition at Yale, see especially Frank Hugh Foster, "The Later New Haven Theology," in *A Genetic History of the New England Theology* (Chicago, 1907), 401–29; and Louise L. Stevenson, *Scholarly Means to Evangelical Ends: The New Haven Scholars and the Transformation of Higher Learning in America, 1830–1890* (Baltimore: Johns Hopkins University Press, 1986).

29. Theodore T. Munger, "Dr. Nathaniel W. Taylor—Master Theologian," *Yale Divinity Quarterly* 5 (February 1909): 240. On this theme, much else could be cited. But see especially the insightful comments of Taylor's younger colleagues at Yale: Fisher, "Historical Address," 21–24; Noah Porter, "Dr. Taylor and His Theology," in *Semi-Centennial Anniversary of the Divinity School of Yale College*, 98; and Fisher, *History of Christian Doctrine*, 437.

the eighteenth century and not for the reasons usually suggested. Rather, it flourished in the northeast during the first half of the nineteenth century, becoming America's first indigenous theological movement—perhaps the most popular movement of indigenous theology in American evangelical history. Its great success proved a two-edged sword, however, as the Edwardsians eventually grew so large and diverse that they tore themselves apart, leaving their culture too weak to sustain a vital tradition of religious reflection.

To be sure, external forces also contributed to their demise, forces recognized by the successors of Taylor, Beecher, Tyler, and Nettleton. But these forces neither co-opted nor overwhelmed New England's Edwardsians. Rather, the problem was that these ministers failed to engage them much at all. Indeed, one looks in vain to the New England theology for any serious, sustained analysis of the challenges that proved most pressing to Christian ministers in the mid–nineteenth century. The Edwardsians largely neglected the new opportunities for urban ministry. They proved more lethargic than Baptists and Methodists in planting churches on the frontier. They disrespected German idealism, even as many of their students devoured Coleridge. And by 1859, when Darwin published *The Origin of Species* and higher criticism began to make inroads into American theological studies, both Taylor and Tyler were dead, their movement was disintegrating, and their followers were struggling simply to hold on to what was left.

In his important recent work on the long history of the New England theology, American historian Bruce Kuklick attributes the Edwardsians' eventual extinction to the intellectual commitments of their leaders. One of the few major interpreters to take the later Edwardsians seriously, Kuklick argues that they declined in the face of indomitable critical challenges. In short, according to Kuklick, Darwin undermined the Edwardsians' traditional dependence on British empiricism and especially on the psychology and epistemology of Common Sense Realism. Or in Kuklick's own words, evolutionary theory "made untenable commitments to a Christian philosophy based on Scottish thought," and thus "[destroyed] . . . the philosophical basis of all American religious orthodoxy."[30] While this is not the place for a full-fledged response to Kuklick's argument, perhaps it is the place to point out that many religious philosophers today espouse a

30. See Bruce Kuklick, *The Rise of American Philosophy: Cambridge, Massachusetts 1860–1930* (New Haven: Yale University Press, 1977), 24–25; and Bruce Kuklick, *Churchmen and Philosophers: From Jonathan Edwards to John Dewey* (New Haven: Yale University Press, 1985), 223.

version of Scottish Realism,[31] and religious orthodoxies of many kinds continue to thrive. The Edwardsians never expressed much fear or confusion regarding Darwin. In fact, they largely ignored the new science, underestimating its eventual influence.

No, the Edwardsians were not the losers of the mid-nineteenth-century culture wars. The fact of the matter is that they hardly entered them at all. The New England theology did not wilt in the face of insurmountable obstacles. Rather, it declined primarily because its leaders had long ago become self-absorbed, expending most of their energy on internal struggles for control of their movement's vast resources. As a result, they failed to respond effectively to the changing needs of the world around them. And, after a while, that changing world just passed them by.

31. For only the most recent example, see Nicholas Wolterstorff, *Thomas Reid and the Story of Epistemology* (New York: Cambridge University Press, 2001).

11

"HE CUTS UP EDWARDSISM BY THE ROOTS"

Robert Lewis Dabney and the Edwardsian Legacy in the Nineteenth-Century South

Sean Michael Lucas

In a eulogy written shortly after Robert Lewis Dabney died in 1898, T. C. Johnson paid tribute to Dabney's mental energy and theological conservatism. After comparing Dabney to the usual heroes of Old School Presbyterianism—James Henley Thornwell, Charles Hodge, A. A. Hodge, and Archibald Alexander—Johnson claimed that "for sheer mental might we suppose that old Jonathan Edwards was more nearly Dr. Dabney's equal." After noting that Edwards founded a theology, made a "great name," and gained a following, Johnson observed that Edwards' power was primarily due "to his peculiar teachings" and to the fact that Edwards changed "the theological system which he wished to defend." By contrast, Dabney demonstrated "his great power while walking in old paths." While Edwards was not afraid of theological innovation—which Johnson characterized as "doubtful and ultimately insufficient, even if profound looking, shifts" from the Westminster Standards—Dabney was truly conservative in his support for the Reformed tradition. He defended "fearlessly our standards received from the great Assembly at Westminster." Johnson even claimed that Dabney "cuts up Edwardsism by the roots," demonstrating that the New Englander's innovations were "untrue and to be repudiated."[1]

Contemporary theologians and historians have spent a great deal of energy tracing Edwards' legacy and the rise and fall of the New Divinity in New England and the mid-Atlantic states. The aim has been to determine the continuity of Edwards' thought with the revivalism and social reform of the Second Great Awakening. Likewise, some historians have considered the major theological battle for Edwards' cultural authority between Princeton and the northern New Divinity schools, Yale and Andover, as an avenue for determining Edwards' legacy. Few, however, have considered Edwards' legacy south of the Mason-Dixon line among southern Presbyterians during the nineteenth century.[2] This essay examines Edwards' legacy in the nineteenth-century South by focusing on the criticisms that southern Presbyterians, led by Dabney, made of Edwards' theology. While admitting Edwards' general reputation as a holy minister of the gospel, southern Presbyterians arraigned Edwards' developments of divine causation, freedom of the will, personal identity, the imputation of Adam's sin, and his theory of true virtue as inadequate and ultimately harmful deviations from Reformed orthodoxy. In the end, what distressed southerners like Dabney about Edwards' theology was its innovation. Because Dabney believed that the Reformed faith was best summarized in the Westminster Standards, his view of the theological task was profoundly conservative. Hence, Dabney stood against the "isms" of his day, especially "Edwardsism," to defend the unchanging truth summarized in the Presbyterian confessional standards.

1. T. C. Johnson, "Robert Lewis Dabney—A Sketch," in *In Memoriam: Robert Lewis Dabney*, ed. Charles W. Dabney et al. (Knoxville: University of Tennessee Press, 1899), 8–9.

2. On the northern Calvinist battle for Edwards' legacy, see Mark A. Noll, "The Contested Legacy of Jonathan Edwards in Antebellum Calvinism," in *Reckoning with the Past: Historical Essays on American Evangelicalism from the Institute for the Study of American Evangelicals*, ed. D. G. Hart (Grand Rapids: Baker, 1995), 200–217; Mark A. Noll, "Jonathan Edwards and Nineteenth-Century Theology," in *Jonathan Edwards and the American Experience*, ed. Nathan O. Hatch and Harry S. Stout (New York: Oxford University Press, 1988), 260–87; Allen C. Guelzo, *Edwards on the Will: A Century of American Theological Debate* (Middletown, Conn.: Wesleyan University Press, 1989); Joseph A. Conforti, *Jonathan Edwards, Religious Tradition, and American Culture* (Chapel Hill: University of North Carolina Press, 1995), 108–44. On Edwards' legacy more generally but still ignoring the South, see the essays by Douglas Sweeney and Allen Guelzo in *Jonathan Edwards's Writings: Text, Context, Interpretation*, ed. Stephen J. Stein (Bloomington: Indiana University Press, 1996), 139–58, 159–74.

Early in the nineteenth century, southern Presbyterians had looked to Edwards as a guide, particularly in his defense of revivalism and his discussion of religious affections. Due to the influence of Samuel Davies, the leading Virginia Presbyterian of the eighteenth century, and William Graham, principal of Liberty Hall Academy, Edwards was a respected voice, influencing a generation that included Archibald Alexander. Early in his ministry, Alexander's theology was a mixture of Westminster Presbyterianism, Scottish Realism, and Edwardsianism. However, an extended trip to New England in 1801 convinced Alexander that the New England theology was a dangerous deviation from the Reformed faith; afterwards, his theology began to fix itself "more definitely in the direction of the common Westminster theology." Alexander later grew critical of Edwards' theology, claiming that Edwards' *Treatise concerning Religious Affections* was "too abstract and tedious for common readers." Alexander would shift the prime importance in religious experience from the affections to the mind. Still, Alexander viewed Edwards as a "great and good man" and believed that "few men ever attained, as we think, higher degrees of holiness, or made more accurate observations on the exercises of others."[3]

Old School Presbyterians, North and South, followed Alexander's revised estimate of Edwards. Due to the influence of "Edwards and his school," its relationship to abolitionism, and its influence in the New School branch of the Presbyterian church, southern Presbyterian theologians became increasingly concerned to distance themselves from Edwards and his followers. Southern Presbyterians took steps to ensure that Edwardsian theology was not taught in their schools, for example. When Columbia Seminary was founded in 1829, one of the first professors, George Howe, came from Andover Seminary in New England. Howe developed the curriculum of the seminary and based the theology course on lecture notes from his teacher at Andover, Leonard Woods, a moderate Edwardsian. Due to the influence of Woods' notes, many of the first students later became New School in their sympathies. During the Old School–New School controversy, the seminary's board of directors resolved in 1835 that the seminary sup-

3. Archibald Alexander, *Thoughts on Religious Experience* (1844; reprint, Carlisle: Banner of Truth Trust, 1967), 27, 61, 67; Guelzo, *Edwards on the Will*, 200–207; James W. Alexander, *The Life of Archibald Alexander, D.D.* (New York: Scribner, 1854), 355; Lefferts A. Loetscher, *Facing the Enlightenment and Pietism: Archibald Alexander and the Founding of Princeton Theological Seminary* (Westport: Greenwood, 1983). After Edwards' dismissal from Northampton, Davies tried to persuade him to relocate to Virginia; see Edwards to John Erskine, 7 July 1752, in Jonathan Edwards, *The Works of Jonathan Edwards*, vol. 16, *Letters and Personal Writings*, ed. George S. Claghorn (New Haven: Yale University Press, 1998), 492.

ported the Old School branch in the controversy. Yet, in 1837 the school still was under "suspicions of unsoundness as to its orthodoxy both civil and ecclesiastical . . . [and] its purity from Northern predilections, notions, and influences." As one editorial writer in the Columbia newspaper questioned, "Is [Columbia Seminary] as free from all suspicions of a taint of the new divinity, and of abolitionism as a Southern school ought ever to be? We hazard nothing in saying it is not." Southern ministers had to be free from all heterodoxies, New Divinity and abolitionism.[4] Not surprisingly, southern Presbyterians ultimately sided with the northern Old Schoolers in the division of 1837, believing that the theological, ecclesiological, and social errors of the New School required the radical excising of four synods.[5]

Southern Presbyterians not only barred Edwardsian theology from their seminaries and their church councils, but they also subjected Edwards himself to a thorough critique. One of the first articles on Edwards published in southern Presbyterians' most important theological organ, *The Southern Presbyterian Review*, hammered Edwards' theology on several fronts. The author, noted Old Schooler Samuel Baird, claimed that Edwards ultimately shared the same position on causation as John Taylor, his Arminian opponent in his treatise on *Original Sin*. This faulty view of causation, which claimed that God was the only efficient cause, led Edwards into innumerable inconsistencies and errors. In particular, Baird accused Edwards of embracing a "form of pantheism, which makes God the only real existence" and led to the conclusion that God was the author of sin. Baird also claimed that Edwards "denied the doctrine of imputation," and this led ultimately to Socinianism and Pelagianism, which many New Englanders embraced because they were "entrenched in the false principles of Edwards' philosophy."[6]

4. William C. Robinson, *Columbia Theological Seminary and the Southern Presbyterian Church, 1831–1931* (Decatur: Dennis Lindsey, 1931), 16–21; Morton H. Smith, *Studies in Southern Presbyterian Theology* (Phillipsburg, N.J.: Presbyterian and Reformed, 1987), 109–12; *Southern Times and State Gazette*, 24 February 1837, 2–3 (thanks to Gregory A. Wills for this reference).

5. On the division of 1837, see George M. Marsden, *The Evangelical Mind and the New School Presbyterian Experience: A Case Study of Theology in Nineteenth-Century America* (New Haven: Yale University Press, 1970); Sean Michael Lucas, "Hold Fast That Which Is Good: The Public Theology of Robert Lewis Dabney" (Ph.D. diss., Westminster Theological Seminary, 2002), 172–75. On the plight of the small New School contingent in the South, see Harold M. Parker Jr., *The United Synod of the South: The Southern New School Presbyterian Church* (Westport: Greenwood, 1988).

6. S. J. Baird, "Edwards and the Theology of New England," *Southern Presbyterian Review* 10 (1858): 574–92. Baird repeated most of these charges in *The Elohim Revealed in the Creation and Redemption of Man* (Philadelphia: Lindsay and Blakiston, 1860).

Baird was not the only representative of the southern Old School Presbyterian perspective to reproach Edwards for his theological shifts and innovations. James Henley Thornwell, one of southern Presbyterianism's leading theologians, also criticized Edwards' theology in several areas. First, Thornwell claimed that Edwards' explanation of the freedom of the will "breaks down" in several ways: it failed to explain human guilt; it did not protect God from being the author of sin; it did "not explain the moral value attached to character"; and it merely accounted for "self-expression, but not self-determination." Thornwell also denounced Edwards' view of personal identity, claiming that the idea that identity consisted in the "arbitrary constitution of God" opposed "the plainest intuitions of intelligence." In addition, the South Carolinian believed that Edwards shared with Augustine the belief that sin was the privation of good. Such an idea was "a mere juggle with words" that had "a strong tendency to dissipate the consciousness of sin." All of these issues led to the errors of the later New England divines, who "made the Bible an appendix to their shallow and sophistical psychology, and to their still shallower and more sophistical ethics." Though Thornwell was not as caustic as Baird, he still registered a decidedly negative opinion about Edwards' theology.[7]

John Girardeau, Thornwell's brightest student, expanded his mentor's basic criticisms of Edwards in a wide-ranging consideration of *The Will in Its Theological Relations*.[8] Girardeau agreed with Thornwell that Edwards' work furnished "an inadequate account of freedom of the will." In particular, Girardeau charged Edwards with holding to

7. James Henley Thornwell, *The Collected Writings of James Henley Thornwell*, ed. J. B. Adger, 4 vols. (1871–73; reprint, Carlisle: Banner of Truth Trust, 1974), 1:250, 350, 381–82, 582. Thornwell, in fact, believed that Baird was too harsh in his criticisms of Edwards. Reviewing Baird's *Elohim Revealed*, Thornwell wrote: "It strikes us as a fault of the book that it betrays something of a captious spirit, a tendency to minute exceptions. Dr. Baird detects an error where others can see only a fault of expression, and belabors opinions with great vehemence which the reader finds it impossible to discriminate from his own. Against Edwards, particularly, he has an inveterate spite" (ibid., 517–18).

8. John L. Girardeau, *The Will in Its Theological Relations* (Columbia: W. J. Duffie, 1891). This book was a reprinting and expansion of a six-installment essay that Girardeau published in the *Southern Presbyterian Review* ("The Freedom of the Will in its Theological Relations," *Southern Presbyterian Review* 29 [1878]: 611–55; 30 [1879]: 51–84; 31 [1880]: 1–45, 323–50, 613–48; 32 [1881]: 63–102). Occasioned by Dabney's exchange with A. T. Bledsoe over Edwards on the will in the prior issues of the *Review*, Girardeau penned the first two installments as his basic position on the matter. However, his essay was criticized by James A. Waddell at the end of 1879 ("Contrary Choice," *Southern Presbyterian Review* 30 [1879]: 516–49). Waddell's critique required four more installments from Girardeau over 1880 and 1881 as a response.

a type of determinism—Edwards' theory of necessity "incompetently ground[ed] human guilt" and led "to the implication of the divine efficiency in the production of sin." Edwards' theory of necessity failed to ground human guilt, Girardeau held, because Edwards claimed that God, by divine fiat, was the sole efficient cause of all things, including Adam's original sin. Adam had no choice, no power to the contrary, in the fall because of a "metaphysical imperfection" that rendered him prone to sin before the fall. Not only did Edwards' position appear to impose "the limitations of human conception upon the products of the divine omnipotence," but it also made God to be "the remote, though not the proximate, efficient cause of sin." This hypothesis, Girardeau believed, was "contradictory to Scripture as interpreted by the consensus of the Church." Girardeau held that the position of Augustine, Calvin, and the Westminster Standards was that Adam had "the power of contrary choice . . . in spiritual things." Adam was a probationer who was able to choose good or evil without moral necessity and with true spontaneity. While the power of contrary choice in spiritual matters was lost in the fall of humankind, Girardeau held that human beings still had the "liberty of spontaneity." Common sense taught that men and women could choose spontaneously and without compulsion as well as discern between contrary choices in the "natural-moral" realm; the Bible taught that the power to choose spiritual good for its own sake instead of evil was lost in the fall. As a result, God was not the author of humankind's first sin; rather, "man, by his first sinful volition, himself unnecessarily determined his mournful captivity to the law of sin and death." Therefore, Girardeau judged Edwards' "theory of determinism" to have been struck down "by the hammer of Scripture, consciousness, and the fundamental beliefs of the race." While Edwards may have been "a wonderful metaphysical genius and of almost angelic saintliness of character," Girardeau believed that "he was no exception to the law of human fallibility," particularly in the area of the will.[9]

Critical to the strength of Girardeau's argument was the support that John Calvin provided. Girardeau held that Edwards' position was "subject to the charge of being uncalvinistic." Calvin held that "sin did

9. Girardeau, "Freedom of the Will," *Southern Presbyterian Review* 29 (1878): 612–13, 623, 636–38; 30 (1879): 82–83; 31 (1880): 6–7, 10–11. A convenient summary of Girardeau's lengthy argument can be found in *The Will in Its Theological Relations*, 401–9. It should be noted that, while Girardeau believed he scored significant points on Edwards, particularly in scouting Edwards' determinism, it does not appear that his final solution to the problem of the will was much different from Edwards' own; compare with Guelzo, *Edwards on the Will*, 54–86; and Stephen J. Nichols, *Jonathan Edwards: A Guided Tour of His Life and Thought* (Phillipsburg, N.J.: P&R, 2001), 173–87.

not result from man's original nature"; nor was "the moral necessity of sinning" from humankind's original condition but was "now from his corrupt nature." In addition, Calvin did not hold to a distinction between the freedom of man and a separate freedom of the will as did some of "the school of Edwards"; instead, Calvin's common sense taught that "the ability of man is exactly the ability of the will." Further, Girardeau claimed that "Calvin affirmed for man in innocence the power of contrary choice—the liberty of inclining to either of opposing alternatives. He plainly—*in terminis*—declares that, although Adam freely elected to sin, he might have done otherwise—he might have elected to stand. If this be Determinism, white is black, or we are dazed." As a result, Girardeau claimed that "we derived our doctrine from him, in great measure, and have faithfully stuck to him until this hour. . . . We would sooner part with most things than our good Calvinistic name." By claiming Calvin's authority for his position, Girardeau was doing more than simply balancing one cultural authority with another. He was signaling Edwards' deviation from the Reformed tradition through doctrinal novelty. Although Edwards might innovate by borrowing the logic and language of determinism, Girardeau pledged, "We go with Calvin; and we have gone with him all along."[10]

While Baird, Thornwell, and Girardeau indicated southern Presbyterians' discomfort and displeasure with the Edwardsian tradition of theological innovation, Dabney was the most wide-ranging critic of Edwards and the best example of southern Presbyterian response to the New England divine. Though Dabney clearly respected the power of Edwards' intellect, he was troubled at several points by Edwards' theological innovation. He most often charged the New England minister with veering off into impractical metaphysical speculation. For example, in a rebuttal of Plymouth Brethren theology, Dabney generally agreed with their assessment of Edwards' *Treatise concerning Religious Affections*. "When they object to the intricacy and impractical character of much of Edwards' analysis, for the unlearned Christian," Dabney observed, "we assent again, remembering the sagacious remark of old Dr. Alexander, that the work of Edwards is 'too anatomical.'" As was typical with Dabney, he preferred the less intricate analysis of Francis Turretin, the seventeenth-century Reformed theologian who authored the *Institutes of Elentic Theology,* which served as Dab-

10. Girardeau, "Freedom of the Will," *Southern Presbyterian Review* 31 (1880): 11–12, 18, 19, 23, 33. Interestingly, Girardeau identified Old School Calvinists Archibald Alexander and Charles Hodge as part of this "Edwardsian school" on the will along with the New Divinity coterie ("Freedom of the Will," *Southern Presbyterian Review* 29 [1878]: 624).

ney's main theology textbook, to Edwards on the matter of assurance of faith.[11]

Another example of Dabney's general criticism of Edwards came by way of a lengthy engagement with the southern Episcopalian A. T. Bledsoe, a longtime antagonist and editor of the *Southern Review*. Bledsoe cherished an intense interest in theology throughout his life and at one time served as assistant to the Episcopal bishop of Kentucky. In 1845 Bledsoe had authored a book-length attack upon Edwards' defense of the Calvinist teaching on freedom of the will. The first engagement that Dabney and Bledsoe had was when Dabney reviewed Bledsoe's *A Theodicy; or, Vindication of the Divine Glory* in 1853 for the *Presbyterial Critic*. Dabney claimed that Bledsoe's discussion of the will could only be sustained by "a materialistic phrenology" that led logically to either atheism or pantheism. Dabney later reviewed Bledsoe's 1856 book *An Essay on Liberty and Slavery*. Though Dabney's review was generally positive—he applauded Bledsoe as "a strong man tearing away the defences of his helpless adversary, rending them into almost invisible shreds, and spurning them as the driven stubble before his bow"—Dabney later blamed Bledsoe for sabotaging Dabney's own book on slavery by preventing its publication in England during the Civil War. After the war, Bledsoe began the *Southern Review* and renewed the theological battle between himself and Dabney by answering Dabney's eighteen-year-old objections to his earlier work on the problem of evil. Bledsoe also penned several articles that constituted a major attack upon Reformed theology in general and the *Southern Presbyterian Review* in particular.[12]

Dabney rushed to defend the Reformed faith, claiming, "We have a long score to settle with Dr. Bledsoe." In two articles spread over ninety pages, Dabney defended his Reformed understanding of hu-

11. Dabney, "Theology of the Plymouth Brethren," in *Discussions*, ed. C. R. Vaughan, 4 vols. (Richmond, Va.: Presbyterian Committee of Publication, 1890–97), 1:175–76; Lucas, "Hold Fast That Which Is Good," 54–56.

12. A. T. Bledsoe, *Examination of President Edwards' "Inquiry into the Freedom of the Will"* (Philadelphia: H. Hooker, 1845); A. T. Bledsoe, *A Theodicy; or, Vindication of Divine Glory* (New York: Carlton and Phillips, 1853); Robert Lewis Dabney, "A Theodicy; or, Vindication of Divine Glory," *Presbyterial Critic* 1 (1855): 13–20; A. T. Bledsoe, *An Essay on Liberty and Slavery* (Philadelphia: J. B. Lippincott, 1856); Robert Lewis Dabney, "Liberty and Slavery," *Discussions*, 3:61–69; Theodrick Pryor to Robert Lewis Dabney, 4 June 1873, Dabney Papers, Archives, Union Theological Seminary, Richmond, Va. Dabney, in his "The Philosophy of Dr. Bledsoe" (*Discussions*, 3:181), claims that he wrote two reviews of *A Theodicy*; however, I could find only one in the two volumes of the *Presbyterial Critic*. For discussion on Bledsoe, see Richard Weaver, "Albert Taylor Bledsoe," in *The Southern Essays of Richard M. Weaver*, ed. George M. Curtis III and James J. Thompson Jr. (Indianapolis: Liberty Fund, 1987), 147–58.

man agency against Bledsoe's "Pelagianism." In the midst of those pages, Edwards became a contested character, someone Dabney had to defend while expressing his own criticisms of the Edwardsian theology. Dabney acknowledged that Edwards had "demolished" the Arminian scheme of human agency with several "unanswerable" arguments and that though Bledsoe tried to avoid Edwardsian objections, he failed to refute the American theologian. In addition, Dabney praised Edwards for being "too clear a thinker to have his mind haunted with any phantom of a *choice* which is *compelled*."[13] That being said, Dabney claimed, "We do not regard President Edwards as infallible, and did not before Dr. Bledsoe assailed him." Particularly, Dabney claimed that Edwards' defense of the Reformed view of human agency was "too much under the influence of the pious Locke; and hence his usually clear vision is sometimes confused by the shallow plausibilities of the sensationalist psychology." Hence, Edwards confused "objective inducement with subjective motive" and failed to distinguish carefully between broad and narrow uses of the word "will." Still, these were only "excrescencies and blemishes" and did not affect the "indestructible" structure of Edwards' argument. Though Dabney was uncomfortable in defending Edwards, he closed ranks with the New England divine against the attacks of Bledsoe.[14]

Dabney advanced more significant theological objections when he addressed Edwards' teaching on personal identity and imputation and on the nature of true virtue. In dealing with the question of whether it was just to impute Adam's sin to his posterity, Dabney summarized Edwards' solution. Edwards claimed that "our federal oneness with Adam is no more arbitrary, in that it was constituted by God's fiat, than our own personal identity: for that also is constituted only by God's institution." Edwards held that personal identity was established by a "perpetual recreation" in which "one moment's existence does not cause or produce a succeeding moment's, not being coexistent with it, as cause and effect must always be." As a result, Edwards claimed that "our continued identity is nothing else than a result of the will of God, sovereignly ordaining to restore our existence out of *nihil*, by a perpetual recreation, at the beginning of each new moment, and to cause in us a consciousness which seems to give sameness." Dabney condemned Edwards' continuous creation view of personal identity as "worthless." Dabney wrote, "I will venture the opinion that no man, not Edwards himself, ever satisfied himself, by his argument,

---

13. Dabney, "Philosophy of Dr. Bledsoe," 184, 187; Dabney, "The Philosophy of Volition," *Discussions*, 3:238.

14. Dabney, "Philosophy of Volition," 237, 239.

that his being had not a true, intrinsic continuity, and a real, necessary identity, in itself." Edwards' speculation contradicted "universal common sense" and "our own intuitions." Belief in personal identity was an "*a priori* intuition" and a "necessary conception" of human consciousness. Common sense demonstrated that Edwards' view of personal identity was "sophistical."[15]

Dabney also conjectured that Edwards' view of true virtue was deviant as well. Dabney classified Edwards' theory of virtue with "the infidel, utilitarian school" because it taught that "virtue is identical with benevolence." Edwards and his most prominent disciple, Samuel Hopkins, held that virtue consisted of "benevolence to being in general—meaning, of course, rational beings—or love to being in general." The being that had "the greatest *quantum* of existence" deserved "the largest share of this benevolence." The conclusion was that human beings must love God more than other creatures "because he is infinite in the dimensions of his existence," and humans must love "a great and good man proportionally more than one less able and full of being." Edwards rested this conclusion on the grounds that "every judgment of beauty of every kind is analyzable into a perception of order and harmony; but the most beautiful and lofty of all rational harmonies is the consent or benevolence of an intelligent being to all being."[16]

Dabney believed that Edwards' original position was "plausible" but also a "most sophistical speculation." Hopkins and Edwards' son, Jonathan Edwards Jr., had transformed Edwards' position into a "utilitarian scheme." These New Divinity theologians shifted love of being in general into "simply the affection of benevolence." The result was that "benevolence is all virtue and all virtue is benevolence." This position differed little in Dabney's estimation from beneficence as "the practical expression of benevolence." As such, Edwards' view was the equivalent of utilitarianism. By reducing virtue to love, New Divinity theologians were forced to affirm the corollary, that selfishness was the essence of sin. The only way the New Divinity could sanctify native human self-interest was to merge individuals into an "impersonal

15. Robert Lewis Dabney, *Syllabus and Notes of the Course of Systematic and Polemic Theology*, 2d ed. (1878; reprint, Carlisle: Banner of Truth, 1996), 338–39. Dabney refused to condemn Edwards for his alleged "mediate imputation." Dabney believed that Charles Hodge accused Edwards erroneously (Dabney, "Hodge's Systematic Theology," *Discussions*, 1:258) and that Hodge's accusation was picked up and repeated as true. Dabney himself believed that "this distinction between 'mediate,' and 'immediate' imputation should have never been made" (Dabney, *Syllabus and Notes*, 342).

16. Robert Lewis Dabney, *The Practical Philosophy, Being the Philosophy of the Feelings, of the Will, and of the Conscience, with the Ascertainment of Particular Rights and Duties* (1897; reprint, Harrisonburg, Va.: Sprinkle, 1984), 219–21. Dabney covered the same material in condensed form in his *Syllabus and Notes*, 100–104.

general being." This would allow an individual the "right to pursue his own selfish interests supremely" as part of a general benevolence to being in general.[17]

Dabney objected to the Edwardsian theory of virtue on several grounds. First, Dabney claimed that Edwards' "grounding of moral virtue in a harmony or order perceived is utterly invalid as a support of his theory unless he holds that aesthetic beauty, logical propriety and moral praiseworthiness are all generically the same beauty, differing only in degree." However, Dabney held that there was a basic difference between moral beauty and aesthetic and logical beauty, rooted in the a priori intuitions of conscience. Dabney also objected that Edwards' theory transformed "virtuous affections" into "a mere abstraction, a general idea." This, too, was false to common-sense intuitions that taught moral virtue was personal. Human beings extended love to persons, not to abstract existence. Moreover, benevolence to those who had the greatest amount of existence led to all sorts of impossibilities and absurdities: the rescue of "a great and gifted stranger" instead of one's own father because "the great man presented to his love a greater quantum of existence" or the prohibition of a peasant mother from nursing a sick and dying child until she properly "calculated the preponderance of the resultant general benefit of the nursing over the industry." Another objection Dabney raised was that Edwards' grounded love to God in ontology, the fact that God had infinite existence and thus deserved humankind's benevolence. This, Dabney argued, ignored that the Bible based human worship "expressly upon God's moral perfections." Worship based on divine ontology was worthless because "God is infinitely blessed. His good cannot be promoted by creatures." Finally, Dabney assailed Edwards for the logical conclusion of his theory that self-love was the essence of sin. Edwards held that benevolence united individuals to general existence. To turn from love for being in general toward oneself in self-love "disunites the man's own being within itself." Self-love produced "the judgment and pain of remorse" because self-love moved the human being away from his or her chief object, which was love to general existence instead of one's own affairs. It followed that any breach of disinterested benevolence to general existence caused by a concern on individual and local matters was, by definition, sinful. Thus, the essence of sin was self-love. While Edwards himself was "too shrewd to adopt" what "his premises should have taught

17. Dabney, *Practical Philosophy*, 221, 228. Dabney probably followed Princetonians Archibald Alexander and Lyman Atwater in charging Edwards with utilitarianism; Noll, "Contested Legacy of Jonathan Edwards in Antebellum Calvinism," 209–10.

him," his followers were not so restrained and boldly reduced sin to self-love.[18]

Dabney's opposition to Edwards' theories of virtue and personal identity found its strongest basis in his commitment to Scottish Realist epistemology. Over and again, Dabney pointed out that Edwards' speculations were "sophistical" and violated "common sense." In fact, he invoked common sense as the standard by which to judge any "scientific hypothesis" or philosophical statement: "When any scientific hypothesis conflicts thus with universal common sense, it is sophistical" and to be "repudiated." But even more than a simple appeal to universal common sense, Dabney and the other southern Presbyterians rejected Edwards as a result of a conflict in epistemologies. Dabney believed that Edwards was hopelessly indebted to Locke, while Girardeau identified him with Berkeley. Regardless of which identification was correct—a matter of great debate among scholars of Edwards to this day—the important matter was that both identified Edwards as an idealist and, through guilt by association, as an opponent of the great Realist philosopher Thomas Reid. Thus, when Dabney (or other southern Presbyterians) made an appeal to consciousness or universal common sense, they appealed to a different way of knowing from Edwards' idealism.[19]

Dabney certainly believed that a simple appeal to consciousness was more than sufficient to contradict Edwards or any other false theory. In discussing various theories of the will, Dabney wrote, "Now, in answer to all this, it would be enough to say, that our consciousness contradicts it. There can be no higher evidence than that of consciousness." Edwards' innovations in *Original Sin* and *The Nature of True Virtue* were philosophical in nature, supported lightly by Scripture; Dabney was comfortable to reject them on philosophical grounds. Interestingly enough, southern Old School Presbyterians agreed with Princeton on many of these criticisms by rooting them in Common

18. Dabney, *Practical Philosophy,* 222–25. Joseph Conforti, in his study of Samuel Hopkins, demonstrated that Hopkins believed Edwards' account of true virtue was faulty for similar reasons to Dabney: "Not only did it make unnecessary concessions to rational moral philosophers, but it tended toward abstraction, mixed aesthetics with ethics, and did not provide an adequate spur to social action." Conforti also confirmed Dabney's understanding of the way Hopkins developed the relationship between disinterested benevolence and self-love (Joseph Conforti, *Samuel Hopkins and the New Divinity Movement* [Grand Rapids: Christian University Press, 1981], 110, 119–23).

19. Dabney, *Syllabus and Notes,* 78–110, 339. Mark Noll observed that Old School Presbyterians appealed to the same universal moral sense for ethical formulation as Francis Hutcheson, the philosopher that Edwards attempted to answer in *The Nature of True Virtue* (Noll, "Contested Legacy of Jonathan Edwards in Antebellum Calvinism," 214–15).

Sense Realism. Princeton theologians were particularly uncomfortable with Edwards' theory of true virtue and argued that it did not represent the heart of Edwards' theology. Unlike the Princetonians, however, southern Presbyterians felt no need to claim Edwards' cultural authority by attempting to divorce Edwards from the Edwardsians the way Charles Hodge and others did. Still, Old School Presbyterian disagreement with Edwards on the nature of true virtue was shared on both sides of the Mason-Dixon line and was rooted in differing epistemologies.[20]

However, one suspects that there was another implicit reason for Dabney's opposition to the Edwardsian theory of virtue. Hopkins and later New Divinity theologians used the logic of disinterested, universal benevolence to hammer the slave trade in New England as well as to motivate northerners to support a general abolition of slavery. Though not as radical as the Unitarian and transcendental developments of New England thought, as far as Dabney was concerned, the result was the same. And Dabney was none too friendly to Boston Unitarians or abolitionists: "Modern abolitionism in America had, in fact, a Socinian birth, in the great apostasy of the Puritans of New England to that benumbing heresy, and in the pharisaism, shallow scholarship, affectation, conceit and infidelity of the Unitarian clique in the self-styled American Athens, Boston." Likewise, Dabney crossed swords repeatedly with New School Presbyterian Albert Barnes and New Divinity Baptist Francis Wayland in his book-length defense of slavery. Dabney certainly would have made the connection between theological and social "error"—between New Divinity and abolition— and he certainly would have despised both errors. It would only be natural for Dabney to trace the errors back to the fountainhead, back to Edwards himself.[21]

Ultimately, Dabney and other southern Presbyterians correctly recognized both Edwards' genius and the undoing of his genius, his willingness to innovate theologically, to adapt Calvinism to the thought

20. Dabney, *Syllabus and Notes*, 121; J. Ligon Duncan, "Common Sense and American Presbyterianism: An Evaluation of Scottish Realism on Princeton and the South" (master's thesis, Covenant Theological Seminary, 1987); Noll, "Contested Legacy of Jonathan Edwards in Antebellum Calvinism," 206, 209, 214–17. For a discussion of Dabney's commitment to Scottish Realism, see Lucas, "Hold Fast That Which Is Good," 45–52.

21. Conforti, *Samuel Hopkins and the New Divinity Movement*, 125–41; Robert Lewis Dabney, *A Defence of Virginia (and through Her, of the South)* (1867; reprint, Harrisonburg, Va.: Sprinkle, 1991), 131, 132, 155, 163, 165, 172, 175, 182, 184; Deborah Vingham Van Broekhoven, "Suffering with Slaveholders: The Limits of Francis Wayland's Antislavery Witness," in *Religion and the Antebellum Debate over Slavery*, ed. John R. McKivigan and Mitchell Snay (Athens: University of Georgia Press, 1998), 196–220.

forms of the age. For Dabney, intentional theological innovation was simply unacceptable. To submit scriptural interpretation to prevailing intellectual canons, rather than judge those canons by Scripture, was nothing short of rationalism. As a result, Dabney approved of Archibald Alexander's conviction that "the Reformed Protestant theology reached its zenith in the seventeenth century." Since that time, the rationalism of German idealists, evolutionists, Socinians, and abolitionists all had chipped away at the doctrinal foundations of the church; all these submitted Scripture to reason rather than the other way around.

Furthermore, Dabney exalted the Westminster Standards as the most correct summary of Christian truth. Because the Standards were built upon the Bible alone and not upon "ever changing" human philosophies, Dabney believed that the Westminster Confession was as relevant and correct in his day as it was when it was written. "It is for this reason," Dabney held, "that the Confession will need no amendment until the Bible needs to be amended." The Confession did not employ "extra-scriptural distinctions" such as those countenanced by Edwards, nor were the Standards based on human philosophies as the Edwardsian shifts were. What was required of Reformed teachers, then, was not theological creativity; rather, Dabney held that "our supreme wisdom will be 'to let well enough alone,' and humbly teach our scriptural creed, instead of attempting vainly to tinker it."[22]

Ironically, it may be that the Edwardsian legacy in the South was better preserved, not by southern Presbyterians, but by southern Baptists. Largely unfettered by historic commitments to confessionalism or a doctrinal battle over New School influence, Baptists in the South were free to adopt and adapt New Divinity modes of thought. Several ministers, led by one of the founders of the Southern Baptist Convention, William B. Johnson, articulated views on imputation, the atonement, and election that paralleled northern New Divinity theologians. The influence of Edwards and the New Divinity on southern Baptists also came through English Baptist Andrew Fuller, who used Edwards' work on the will to forge a distinctive theology that legitimated revivalism. Though an "Old School" Princeton stream existed in nineteenth-century southern Baptist life as well, particularly through Southern Baptist Theological Seminary founders James P. Boyce and Basil Manly Jr., Edwards' commitment to revivalism and "moderate"

22. Dabney, *Syllabus and Notes*, 138–39; Robert Lewis Dabney, "The Doctrinal Contents of the Confession—Its Fundamental and Regulative Ideas, and the Necessity and Value of Creeds," in *Memorial Volume of the Westminster Assembly, 1647–1897* (Richmond: Presbyterian Committee of Publications, 1897), 92, 95, 99, 101–2.

Calvinism made him a beloved southern Baptist hero well into the twentieth century. Edwards may have been chagrined that his best disciples in the nineteenth-century South were Baptists and not Presbyterians. But he probably would have preferred their fellowship to Dabney and his brethren, who sought to "cut up Edwardsism by the roots."[23]

23. Gregory A. Wills, "Forum: Neglected Theological Influences," *Southern Baptist Journal of Theology* 3 (spring 1999): 87–91; Phil Roberts, "Andrew Fuller," in *Baptist Theologians*, ed. David Dockery and Timothy George (Nashville: Broadman, 1990), 125–26, 131; A. James Fuller, *Chaplain to the Confederacy: Basil Manly and Baptist Life in the Old South* (Baton Rouge: Louisiana State University Press, 2000), 62–64; Thomas J. Nettles, *By His Grace and for His Glory* (Grand Rapids: Baker, 1986), 128–30, 187–205; R. E. Neighbor, "Shall We Read Jonathan Edwards?" *Review and Expositor* 15 (1918): 148–56. W. B. Johnson penned a lengthy but important series of essays that defended the New Divinity position on imputation: see *Southern Baptist*, 7 March 1849–18 April 1849.

PART 4

⊠ ⊠ ⊠

REFLECTIONS

12

☆

TRANSCRIBING A DIFFICULT HAND

Collecting and Editing Edwards' Letters
over Thirty-Five Years

George S. Claghorn

Jonathan Edwards made a great impression on me from the time I first started studying American philosophy. For me, he was the major colonial American thinker. This was demonstrated by the popularity and influence of his books: *Faithful Narrative,* a powerful incentive for revival, which won him the title "Father of the Great Awakening"; *Religious Affections,* a thoughtful analysis of religious experience; and *Life of Brainerd,* the biography that aroused wide interest in Native Americans and missions. Edwards' writings gave fresh insight into the nature of God, humankind, and their relation; his spirit was heart-warming.

It was, therefore, a shock for me to read, one day in 1959, that his letters were still uncollected.[1] "Life and letters" of any leader go hand in hand, but could it be that those of this distinguished figure had not been assembled, over 250 years after his birth? It was unbelievable.

To find whether this was still so, I immediately inquired of Perry Miller, Cabot Professor of American Literature at Harvard. He had

1. Robert E. Spiller et al., eds., *Literary History of the United States: Bibliography Supplement,* ed. Richard M. Ludwig (New York: Macmillan, 1959), 110.

been appointed general editor of a new series of *The Works of Jonathan Edwards*, to be published by the Yale University Press. Almost before I knew what was happening, the editorial board designated me editor of the *Letters* volume. In the summer of 1960, I found myself in the Sterling Library at Yale, facing a box of precious original letters in Edwards' own hand. It was the beginning of a long journey. Little did I dream that it would last thirty-five years.

Most of the letters are now part of the Edwards Collection of the Beinecke Rare Book and Manuscript Library at Yale. These originally came from materials gathered by Edwards A. Park, a nineteenth-century theologian, for a biography of Edwards that was never written. The bulk of Edwards' manuscript sermons is also at Yale. The greater part of the remainder are located in the Trask Library of the Andover-Newton Theological School at Newton Centre, Massachusetts. In the late 1950s, the latter were loaned to Yale for research but in 1974 were returned to the Trask Library, where they are presently housed. In addition to the letters, the collection there includes many letters to Edwards, family letters, transcripts of Sereno Dwight, and oversized sermons.

At the outset, a census was made of all known Edwards letters, found through notices in national book reviews and questionnaires sent to approximately five hundred historical societies, state libraries, colleges, and universities coast to coast. Further, I personally visited libraries throughout New England, the Middle Atlantic states, Washington, D.C., and Virginia. Later I checked the Huntington Library in California and libraries in Scotland and England. Eventually, the number of letters copied came to 458, plus many collateral documents.

The completed volume, *Letters and Personal Writings*, volume 16 in the Yale edition, was finally published in 1998. It consists of 236 letters, all the extant ones known to be written *by* Edwards. This is the most chronologically comprehensive volume of the Yale series and contains 116 letters never before published. The book includes a biographical glossary of all persons named in the letters, a list of fragmentary letters by Edwards, and a register of all known letters *to* him. Each edited letter has an introduction, as do the "Personal Writings," printed there in full text.

For decades, the Edwards series had no permanent staff or office location, unlike the more affluent research "factories." Editors were largely on their own expense, yet the work went steadily on. Library support was most helpful, and in particular that of Margery G. Wynne, research librarian of the Beinecke Library at Yale, who provided special places to work and took a personal interest in the project at all times. After the untimely death of Perry Miller in 1963, he was succeeded as general editor by John E. Smith, Clark Professor of Philosophy at Yale, who gave unstinting help, support, and encouragement in that post for twenty-five years. Harry S. Stout, Jonathan Edwards Professor of American Christianity, likewise of Yale, became general editor in 1991 and continues to the present. His gifted leadership has brought the Edwards edition ever closer to completion.

Editing the Edwards letters was a labor of love, replete with colorful experiences. For example, early in the search, I was invited by two generous sisters in Montclair, New Jersey, to check out their manuscript of a "Diary and Account Book" of Timothy Edwards, father of Jonathan. One of the women said, "My sister and I were talking about this book, and if you are going up to Yale sometime, we would like to give it to them."

I replied at once, "If you are willing to give it to Yale, I will take it up now!" Then and there, they presented it to me, and off I went to New Haven. On arrival late that Saturday afternoon, I found the library closed, but I was able to find open the office of Norman Holmes Pearson. He was the redoubtable chair of American studies at Yale and a member of the Edwards board, so I safely delivered it to his care.

Another time, through a librarian at Stockbridge, Massachusetts, I learned of a woman in Honeoye Falls, New York, who had an unknown original account book of Jonathan Edwards. I was able to visit her, authenticate the work, and make notes. She told me that she and a member of the family had wanted to donate the book to Harvard and had even driven to Cambridge with it. As it happened, the weather was rainy, and they could not find a parking place, so they returned home, still holding the book. Today it is part of the Beinecke collection.

A third interesting experience was finding a facsimile letter of Jonathan Edwards. It seems that Jeremiah Eames Rankin, president of Howard University, Washington, D.C., and author of "God Be with You Till We Meet Again," was an avid researcher of Jonathan Edwards. One way he expressed this was to make printed copies of Edwards' letter of March 14, 1756, in Edwards' own hand.[2] He distributed these to scattered libraries, and even though it was duplicated on sulphite, rather than on colonial rag paper, some still think it is an original.

Other memorable moments include discovering the fair copy of the famous Spider Letter, previously unknown to the Yale editors, in the

2. Edwards to Aaron Burr, 14 March 1756, in Jonathan Edwards, *The Works of Jonathan Edwards*, vol. 16, *Letters and Personal Writings*, ed. George S. Claghorn (New Haven: Yale University Press, 1998), 682–84. If a collection of Rankin papers still exists somewhere, it may contain the original.

library of the New York Historical Society; passing through a secret door in the Firestone Library at Princeton University to find an Edwards original letter not listed in the university card catalog; copying a letter[3] in that same library from an extremely rare book—in pencil, because photocopies were forbidden—under the watchful eye of a guard, one on one, while I had to wear white gloves; noting missing letters, lamentably lost in fire or consciously destroyed; unearthing a diary in the Library of Congress by a Northampton parishioner, which supplied needed dates for some early Edwards sermons; and furnishing photocopies, when originals of Edwards letters were lost by owners, so that they would know the objects of their search.

Serious researchers have repeatedly asked why no critical edition of Edwards' letters was produced until now. The answer is simple: because of the incredible difficulty of reading Edwards' handwriting, which approaches "an almost indecipherable cryptography."[4]

Edwards had two kinds of handwriting, one for his friends and the other for himself. The former could be large, clear, and sometimes elegant. The latter was written rapidly, with the customary quill pen, full of unfinished words, abbreviations, and frequent shifts of text, back and forth. The private hand was often so small that some folio sheets are estimated to contain over 3,500 words. The samples shown in the first "Miscellanies" volume of the Yale *Works* do not begin to approach the height of reading hurdles in many letter drafts. Light tables, ultraviolet lights, magnifying glasses, and high-powered microscopes were all employed in the quest.[5]

The pioneer in transcribing Edwards manuscripts in recent times is Thomas A. Schafer, editor of the *Miscellanies* and professor of church history at McCormick Theological Seminary, whose career spans half a century, from 1945 to 1995. His assistance to me and countless others was of inestimable value. Besides transcribing the "Miscellanies," he performed many other services for the Edwards project, one of which was cataloging 1,200 manuscript sermons of Edwards at Yale, putting them into envelopes, and arranging them by text in canonical

    3. Edwards to John Erskine, 25 July 1757, ibid., 705–18.
    4. Thomas A. Schafer, "Manuscript Problems in the Yale Edition of Jonathan Edwards," *Early American Literature* 3 (1968): 165.
    5. On the notorious Edwards scrawl, see the following: Sereno E. Dwight, *The Life of President Edwards* (New York: Carvill, 1830), 34; Edwards' MS of the Spider Letter, New York Historical Society; Jonathan Edwards, *The Works of Jonathan Edwards*, vol. 6, *Scientific and Philosophical Writings*, ed. Wallace E. Anderson (New Haven: Yale University Press, 1980), 163–69; Schafer, "Manuscript Problems," 166; Schafer, "The Evolution of Edwards' Early Handwriting," in *The Works of Jonathan Edwards*, vol. 13, *The "Miscellanies," a–500*, ed. Thomas A. Schafer (New Haven: Yale University Press, 1994), 562–66.

order—a monumental task. Another effort, his work in dating Edwards' manuscripts, is magisterial and has been followed by all subsequent scholars.[6]

Schafer also listed many characteristics of Edwards' handwriting in the manuscripts. For example, Edwards customarily wrote the vowels *a, e,* and *o* as dots or loops indistinguishable from one another. The endings of words, such as "ing," "ian," or "ary," are likely to be straight lines, "maddeningly similar." Consonants like *s, f,* and *t* commonly resemble each other in words such as "savour," "favour," and "tenour," calling for reference to the context.[7] Words are often little more than horizontal squiggles. The redeeming factor is Edwards' steady, purposeful exposition, a logical delight and a spiritual inspiration.

In bringing the text from raw manuscript to finished product, the first aim of the Yale edition has been *accuracy,* fidelity to Edwards' own words. Secondarily, the goal has been *readability,* extending abbreviations and using, for the most part, modern spelling. *Usability* for contemporary readers is a third major objective.[8]

The best text for a letter is the autograph letter signed (ALS), or "fair copy." When this was not available, Yale editors used the next-highest accessible text, in descending order of priority, as follows: writer's copy; writer's draft; contemporary written copy by recipient or others; contemporary printed copy; later written copy (e.g., Sereno Dwight transcript); later printed copy (e.g., by Samuel Hopkins or Dwight).

Another editorial convention has been to place dates uniformly at the beginning of each letter. Under the Julian calendar, the new year began on March 25, so all dates between January 1 and March 24, inclusive, are listed both with the old year ("Old Style") and the year under our present system (Gregorian calendar or "New Style"). This applies to all years through 1752, when the new calendar went into effect in September throughout the British Empire.

One case that illustrates the formidable task of transcribing the letters is Edwards' communication to Speaker Thomas Hubbard of March 30, 1752.[9] I once spent an entire week at Andover-Newton, working on part of this letter. A "map" spanning a page and a half records my reconstruction of the text, following Edwards' system of

6. Schafer, "Manuscript Problems," 164; Schafer, "Introduction," in *Works,* 13:59–109.

7. Schafer, "Manuscript Problems," 166.

8. Jonathan Edwards, *The Works of Jonathan Edwards,* vol. 1, *Freedom of the Will,* ed. Paul Ramsey (New Haven: Yale University Press, 1957), 118–28.

9. Edwards to Thomas Hubbard, 30 March 1752, *Letters and Personal Writings, Works,* 16:460–70.

twelve symbols, with random references to eleven columns of documents, located in two libraries. Here is a paragraph I wrote for the headnote, which does not appear in the printed edition: "The draft is in a rapid hand, with crossouts, duplications, and omissions. Sentences are often long, with many ampersands, as though Edwards is speaking in continuous fashion, without pausing for a breath. A complex system of symbols refers back and forth to various parts of the ms." In preparing this letter for publication, I was fortunate to have the skilled assistance of Kenneth P. Minkema, executive editor of the Yale Edwards series, who was indispensable in completing the transcription and in many other ways as well.

A persistent roadblock to editing was the quality of paper on which letters were written. Good paper was of high quality. As this was at the same time expensive, Edwards salvaged for his own use every possible scrap, including envelopes, letters received, broadsides, and commencement announcements, some of which were quite rough. On occasion his drafts, which were cut up and made part of other documents, had to be ferreted out and reassembled for publication. To make matters worse, some recipients of Edwards' letters recycled them for their own use and wrote over his script, making it almost illegible.[10]

No account of the transcriptions of Jonathan Edwards' manuscripts would be complete without mention of three names: Hopkins, Dwight, and Grosart. Samuel Hopkins (1721–1803) was Edwards' protégé and confidant. During the time Edwards lived in Stockbridge, from 1751 to 1758, Hopkins was his nearest ministerial neighbor, at Great Barrington, only seven miles away. They visited each other often. Hopkins later became a prominent theologian, in the forefront of the New Divinity movement. After Edwards' death in 1758, his manuscripts were entrusted for several years to this friend, who published the first lengthy biography of his mentor. His transcriptions from the manuscripts are regarded generally as reliable and meticulous.[11]

After Hopkins came Jonathan Edwards, Jr., who held the manuscripts until 1801. He, in turn, published two volumes of excerpts from

---

10. Jonathan Edwards, *The Works of Jonathan Edwards*, vol. 8, *Ethical Writings*, ed. Paul Ramsey (New Haven: Yale University Press, 1989), 634–35; Edwards to Isaac Chauncy, 18 February 1739/40, *Letters and Personal Writings*, *Works*, 16:81–82; Edwards to Thomas Foxcroft, 13 April 1753, ibid., 593; Edwards to Thomas Foxcroft, 24 May 1753, ibid., 595–96; Edwards to Thomas Foxcroft, 6 March 1754, ibid., 624–25; Edwards to Thomas Foxcroft, 8 March 1755, ibid., 658–59.

11. Samuel Hopkins, *The Life of the Late Reverend, Learned, and Pious Mr. Jonathan Edwards* (Boston, 1765); Wilson H. Kimnach, "Introduction," in Jonathan Edwards, *The Works of Jonathan Edwards*, vol. 10, *Sermons and Discourses, 1720–1723*, ed. Wilson H. Kimnach (New Haven: Yale University Press, 1992), 207.

the "Miscellanies" and three volumes of sermons.[12] Then in 1817, the manuscripts were transferred to Sereno E. Dwight (1786–1850), Edwards' great-grandson, who was pastor of Park Street Church in Boston and later president of Hamilton College. He carried out a massive search and transcription effort for more than a decade, culminating in his biography, *The Life of President Edwards*, and nine other volumes of Edwards' works. Dwight's methods and thoroughness are revealed in his letter to Jonathan W. Edwards, Esq.[13] The large collection of Dwight transcripts, presently at Andover-Newton, is a tribute to his energetic dedication. It constitutes a major, sometimes the only, source of many texts. The usefulness of these transcripts, however, is to some degree impaired by omissions, rephrasings, and erroneous datings. Among the letters, Dwight often makes such radical revisions of the text that his transcripts must be tested by manuscripts, whenever available. Crossouts on his transcripts, of material he deemed inappropriate, are a continuing source of frustration to editors. A characteristic trademark of these takes the appearance of bunches of grapes.[14] Dwight explicitly stated that he changed some of the names he transcribed: "I have regarded the use of the *antonomasia* as correct, in this, and some other quotations." Examples of this are these substitutions: "resident trustee" for Colonel Joseph Dwight; "mistress of the school" for Mrs. Abigail Sergeant Dwight; and "the former teacher" for Captain Martin Kellogg. An instance of these may be found in the letter of Jonathan Edwards to Andrew Oliver, October 1752.[15]

In 1847 most of the manuscripts were turned over to Tryon Edwards, great-grandson of Jonathan Edwards Jr. and minister at New London, Connecticut. Shortly before mid-century, a Scottish firm planned a biography of Edwards and collected works. The biography never materialized, but as part of this project, author and editor

12. Thomas A. Schafer, "Previous Publication of the 'Miscellanies,'" in *"Miscellanies," a–500, Works*, 13:545–46; Jonathan Edwards, *Practical Sermons* (Edinburgh, 1788); Jonathan Edwards, *Miscellaneous Observations on Important Theological Subjects* (Edinburgh, 1793); Jonathan Edwards, *Remarks on Important Theological Controversies* (Edinburgh, 1796).

13. Schafer, "Previous Publication," 547; Dwight, *Life of Edwards;* Sereno Dwight to Jonathan W. Edwards, Esq., 15 December 1818, MS, Beinecke Library, Yale University.

14. Jonathan Edwards, *The Works of Jonathan Edwards*, vol. 2, *Religious Affections*, ed. John E. Smith (New Haven: Yale University Press, 1959), 75–77; Schafer, "Introduction," in *Works*, 13:59–60. Dwight, *Life of Edwards*, 527–31, is an example of his sometimes cavalier rewriting of Edwards. He also omits the first paragraph entirely. Compare with Edwards to Andrew Oliver, 12 April 1753, *Letters and Personal Writings, Works*, 16:580–86.

15. Dwight, *Life of Edwards*, 494, 504–6; Edwards to Andrew Oliver, October 1752, *Letters and Personal Writings, Works*, 16:533–37.

Alexander B. Grosart (1827–99) came to New London and copied various manuscripts. In addition, according to Tryon, he surreptitiously took several manuscripts back to Scotland with him. Grosart published some works from this collection and returned several items.[16] While to this day there remains a lingering suspicion that missing Edwards manuscripts may still lurk in some cache abroad, repeated efforts to find them have proved fruitless.

In reading the *Letters and Personal Writings,* one cannot fail to note the audiences addressed, topics chosen, and approaches made. Edwards wrote to a wide variety of people, starting with his family and extending to ministers, government leaders, educators, and others, including the plainest of individuals. For each level, his language was clear and understandable. A person can be identified by the type of people he or she attracts. Edwards found in Boston ministers a solid base of support: first, Benjamin Colman of Brattle Street Church in the 1730s, then Thomas Foxcroft of First Church and Thomas Prince of Old South (Third) in the 1740s and 1750s. Clergy in Scotland rallied to his cause: William McCulloch, James Robe, Thomas Gillespie, and, most notably, John Erskine. Isaac Watts and John Guyse sponsored publication of his *Faithful Narrative* in London, and Edwards welcomed George Whitefield into his pulpit twice.[17]

Among colonial worthies, Edwards corresponded regularly with Thomas Hubbard, Speaker of the Massachusetts House of Representatives; Andrew Oliver, lieutenant governor of the province; and Jonathan Belcher, governor of Massachusetts and New Jersey. Sir William Pepperrell, conqueror of Louisburg, knew Edwards well from visits and letters.[18]

Many young ministers also came to Edwards for instruction and guidance. He was in demand as a speaker at ordinations and installations, as for Jonathan Judd, Robert Abercrombie, Samuel Buell, Job Strong, and the heroic Edward Billing. His closest disciples were Samuel Hopkins, mentioned above, and the distinguished Joseph Bellamy, to whom he wrote more extant letters than to anyone else.[19]

16. Schafer, "Manuscript Problems," 161; Tryon Edwards to A. V. G. Allen, 8 November 1889, MS, Beinecke Library, Yale University; Alexander B. Grosart, *Selections from the Unpublished Works of Jonathan Edwards of America* (Edinburgh, 1865).

17. Edwards to Benjamin Colman, 30 May 1735, *Letters and Personal Writings, Works,* 16:48–58; Edwards to George Whitefield, 14 December 1740, ibid., 87; Edwards to Friends in Scotland, after 16 September 1745, ibid., 174–79.

18. Edwards to William Pepperrell, 28 November 1751, ibid., 406–14; Edwards to John Erskine, 23 November 1752, ibid., 540.

19. Thomas H. Johnson, *The Printed Writings of Jonathan Edwards, 1703–1758, a Bibliography* (Princeton, N.J., 1940), nos. 94, 95, 96, and 173; John L. Sibley et al., *Sibley's Harvard Graduates; Biographical Sketches of Those Who Attended Harvard College* (Cambridge, 1873), 9:22–28.

The themes of the letters were also diverse. One has only to read the letter to Deborah Hatheway, often republished as "Advice to Young Converts," to sense its wisdom and charm. Edwards' letter to John Brainerd reveals his orderly method of research for his biography of David Brainerd. The missive to Elnathan Whitman shows his pastoral, reconciling nature. His letter to the Princeton trustees never ceases to amaze us with its recital of his own weaknesses. Surely this is the most improbable letter for a college board of trustees to receive in response to an invitation to become president.[20]

An outstanding letter, still preserved in a copy at the Lambeth Palace in London, is addressed to Joseph Paice. In it Edwards presents a broad survey of the political situation in America and outlines his plan for educating and Christianizing the Indians at Stockbridge. In another communication, he appeals to Edward Wigglesworth, Hollis Professor of Theology at Harvard, to defend the doctrine of the Trinity. As subsequent events proved, Edwards' request was a prescient one.[21]

The letters express Edwards' perennial love for books. It was fostered at Yale, where he early helped organize the college library, as his grandfather, the venerable Stoddard, had at Harvard while a student there. Edwards was tireless in requisitioning, reading, and recommending books. He sponsored the library for ministers of the Hampshire Association, a "continuing education" program of its time. Later he distributed Bibles wherever he could.[22]

Another motif repeated in the letters is Edwards' love of the Indians. He informed Eleazer Wheelock in 1744 of his commitment to the Stockbridge Native Americans. This began much earlier and grew with his unanimous call to be missionary and pastor there in 1751. He enjoyed the full support of the Indians by preaching and performing many other services, such as writing petitions for them. His circle of concern was constantly expanding. He won the respect and cooperation of famous chiefs among them, such as Nicholas and Hendrick.[23]

The golden thread that runs though the letters from beginning to end is *conversion*, the necessity of a life-changing experience through

20. Edwards to Deborah Hatheway, 3 June 1741, *Letters and Personal Writings, Works,* 16:90–95; Edwards to John Brainerd, 14 December 1747, ibid., 241–44; Edwards to Trustees of the College of New Jersey, 19 October 1757, ibid., 725–30.

21. Edwards to Joseph Paice, 24 February 1751/52, ibid., 434–47; Edwards to Edward Wigglesworth, 11 February 1757, ibid., 697–700.

22. Edwards to Jacob Wendell, 8 August 1737 and 23 August 1737, ibid., 70–71; Ola Winslow, *Jonathan Edwards, 1703–1758: A Biography* (New York: Macmillan, 1940), 92, 119–22; Sibley, *Sibley's Harvard Graduates,* 2:112; Jonathan Edwards, "Diary and Account Book," MS, Beinecke Library, Yale University.

23. Edwards to Thomas Price, 27 July 1744, *Letters and Personal Writings, Works,* 16:145–46; Edwards to Thomas Hubbard, 31 August 1751, ibid., 394–405.

personal encounter with God.[24] Edwards later added themes, such as human motivation; the will; biblical, historical, and apocalyptic studies; the concert for prayer; and others. The stream widened and deepened, but Edwards' letters remained in the central channel.

In the *Letters and Personal Writings* are treasures. The apostrophe "On Sarah Pierpont" relates his early admiration for her religious stance. This often-quoted tribute marks the inception of a romance that blossomed into the marriage of two lives, spent together in devoted ministry.[25] The "Personal Narrative," considered by many to be the most eloquent statement of his faith, is the best place to start reading Edwards. Next should be the letter to Deborah Hatheway, mentioned above. The "Narrative" tells how his conversion came about, the manner in which it transformed him, and the power it became in his life. God spoke to him through nature, as never before. Above all, he heard the divine voice in the Bible.

> I had then, and at other times, the greatest delight in the holy Scriptures, of any book whatsoever. Oftentimes in reading it, every word seemed to touch my heart. I felt an harmony between something in my heart, and those sweet and powerful words. I seemed often to see so much light, exhibited in every sentence, and such refreshing ravishing food communicated, that I could not get along in reading. Used oftentimes to dwell on one sentence, to see the wonders contained in it; and yet almost every sentence seemed to be full of wonders. . . . Sometimes only mentioning a single word, causes my heart to burn within me; or only seeing the name of Christ, or the name of some attribute of God.[26]

He further tells of his communion with the Most High through prayer and of his praise of the attributes of God and the doctrines of the gospel:

> Heaven appeared to me exceeding delightful as a world of love. It appeared to me, that all happiness consisted in living in pure, humble, heavenly, divine love. . . . I have loved the doctrines of the gospel: they have been to my soul like green pastures. The gospel has seemed to me to be the richest treasure; the treasure that I have most desired, and longed that it might dwell richly in me. The way of salvation by Christ, has appeared in a general way, glorious and excellent, and most pleasant and beautiful.[27]

24. Jonathan Edwards, "Personal Narrative," in ibid., 792–95.
25. "On Sarah Pierpont," in ibid., 745–47, 789–90.
26. "Personal Narrative," ibid., 747–50, 790–804 (quotation, 797, 800).
27. Ibid., 796, 799.

In sum, transcribing the manuscripts of Jonathan Edwards led me to know better a man who walked with God, one who was focused, fearless, and faithful. *Focus* is displayed in the "Resolutions," his platform for living, a well-defined set of objectives that he pursued with intensity all his life.[28] Edwards' *fearless* nature is expressed in his refusal to be intimidated by the almost overwhelming opposition he often faced. He confidently stood toe to toe, argument to argument, with the rector of Yale or the Massachusetts General Assembly. Even when he felt as if "casting himself from a precipice," he was convinced he would be sustained through God's grace.[29] The term *faithful* honors his consistency over the years. Edwards remained true to his mission and endeavored to extend it to every area of his life. His regular practice of spending thirteen hours a day in the study was only one example of that. He stands as a model of steadfastness to faith.[30]

My rewards in terms of insights and satisfactions from transcribing Jonathan Edwards across the years are beyond measure. These riches are now available to everyone who reads his magnificent works.

28. "Resolutions," in ibid., 741–45, 753–59.

29. Edwards to "A Friend," 4 February 1744/45, ibid., 153–62; Edwards to Thomas Clap, 20 May 1745, ibid., 163–72; Edwards to Thomas Hubbard, 19 March 1753, ibid., 563–76; Edwards to Thomas Foxcroft, 24 May 1749, ibid., 284.

30. Hopkins, *Life of the Late Reverend, Learned, and Pious Mr. Jonathan Edwards,* 40.

13

JONATHAN EDWARDS BETWEEN CHURCH AND ACADEMY

A Bibliographic Essay

Sean Michael Lucas

All too often, the Christian church acts unaware of the academy's best work, while conversely the academy often appears unconcerned about the needs of the church. While especially the case in biblical studies and systematic theology, this observation also is true when applied to historical studies generally and the study of Jonathan Edwards particularly. Over the past ten years, evangelical publishing houses have produced a mass of books on Edwards that the academy has taken little notice of. Conversely, as the study of Edwards within the academy moves increasingly in trendy directions, church ministers and intelligent laypeople believe the academy's Edwards to be far from what they themselves find when they read the Northampton divine. In keeping with the purpose of the book, this bibliographic essay proposes to bridge the wide chasm between church and academy, first by pointing out several important and worthy studies for evangelical pastors and laypeople. Some evangelicals may be approaching the study of Edwards for the first time and need some direction; likewise, pastors might be interested in Edwards' contributions to preaching, biblical studies, and ministry. Thus, the first section of this essay highlights several studies that orient beginning Edwards students to the lay of the land. In addition, this bibliographic essay also seeks to update M. X. Lesser's marvelous bibliographies of Edwards studies by surveying most of the relevant scholarly literature that appeared from 1994 to 2000.[1] The hope is that both church and academy will find several items in this essay to assist in navigating the ever-increasing web of information on Jonathan Edwards.[2]

Edwards for the Church

The best way to start learning about Edwards is to read Jonathan himself. Until recently, the choices were either the two-volume set of Edwards' works produced by Banner of Truth Trust (and now Hendrickson Publishers) or the (soon-to-be) twenty-seven volume critical edition from Yale University Press.[3] The Banner of Truth edition, a reprint of an 1834 set edited by Edward Hickman and based on Sereno Dwight's 1829 edition, contains all of the published treatises, many sermons and "miscellanies," and Samuel Hopkins' *Life of Edwards*. However, the text is uncritical, unreliable, and at times almost unreadable due to the miniscule font. The Yale University Press edition, of which more will be said, is expensive and may be too much for the beginner. Now, however, another option exists whereby a student or pastor can study Edwards with reliable, critical texts. The Works of Jonathan Edwards project at Yale University issued two readers to introduce Edwards to a wider audience. *A Jonathan Edwards Reader* (1995) selects from many of the most important Edwards writings—sermons such as "Sinners in the Hands of an Angry God"; essays such as *A Treatise concerning Religious Affections, Freedom of the Will*, and *The Nature of True Virtue*; and personal writings and letters.[4] In this

1. M. X. Lesser, *Jonathan Edwards: A Reference Guide* (Boston: G. K. Hall, 1981); M. X. Lesser, *Jonathan Edwards: An Annotated Bibliography, 1979–1993* (Westport: Greenwood, 1994). Unlike Lesser's volumes, this essay does not cover book reviews published during the period surveyed.

2. Three recent surveys of Edwardsiana are David Owen Filson, "Jonathan Edwards for Pastors: A Bibliographic Essay," *Presbyterion* 24 (1998): 110–18; Michael J. McClymond, "The Protean Puritan: The Works of Jonathan Edwards, Volumes 8 to 16," *Religious Studies Review* 24 (1998): 361–67; and Roland A. Delattre, "Recent Scholarship on Jonathan Edwards," *Religious Studies Review* 24 (1998): 369–75.

3. Jonathan Edwards, *The Works of Jonathan Edwards*, ed. Edward Hickman, 2 vols. (1834; reprint, Edinburgh: Banner of Truth Trust, 1974); Edwards, *The Works of Jonathan Edwards*, general editors, Perry Miller, John E. Smith, and Harry S. Stout, 19 volumes to date (New Haven: Yale University Press, 1957–).

4. Jonathan Edwards, *A Jonathan Edwards Reader*, ed. John E. Smith, Harry S. Stout, and Kenneth P. Minkema (New Haven: Yale University Press, 1995).

one inexpensive, accessible volume, the vast corpus of Edwards' thought can be surveyed. Even better, the texts are all drawn from the larger, critical Yale edition, so students know they are reading accurate transcriptions of what Edwards actually wrote and saw through to press. *The Sermons of Jonathan Edwards: A Reader* (1999) reproduces several familiar sermons as well as four previously unpublished sermons to readers in another inexpensive volume.[5] Arranged to emphasize the cycle of the Christian life, this collection draws sermons from every period of Edwards' preaching life—from his earliest ministries in New York City and Bolton, Connecticut, to Northampton to his mission work at Stockbridge. What emerges is an Edwards who is much more than the hellfire preacher so well known from "Sinners." Rather, he was ravished by the beauty and glory of Jesus Christ and longed to move his auditors into a vital relationship with God.

Though not as reliable as the critical transcriptions of the Yale edition, other small publishers have reproduced Edwards' writings in inexpensive formats. For example, Soli Deo Gloria Publishers, a reprint company in western Pennsylvania, has published five volumes of Edwards' writings, using and improving the same text that is found in the Banner of Truth set.[6] Another publisher, P&R Publishing in Phillipsburg, New Jersey, has produced two pamphlets containing Edwards' writings—*Jonathan Edwards' Resolutions: An Advice to Young Converts* and *Sinners in the Hands of an Angry God.*[7] Banner of Truth Trust also has several volumes in trade paperback format, including *Charity and Its Fruits* and *The Religious Affections.*[8] In addition, Baker Book House has reprinted *The Life and Diary of David Brainerd.*[9] Calvary Press, a Calvinistic Baptist press in Amityville, New York, also re-

5. Jonathan Edwards, *The Sermons of Jonathan Edwards: A Reader,* ed. Wilson H. Kimnach, Kenneth P. Minkema, and Douglas A. Sweeney (New Haven: Yale University Press, 1999).

6. Soli Deo Gloria's Edwards offerings include *Freedom of the Will, Justification by Faith Alone,* and three collections of sermons—*Pressing into the Kingdom: Jonathan Edwards on Seeking Salvation, The Wrath of Almighty God: Jonathan Edwards on God's Judgment against Sinners,* and *Altogether Lovely: Jonathan Edwards on the Glory and Excellency of Jesus Christ.*

7. Jonathan Edwards, *Jonathan Edwards' Resolutions: An Advice to Young Converts,* ed. Stephen J. Nichols (Phillipsburg, N.J.: P&R, 2001); Jonathan Edwards, *Sinners in the Hands of an Angry God* (Phillipsburg, N.J.: P&R, n.d.). "Sinners" also was reprinted by Whitaker House (1997) and Sword of the Lord Publishers (n.d.).

8. Jonathan Edwards, *Charity and Its Fruits* (Carlisle: Banner of Truth, 1978); Jonathan Edwards, *Jonathan Edwards on Revival* (Carlisle: Banner of Truth, 1984); Jonathan Edwards, *Jonathan Edwards on Knowing Christ* (Carlisle: Banner of Truth, 1990); Jonathan Edwards, *The Religious Affections* (Carlisle: Banner of Truth, 1986).

9. Jonathan Edwards, *The Life and Diary of David Brainerd* (Grand Rapids: Baker, 1989).

cently republished the sermon "Heaven Is a World of Love" in a small paperback format.[10] Clearly, the evangelical pastor or layperson can find versions of Edwards at an inexpensive price. Tellingly, the Edwards' volumes that are being reprinted by evangelical publishing houses are those that emphasize his piety or defend Calvinism.

Though Edwards' writings are available in seeming abundance, the same cannot be said for studies of Edwards' life. Currently, the only biography in print is Iain Murray's *Jonathan Edwards: A New Biography* (1987).[11] Murray's work is a fairly comprehensive telling of Edwards' life, with careful attention paid to Edwards' theology. At times, however, Murray's account appears filiopietistic; at other times, he seems to use Edwards for his own apologetic purposes (the maintenance of a "pure" evangelical Calvinism). Above all, Murray has a strange animus against Perry Miller and the entire Works of Jonathan Edwards project at Yale University, chiding the project participants for their "naturalistic" bias. Before Murray, the standard biographies were Ola Winslow's Pulitzer Prize–winning *Jonathan Edwards, 1703–1758: A Biography* (1940) and Perry Miller's seminal intellectual biography, *Jonathan Edwards* (1949).[12] All three will be superseded in 2003 when George Marsden's biography of Edwards appears from Yale University Press. Two other works, while not strictly historical, ought to be mentioned here. Both Edna Gerstner and Elisabeth Dodds highlight the "uncommon union" of Jonathan and his wife, Sarah; both books, however, are fictional accounts based on some primary research.[13]

First-time readers of Edwards may need further assistance. One place to start is Stephen Nichols' splendid guide to Edwards' life and thought.[14] After offering a brief overview of Edwards' life, Nichols summarizes several key Edwardsian writings, pointing out highlights and themes perhaps imperceptible to the uninitiated. Also useful are several books that resulted from the national symposiums on Jonathan Edwards sponsored

10. Jonathan Edwards, *Heaven—A World of Love* (Amityville, N.Y.: Calvary Press, n.d.).

11. Iain H. Murray, *Jonathan Edwards: A New Biography* (Carlisle: Banner of Truth, 1987). See the particularly negative review by Stephen J. Stein in *Church History* 59 (1990): 564–65.

12. Ola Winslow, *Jonathan Edwards, 1703–1758: A Biography* (New York: Macmillan, 1940); Perry Miller, *Jonathan Edwards* (New York: William Sloane, 1949).

13. Elisabeth D. Dodds, *Marriage to a Difficult Man: The "Uncommon Union" of Jonathan and Sarah Edwards* (Philadelphia: Westminster, 1971); Edna Gerstner, *Jonathan and Sarah: An Uncommon Union* (Morgan, Pa.: Soli Deo Gloria, 1995). See also Avihu Zakai, "The Conversion of Jonathan Edwards," *Journal of Presbyterian History* 76 (1998): 127–38.

14. Stephen J. Nichols, *Jonathan Edwards: A Guided Tour of His Life and Thought* (Phillipsburg, N.J.: P&R, 2001).

by the Works of Jonathan Edwards project at Yale University. The best of these collections is *Jonathan Edwards and the American Experience* (1988).[15] In this one volume, most of the major issues that have occupied Edwards scholars over the past decade were addressed in seminal fashion—Edwards' metaphysics, preaching, and eschatology, as well as his connection with earlier Puritans and later disciples. This is one of the most essential volumes of secondary literature on Edwards.[16]

Evangelicals approaching Edwards are sure to be interested in his theology. Unfortunately, there are few worthwhile summaries of it. The most helpful single volume remains Conrad Cherry's foundational *The Theology of Jonathan Edwards: A Reappraisal* (1966).[17] Cherry revolutionized Edwards studies by returning scholarly focus to Edwards' theological milieu, namely, scholastic Calvinism. Using the themes of faith and covenant as organizing principles, Cherry helpfully navigates a large portion of the Edwardsian theological corpus. Others might find John Gerstner's massive *The Rational Biblical Theology of Jonathan Edwards* (1991–93) useful.[18] Gerstner's three-volume work, a labor of love (and perhaps revenge on Yale University Press), draws heavily on his work as the former editor of the sermon volumes that were to appear in the Works of Jonathan Edwards edition. Unfortunately, the work is marred by Gerstner's heavy-handed attempt to make Edwards an evidential apologist and a thoroughgoing rationalist. More useful for students wanting Gerstner's take on Edwards' theology is his *Jonathan Edwards: A Mini-Theology* (1987).[19] Another volume that summarizes Edwards' theology and seeks to recommend him to a broader intellectual community is Robert Jenson's *America's Theologian: A Recommendation of Jonathan Edwards* (1988).[20] Jenson uses Edwards' critique of religious hypocrisy and ap-

15. Nathan O. Hatch and Harry S. Stout, eds., *Jonathan Edwards and the American Experience* (New York: Oxford University Press, 1988). These were papers from the 1984 conference hosted by Wheaton College.

16. The other collections were Barbara B. Oberg and Harry S. Stout, eds., *Benjamin Franklin, Jonathan Edwards and the Representation of American Culture* (New York: Oxford University Press, 1993); Stephen J. Stein, ed., *Jonathan Edwards's Writings: Text, Context, Interpretation* (Bloomington: Indiana University Press, 1996); and Sang Hyun Lee and Allen C. Guelzo, eds., *Edwards in Our Time: Jonathan Edwards and the Shaping of American Religion* (Grand Rapids: Eerdmans, 1999).

17. Conrad Cherry, *The Theology of Jonathan Edwards: A Reappraisal* (Garden City: Anchor Books, 1966; reprint, Bloomington: Indiana University Press, 1990).

18. John H. Gerstner, *The Rational Biblical Theology of Jonathan Edwards*, 3 vols. (Orlando: Ligonier, 1991–93).

19. John H. Gerstner, *Jonathan Edwards: A Mini-Theology* (Wheaton: Tyndale House, 1987; reprint, Morgan, Pa.: Soli Deo Gloria, 1996).

20. Robert W. Jenson, *America's Theologian: A Recommendation of Jonathan Edwards* (New York: Oxford University Press, 1988). Jenson also makes thorough use of Edwards in his own *Systematic Theology*, 2 vols. (New York: Oxford University Press, 1997–99).

pearance to explore American theology's marriage of the nation and deity. While some might rebel against the sometimes Barthian Edwards in Jenson's account, the work is undeniably important and useful. Two recent volumes that attempt an "approach" to Edwards' theology are Michael McClymond's *Encounters with God* (1998) and Stephen Holmes, *God of Grace and God of Glory: An Account of the Theology of Jonathan Edwards* (2001).[21]

Specific doctrines from an Edwardsian perspective are also treated in a popular format. Perhaps the most important popularizer of Edwards is John Piper, pastor of Bethlehem Baptist Church in Minneapolis, Minnesota. Piper introduced evangelicals to Edwards in a trilogy of books written between 1986 and 1991: *Desiring God: Meditations of a Christian Hedonist* (1986); *The Supremacy of God in Preaching* (1990); and *The Pleasures of God* (1991).[22] More recently, Piper drew on Edwardsian eschatology in *The Purifying Power of Living by Faith in Future Grace* (1995), and he introduced and edited a version of Edwards' *Concerning the End for Which God Created the World*.[23] Though some might disagree with Piper's summary of Edwards' legacy for evangelical theology—"God is most glorified when we are most satisfied in him"—still it is the case that Piper may be the most influential popularizer of Edwards for evangelicals today. That does not mean he is alone. R. C. Sproul has sought the wisdom of Edwards in discerning the nature of true revival; he has also offered Edwards as the classic formulator of the Reformed position on freedom of the will.[24] Likewise, Gerstner summarized Edwards' teaching on heaven and hell as well as on evangelism in short, popular treatments.[25] In the book *See-*

21. Michael J. McClymond, *Encounters with God: An Approach to the Theology of Jonathan Edwards* (New York: Oxford University Press, 1998); Stephen R. Holmes, *God of Grace and God of Glory: An Account of the Theology of Jonathan Edwards* (Grand Rapids: Eerdmans, 2001).

22. John Piper, *Desiring God: Meditations of a Christian Hedonist* (Sisters, Ore.: Multnomah, 1986; 2d ed., 1996); John Piper, *The Supremacy of God in Preaching* (Grand Rapids: Baker, 1990); and John Piper, *The Pleasures of God* (Sisters, Ore.: Multnomah, 1991; 2d ed., 2000).

23. John Piper, *The Purifying Power of Living by Faith in Future Grace* (Sisters, Ore.: Multnomah, 1995); John Piper, *God's Passion for His Glory: Living the Vision of Jonathan Edwards* (Wheaton: Crossway, 1998).

24. Archie Parrish and R. C. Sproul, *The Spirit of Revival: Discovering the Wisdom of Jonathan Edwards* (Wheaton: Crossway, 2000); R. C. Sproul, *Willing to Believe: The Controversy over Free Will* (Grand Rapids: Baker, 1997). See Allen Guelzo's trenchant critique of Sproul's use of Edwards (*Christianity Today* 42 [2 March 1998]: 59–61).

25. John H. Gerstner, *Jonathan Edwards on Heaven and Hell* (Grand Rapids: Baker, 1980; reprint, Morgan, Pa.: Soli Deo Gloria, 1999); John H. Gerstner, *Jonathan Edwards, the Evangelist* (Morgan, Pa.: Soli Deo Gloria, 1995; previously titled *Steps to Salvation: The Evangelistic Message of Jonathan Edwards*).

ing God (1995), Edwards scholar Gerald McDermott offered a popular retelling and application of Edwards' *Treatise concerning Religious Affections*.[26] And the classic evangelical use of Edwards is Richard Lovelace's *Dynamics of Spiritual Life* (1979), where he connects the Puritan divine with the 1970s Jesus people.[27]

Surprisingly, there are not many studies of Edwards as preacher.[28] Four worthy of mention are Stephen Yarbrough's *Delightful Conviction: Jonathan Edwards and the Rhetoric of Conversion* (1993), Piper's *Supremacy of God in Preaching*, Ralph Turnbull's *Jonathan Edwards the Preacher* (1958), and Perry Miller's essay "The Rhetoric of Sensation."[29] In addition, Jim Ehrhard has examined the tradition that Edwards was a manuscript preacher, concluding that the evidence indicates otherwise. It turns out that Edwards preached extemporaneously, using full outlines.[30] Likewise, not much attention has been given to Edwards' view of the ministry or work as pastor.[31] Two useful books along this line are Patricia Tracy's *Jonathan Edwards, Pastor* (1980) and Helen Westra's *The Minister's Task and Calling in the Ser-*

26. Gerald R. McDermott, *Seeing God: Twelve Reliable Signs of True Spirituality* (Downers Grove, Ill.: InterVarsity, 1995). This book was recently reprinted as *Seeing God: Jonathan Edwards and Spiritual Discernment* (Vancouver: Regent College Press, 1999).

27. Richard Lovelace, *Dynamics of Spiritual Life: An Evangelical Theology of Renewal* (Downers Grove, Ill.: InterVarsity, 1979).

28. But see Wilson Kimnach's wonderful introduction in Jonathan Edwards, *The Works of Jonathan Edwards*, vol. 10, *Sermons and Discourses, 1720–1723*, ed. Wilson H. Kimnach (New Haven: Yale University Press, 1992), 1–258. This introduction is a major study of Edwards' preaching that sets the groundwork for all future investigation.

29. Stephen R. Yarbrough, *Delightful Conviction: Jonathan Edwards and the Rhetoric of Conversion* (Westport: Greenwood, 1993); Piper, *Supremacy of God in Preaching*; Ralph G. Turnbull, *Jonathan Edwards the Preacher* (Grand Rapids: Baker, 1958); and Perry Miller, "The Rhetoric of Sensation," in *Errand into the Wilderness* (Cambridge: Harvard University Press, 1956), 167–83. There are several doctoral dissertations and master's theses that deal with this topic; see, for example, William T. Flynt, "Jonathan Edwards and His Preaching" (Th.D. diss., Southern Baptist Theological Seminary, 1954); and Audrey Pugh Granade, "The Devotional Preaching of Jonathan Edwards" (Th.M. thesis, Southern Baptist Theological Seminary, 1950). Also see the article edited by Kenneth P. Minkema and Richard A. Bailey, "Reason, Revelation, and Preaching: An Unpublished Ordination Sermon by Jonathan Edwards," *The Southern Baptist Journal of Theology* 3.2 (summer 1999): 16–33.

30. Jim Ehrhard, "A Critical Analysis of the Tradition of Jonathan Edwards as a Manuscript Preacher," *Westminster Theological Journal* 60 (1998): 71–84. See also Christopher Grasso, *A Speaking Aristocracy: Transforming Public Discourse in Eighteenth-Century Connecticut* (Chapel Hill: University of North Carolina Press, 2000), 86–143.

31. A volume of sermons, never before published and freshly transcribed, was published by Crossway Publishers with the blessing of the Works of Jonathan Edwards office at Yale University; see Jonathan Edwards, *The Salvation of Souls: Nine Previously Unpublished Sermons by Jonathan Edwards on the Call of the Ministry and the Gospel*, eds. Gregory A. Wills and Richard A. Bailey (Wheaton: Crossway, 2002).

mons of Jonathan Edwards (1986).[32] Another sparse area in Edwards studies is Edwards as biblical interpreter.[33] Stephen Stein has done the most significant work here. As editor of the Works of Jonathan Edwards volumes on Edwards' apocalyptic writings, his *Notes on Scripture*, and the forthcoming edition of Edwards' "Blank Bible," Stein has overseen the volumes that contain Edwards' ruminations on the biblical text.[34] Further, Stein penned three groundbreaking articles on Edwards' hermeneutics that set the stage for future interpreters.[35] One recent dissertation that does address Edwards' method of biblical interpretation in the broader context of eighteenth-century historical-critical studies is a dissertation by Robert Eric Brown.[36] However, more work clearly needs to be done in this area; the results certainly would be of great value for the church.

Edwards in the Academy

The academic study of Edwards continues to be an industry whose production outpaces several third-world countries. Part of the

32. Patricia J. Tracy, *Jonathan Edwards, Pastor: Religion and Society in Eighteenth-Century Northampton* (New York: Hill and Wang, 1980); Helen Westra, *The Minister's Task and Calling in the Sermons of Jonathan Edwards* (Lewiston, N.Y.: Edwin Mellen, 1986). See also several essays by Westra: "Divinity's Design: Edwards and the History of the Work of Revival," in *Edwards in Our Time*, 131–57; "Jonathan Edwards and 'What Reason Teaches,'" *Journal of the Evangelical Theological Society* 34 (1991): 495–503; "Above All Others: Jonathan Edwards and the Gospel Ministry," *American Presbyterians* 67 (1989): 209–19; "Jonathan Edwards on 'Faithful and Successful Ministers,'" *Early American Literature* 23 (1988): 281–90; "Jonathan Edwards and the Scope of Gospel Ministry," *Calvin Theological Journal* 22 (1987): 68–90; and "Jonathan Edwards' Sermons: Search for 'Acceptable Words,'" *American Theological Library Association: Summary of Proceedings* 38 (1984): 102–16.

33. See Conrad Cherry, "Symbols of Spiritual Truth: Jonathan Edwards as Biblical Interpreter," *Interpretation* 39 (1985): 263–71.

34. Jonathan Edwards, *The Works of Jonathan Edwards*, vol. 5, *Apocalyptic Writings*, ed. Stephen J. Stein (New Haven: Yale University Press, 1977); Jonathan Edwards, *The Works of Jonathan Edwards*, vol. 15, *Notes on Scripture*, ed. Stephen J. Stein (New Haven: Yale University Press, 1998).

35. Stephen J. Stein, "The Quest for the Spiritual Sense: The Biblical Hermeneutics of Jonathan Edwards," *Harvard Theological Review* 70 (1977): 99–113; Stephen J. Stein, "'Like Apples of Gold in Pictures of Silver': The Portrait of Wisdom in Jonathan Edwards's Commentary on the Book of Proverbs," *Church History* 54 (1985): 324–37; Stephen J. Stein, "The Spirit and the Word: Jonathan Edwards and Scriptural Exegesis," in *Jonathan Edwards and the American Experience*, 118–30.

36. Robert Eric Brown, "Connecting the Sacred with the Profane: Jonathan Edwards and the Scripture History" (Ph.D. diss., University of Iowa, 1999). See also Karl Dietrich Pfisterer, *The Prism of Scripture: Studies on History and Historicity in the Work of Jonathan Edwards* (Frankfurt: Peter Lang, 1975).

continued interest is the often-noted ambiguity, or, perhaps better, multifaceted nature, of Edwards' own thought. However, another reason is simply that he looms as a singular historical figure. Indeed, Peter Thuesen recently argued that Jonathan Edwards is a "great mirror" whose size and substance lends itself to the multiplicity of scholarly opinion.[37] And certainly academics see Edwards from a dizzying array of perspectives. For George Marsden, Edwards is the "American Augustine" in opposition to the American Foucault that Stephen Daniel appreciates.[38] Leon Chai believes that the Enlightenment compromised Edwards, while Alvin Plantinga and Stephen Nichols contend that Edwards' theological emphasis of Word and Spirit made him a critic of the Enlightenment.[39] Anri Morimoto praises Edwards' "Catholic" vision of salvation; Gerald McDermott looks to Jonathan's (sometimes) charitable dealings with non-Christian religions; Kenneth Minkema examines Edwards on slavery and the slave trade; and Amy Plantinga Pauw finds in Edwards a theology conducive to social action.[40] Meanwhile, feminist scholars have focused attention on Edwards' view of women and children.[41] Clearly, Edwards scholars seek to discover what Jonathan might say to their own interests and agendas.

37. Lesser, Jonathan Edwards: An Annotated Bibliography, xiii, xxxi; Peter J. Thuesen, "Jonathan Edwards as Great Mirror," Scottish Journal of Theology 50 (1997): 39–60.

38. George M. Marsden, "Jonathan Edwards: American Augustine," Books and Culture 5 (November–December 1999), 10; Stephen H. Daniel, The Philosophy of Jonathan Edwards: A Study in Divine Semiotics (Bloomington: Indiana University Press, 1994).

39. Leon Chai, Jonathan Edwards and the Limits of Enlightenment Philosophy (New York: Oxford University Press, 1998); Alvin Plantinga, Warranted Christian Belief (New York: Oxford University Press, 2000); Stephen J. Nichols, "An Absolute Sort of Certainty: The Holy Spirit and the Apologetics of Jonathan Edwards" (Ph.D. diss., Westminster Theological Seminary, 2000), published in revised form as The Spirit of Truth: The Holy Spirit and the Apologetics of Jonathan Edwards (Phillipsburg, N.J.: P&R, 2003).

40. Anri Morimoto, Jonathan Edwards and the Catholic Vision of Salvation (University Park: Pennsylvania State University Press, 1995); Gerald McDermott, Jonathan Edwards Confronts the Gods: Christian Theology, Enlightenment Religion, and Non-Christian Faiths (New York: Oxford University Press, 2000); Gerald McDermott, "Jonathan Edwards and American Indians: The Devil Sucks Their Blood," New England Quarterly 72 (1999): 539–57; Kenneth P. Minkema, "Jonathan Edwards on Slavery and the Slave Trade," William and Mary Quarterly 54 (1997): 823–34; Amy Plantinga Pauw, "The Future of Reformed Theology: Some Lessons from Jonathan Edwards," in Toward the Future of Reformed Theology: Tasks, Topics, Traditions, ed. D. Wills (Grand Rapids: Eerdmans, 1999), 456–69.

41. Ava Chamberlain, "The Immaculate Ovum: Jonathan Edwards and the Construction of the Female Body," William and Mary Quarterly, 3d series, 57 (2000): 289–322; Catherine Brekus, "Children of Wrath, Children of Grace: Jonathan Edwards and the Puritan Culture of Child Rearing," in The Child in Christian Thought, ed. Marcia J. Bunge (Grand Rapids: Eerdmans, 2001), 300–328.

The most important scholarly contribution in the last decade was the explosion of volumes in the Works of Jonathan Edwards edition published by Yale University Press. From 1994 to 2000, seven volumes appeared; the importance of these volumes can hardly be measured. David Hall's volume of *Ecclesiastical Writings* (1994) contains the documents relating to the final controversy of Edwards' career at Northampton, the controversy over communion.[42] Most importantly, the volume reproduces Edwards' narrative on the controversy as transcribed by one of Sereno Dwight's workers, which Dwight then edited for the published version that appeared in his edition of Edwards' works. Hall collated this transcript with extant letters to produce a full rendering of Edwards' view of the controversy. In the same year, Edwards scholars received another boon when Thomas Schafer produced the first volume of *The "Miscellanies," a–500* (1994).[43] Schafer, the dean of Edwards scholars, personally transcribed all of the "Miscellanies" as a graduate student and junior scholar; this volume was the fruit of almost fifty years with Edwards. A second volume of sermons, edited by Kenneth Minkema and covering the "missing" years of 1723 to 1729, appeared in 1997.[44] Of particular note in this volume are Edwards' master's oration, which was his first public statement on justification by faith alone, as well as sermons from his aborted Bolton pastorate. Stephen Stein contributed once again to knowledge of Edwards' biblical studies with his edition of *Notes on Scripture* (1998).[45] Stein's edition represents the first time that Edwards' biblical notes appeared in their entirety and in the order in which he wrote them; thus, scholars can now discern Edwards' development as an exegete and biblical interpreter. In the same year, the definitive volume of Edwards' letters and personal writings appeared. Edited by George Claghorn, *Letters and Personal Writings* (1998) represented a forty-year labor of love that involved tracking down letters from two continents and transcribing 236 extant letters, including 116 never before published.[46] Mark Valeri's volume of sermons, covering the years 1730 to 1733, marked the third sermons volume to appear and the first from Edwards' ministry as Northampton's sole Congregational pas-

42. Jonathan Edwards, *The Works of Jonathan Edwards*, vol. 12, *Ecclesiastical Writings*, ed. David D. Hall (New Haven: Yale University Press, 1994).

43. Jonathan Edwards, *The Works of Jonathan Edwards*, vol. 13, *The "Miscellanies," a–500*, ed. Thomas A. Schafer (New Haven: Yale University Press, 1994).

44. Jonathan Edwards, *The Works of Jonathan Edwards*, vol. 14, *Sermons and Discourses, 1723–1729*, ed. Kenneth P. Minkema (New Haven: Yale University Press, 1997).

45. Edwards, *Works of Jonathan Edwards*, vol. 15, *Notes on Scripture*.

46. Jonathan Edwards, *The Works of Jonathan Edwards*, vol. 16, *Letters and Personal Writings*, ed. George S. Claghorn (New Haven: Yale University Press, 1998).

tor.[47] Perhaps more than any other interpreter of Edwards, Valeri highlights Edwards' focus on the economic sins of the Northampton citizens in his introduction to the volume. Edwards pointed to the failure
of charity and the competitive climate of Northampton merchants as
evidence of the sinfulness of his people and their need for a divine and
supernatural light to grant their souls salvation and to remake their society into a world of love.[48] Finally, Ava Chamberlain oversaw the production of the second volume of *The "Miscellanies," 501–832* (2000).[49]
It is particularly vital for understanding Edwards' mental universe until the arrival of Whitefield and the beginning of the Great Awakening
in 1740. Chamberlain demonstrates how Edwards focused on several
major themes in these notebooks—justification by faith alone, the history of the work of redemption, spiritual knowledge, the rationality of
Christianity, and the nature of conversion and spiritual life. As the Yale
edition races toward the tercentenary of Edwards' birth in 2003, the final volumes will appear—two more volumes of "Miscellanies," two additional volumes of sermons, the two-volume edition of Edwards'
"Blank Bible," a collection of Edwards' "shorter writings" on grace and
the Trinity, and Edwards' "Catalogue of Reading."[50]

Next to Edwards' own writings, perhaps the most important volumes to appear recently were the two collections of essays arising from
the national symposiums of Jonathan Edwards, sponsored by the
Works of Jonathan Edwards project at Yale University. *Jonathan Edwards's Writings* (1996), the published essays from the 1994 conference
hosted at Indiana University, moved Edwards studies in new directions. Particularly important essays included Ava Chamberlain's investigation of Edwards' unpublished sermon series on the parable of the
wise and foolish virgins, Kenneth Minkema's treatment of Edwards'
unpublished "Harmony of the Old and New Testament," Richard A. S.
Hall's deft handling of the relationship between Edwards and British

47. Jonathan Edwards, *The Works of Jonathan Edwards*, vol. 17, *Sermons and Discourses, 1730–1733*, ed. Mark Valeri (New Haven: Yale University Press, 1999).

48. See also Mark Valeri, "The Economic Thought of Jonathan Edwards," *Church
History* 60 (1991): 37–54; Gerald R. McDermott, "Jonathan Edwards, the City on a Hill,
and the Redeemer Nation: A Reappraisal," *American Presbyterians* 69 (1991): 33–47;
and Gerald R. McDermott, *One Holy and Happy Society: The Public Theology of
Jonathan Edwards* (University Park: Pennsylvania State University Press, 1992), 111–16,
158–59.

49. Jonathan Edwards, *The Works of Jonathan Edwards*, vol. 18, *The "Miscellanies,"
501–832*, ed. Ava Chamberlain (New Haven: Yale University Press, 2000).

50. At the time of this writing, another volume in the edition had appeared:
Jonathan Edwards, *The Works of Jonathan Edwards*, vol. 19, *Sermons and Discourses,
1734–1738*, ed. M. X. Lesser (New Haven: Yale University Press, 2001). This was the
fourth of six sermon volumes.

idealist George Berkeley, and Allen Guelzo's exploration of the Edward-sian influence on Charles Finney and Oberlin perfectionism.[51] The 1996 Edwards Conference papers, published as *Edwards in Our Time* (1999), focused on the contemporary application of Edwards' thought. Highlights of the volume were Guelzo's application of Edwards' under-standing of freedom of the will to contemporary problems, Helen Wes-tra's exploration of revivalism from unpublished Edwards sermons, Robert Jenson's creative use of Edwardsian eschatology, and Gerald McDermott's focus on Edwards' perspective on world religions.[52]

Several of the themes explored at these national conferences found voice in full-length studies. One of the most provocative and impor-tant books was Gerald McDermott's *Jonathan Edwards Confronts the Gods* (2000). McDermott argues that in Edwards' later years, his pri-vate notebooks reveal a thinker who was moving beyond his Re-formed predecessors on several issues: the relationship between rea-son and revelation, the kind of religious knowledge that the "heathen" have, and the possibility of salvation for those who do not have ex-plicit faith in Christ. The catalyst for Edwards' new direction was his encounter with the radical Enlightenment as represented by Deistic thinkers such as Matthew Tindal, Thomas Chubb, and John Toland. Though Edwards reaffirmed the priority of revelation over reason against the Deists, he also drew upon the ancient tradition of the *prisca theologia*, the idea that knowledge of God the Redeemer had come to the nations through general, not special, revelation. Further, McDermott also argues that Edwards' dispositional ontology should have led him to conclude that humans might be saints, having re-ceived a new disposition from God, without confessing faith in Christ immediately or, for some, at all. Though this study was historical in nature, McDermott drew upon this academic study to make a popular application in *Can Evangelicals Learn from World Religions?* (2000).[53]

Another study along the same lines is Anri Morimoto's *Jonathan Ed-wards and the Catholic Vision of Salvation* (1995). Whereas McDermott focuses on the issue of Edwards' potential ecumenicity historically, Morimoto explores Edwards' ecumenical soteriology. Morimoto and McDermott agree that Edwards' dispositional ontology provides the potential for a soteriology that affirms salvation for the unevangelized. Edwards' persistent claim that God infuses grace into the regenerate in

---

51. Stein, ed., *Jonathan Edwards's Writings*, 3–18, 52–65, 100–121, 159–74.

52. Lee and Guelzo, eds., *Edwards in Our Time*, 87–110, 131–57, 161–202.

53. Gerald R. McDermott, *Can Evangelicals Learn from World Religions? Jesus, Rev-elation, and Religious Traditions* (Downers Grove, Ill.: InterVarsity, 2000). Also see Gerald R. McDermott, "Jonathan Edwards, Deism, and the Mystery of Revelation," *Journal of Presbyterian History* 77 (1999): 211–24.

order to transform the human being's existence offers an avenue of rec-
onciliation between Protestant and Roman Catholic views of salvation,
as well as "a remarkable opportunity for reconsidering the salvation of
those who do not explicitly believe in Jesus Christ."[54] Not only do
Morimoto and McDermott share the same conclusion, but they also
share a similar starting point: Sang Hyun Lee's influential *The Philosophical Theology of Jonathan Edwards*. Lee argues that Edwards engaged in a major metaphysical reconstruction in which the classic categories of substance and form were replaced with a conception of
reality as dispositional forces and habits. Thus, Edwards was radically
modern—his focus on ontology enabled him "to reaffirm in the strongest possible terms his theological tradition within a thoroughly modern philosophical framework." Edwards' metaphysical revisioning allowed him to conceive of God as "essentially a perfect actuality as well
as a disposition to repeat that actuality through further exercises"
within the Trinity. As a result, Lee affirms that "Edwards' dispositional
ontology, which underlies his reconception of the divine being, is the
clue to the originality and unity of Edwards' philosophical theology as
a whole."[55] While not nearly as radical a revision of Edwards' theology,
Michael McClymond's *Encounters with God* (1998) also breaks new
ground. McClymond situates Edwards in an eighteenth-century intellectual context and views him as an apologist. Edwards claimed that
the saints' spiritual perception of divine excellency was itself a proof
for the existence of God. Thus, Edwards was "modern, yet with a
twist," according to McClymond. Edwards engaged the high European
culture of his day and appropriated several of its leading ideas. However, he was no mere passive receptor—instead, Edwards reinterpreted
these ideas and made them "subservient to his theological purposes."[56]

54. Morimoto, *Jonathan Edwards and the Catholic Vision of Salvation*, 64–66, 157–
59. See also Anri Morimoto, "Salvation as Fulfillment of Being: The Soteriology of
Jonathan Edwards and Its Implications for Christian Missions," *Princeton Seminary
Bulletin*, n.s., 20 (1999): 13–23.

55. Sang Hyun Lee, *The Philosophical Theology of Jonathan Edwards* (1988; 2d ed.,
Princeton: Princeton University Press, 2000), 3–4, 6–7. This second edition incorporates
Lee's "Jonathan Edwards on Nature," previously published in *Faithful Imagining: Es-
says in Honor of Richard R. Niebuhr* (Atlanta: Scholars, 1995), 39–59.

56. McClymond, *Encounters with God*, 5–7. McClymond incorporated several essays
into this book: "God the Measure: Towards an Understanding of Jonathan Edwards'
Theocentric Metaphysics," *Scottish Journal of Theology* 47 (1994): 43–59; "Sinners in
the Hands of a Virtuous God: Ethics and Divinity in Jonathan Edwards's End of Creation," *Zeitschrift für neuere Theologiegeschichte/Journal for the History of Modern Theology* 2 (1995): 1–22; and "Spiritual Perception in Jonathan Edwards," *Journal of Religion*
77 (1997): 195–216.

Not surprisingly, doctoral students have risen to the challenge and drawn upon these new interpretations of Edwards. The best of these dissertations was already noted: Robert Eric Brown's "Connecting the Sacred with the Profane," the first major study of Edwards' engagement with the rising historical consciousness. Brown expands on McDermott's theme, demonstrating that Edwards primarily was concerned by the Deist attacks on the historical reliability of the Scripture. To refute Deists on their own grounds, Edwards immersed himself in historical study, purchasing and using the best historical sources of his day. In addition, Brown demonstrates that Edwards became increasingly comfortable with a historical approach to theological formulation.[57] In another dissertation, Rachel Stahle interacts with the same themes that interest Sang Lee and Michael McClymond, reinterpreting Edwards' theology from a thoroughly Trinitarian perspective.[58] Allyn Lee Ricketts, through a thorough study of Edwards' epistemology, concludes that Edwards affirmed the priority of revelation over reason in his philosophical theology while also stressing the need for spiritual perception in order to know truth, a position that dovetails nicely with McDermott and McClymond.[59]

Other dissertations take their cues from broader themes in theology, ethics, and historical study. Matthew Todd Mathews took up the possible intersection between Edwards and Schleiermacher's religious affection and anthropology, an exploration suggested in part by Michael McClymond.[60] Another major theological interest for Edwards students is eschatology. Kyoung-Chul Jang treated the destiny of saints in a dissertation under the direction of Sang Hyun Lee.[61] Philosophically, Edwards is coupled together with George Berkeley, Samuel Johnson, and Arthur Collier in Bruce Allen Freeberg's study of "The Problem of Divine Ideas in Eighteenth Century Immaterialism."[62] In another study, Stephen Nichols explores the role of the Holy Spirit in Ed-

57. Brown's dissertation was recently published as *Jonathan Edwards and the Bible* (Bloomington: Indiana University Press, 2002).

58. Rachel S. Stahle, "The Trinitarian Spirit of Jonathan Edwards' Theology" (Ph.D. diss., Boston University, 1999).

59. Allyn Lee Ricketts, "The Primacy of Revelation in the Philosophical Theology of Jonathan Edwards" (Ph.D. diss., Westminster Theological Seminary, 1995).

60. Matthew Todd Mathews, "Toward a Holistic Theological Anthropology: Jonathan Edwards and Friedrich Schleiermacher on Religious Affection" (Ph.D. diss., Emory University, 2000).

61. Kyoung-Chul Jang, "The Logic of Glorification: The Destiny of the Saints in the Eschatology of Jonathan Edwards" (Ph.D. diss., Princeton Theological Seminary, 1995).

62. Bruce Allen Freeberg, "The Problem of Divine Ideas in Eighteenth Century Immaterialism: A Comparative Study of the Philosophies of George Berkeley, Samuel Johnson, Arthur Collier, and Jonathan Edwards" (Ph.D. diss., Emory University, 1999).

wards' idea of assurance of faith and how that relates to contemporary debates over epistemology.[63] Aesthetics was the area of study in Louis Joseph Mitchell's dissertation on Edwards.[64] Stephen Wilson develops an ethics of virtue from Edwards' writings, finding some coherence between the Northampton divine and contemporary theological ethicists such as Stanley Hauerwas.[65] The Stockbridge years receive notice in dissertations addressing Edwards' *Life of Brainerd*, his work with the Mahicans, and his philosophy and work as an educator.[66]

One of the perennial questions of Edwards scholarship is the relationship between Edwards and the Enlightenment. Ever since Perry Miller, scholars have sought to determine the relationship between Locke and Edwards as well as to ascertain whether Miller was correct to tie the two together. In an article in *Journal of Religion*, Robert Brown concludes that Edwards and Locke shared similar estimates about the epistemological status of biblical revelation.[67] William Wainwright also explored the nature of logic and rationality by comparing Richard Swinburne, a contemporary philosopher, with Locke and Edwards to determine whether passion or "the heart" affects the use of reason.[68] These discussions are not restricted to Locke, however. In his provocative book *Jonathan Edwards and the Limits of the Enlightenment* (1998), Leon Chai explores the crisis of knowing that occurred in the work of Locke, Malebranche, and Leibniz and uses

63. Nichols, "An Absolute Sort of Certainty."

64. Louis Joseph Mitchell, "The Experience of Beauty in the Thought of Jonathan Edwards" (Ph.D. diss., Harvard University, 1995).

65. Stephen A. Wilson, "The Virtue of the Saints: Jonathan Edwards on the Nature of Christian Ethics" (Ph.D. diss., Stanford University, 1998). See also Paul Lewis, "'The Springs of Motion': Jonathan Edwards on Emotions, Character, and Agency," *Journal of Religious Ethics* 22 (1994): 275–97.

66. Keely E. McCarthy, "'Reducing Them to Civilitie': Religious Conversions and Cultural Transformations in Protestant Missionary Narratives, 1690–1790" (Ph.D. diss., University of Maryland, College Park, 2000); Rachel Wheeler, "Living upon Hope: Mahicans and Missionaries, 1730–1760" (Ph.D. diss., Yale University, 1998); Donald Edd Stelting, "Edwards as Educator: His Legacy of Educational Thought and Practice" (Ph.D. diss., University of Kansas, 1998). See also Ronald E. Davies, "Jonathan Edwards: Missionary Biographer, Theologian, Strategist, Administrator, Advocate—and Missionary," *International Bulletin of Missionary Research* 21 (April 1997): 60–67; and T. M. Moore, "A Brief Introduction to an Edwardsean View of Christian Instruction," *Presbyterion* 25 (1999): 21–31.

67. Robert E. Brown, "Edwards, Locke, and the Bible," *Journal of Religion* 79 (1999): 361–84.

68. William J. Wainwright, "The Nature of Reason: Locke, Swinburne, and Edwards," in *Reason and the Christian Religion: Essays in Honor of Richard Swinburne*, ed. Alan G. Padgett (Oxford: Clarendon, 1994), 91–118. See also William J. Wainwright, *Reason and the Heart: A Prolegomenon to a Critique of Passional Reason* (Ithaca: Cornell University Press, 1995).

Edwards to determine the nature of rationality and why epistemological questions are worth asking at all. Others, such as Alvin Plantinga, question Chai's basic thesis, believing that Edwards' revelation-centered theology helped him to subvert the effects of the Enlightenment upon his thought.[69] John Smith sought to explore the problem of Puritanism and the Enlightenment through a comparison of the representative eighteenth-century Americans Edwards and Benjamin Franklin.[70] Some, such as Stephen Daniel, even seek to transcend the Enlightenment by viewing Edwards as a postmodern thinker, comparing Edwards' view of language as a sign system with insights of Michel Foucault.[71]

This is not to claim that the best academic work on Edwards has been restricted to philosophy. Some of the most creative work is being done on individual doctrines and themes in Edwards' theology. Amy Plantinga Pauw's dissertation was a trailblazing piece of work, stressing the Trinity as the starting point of his theology. Pauw drew upon her research in a 1995 article in the *Calvin Theological Journal*, where she traced the centrality of the Trinity in Edwards' reflections on heaven.[72] Another theological area that has drawn attention is Edwards' thoughts on spiritual perception and knowledge, as well as his work on religious affections. Michael McClymond translated Miklos Veto's fine article on "Spiritual Knowledge according to Jonathan Edwards," as well as offered his own reflections on spiritual perception in a separate article published in the *Journal of Religion*.[73] Ava Chamberlain drew from her own dissertation to point out Edwards' preoccupation with the theological problem of self-deception in his *Religious Affections*.[74] The enduring Edwardsian problems of original sin

69. Plantinga, *Warranted Christian Belief*, 293–320.

70. John E. Smith, "Puritanism and Enlightenment: Edwards and Franklin," in *Knowledge and Belief in America*, ed. W. Shea (New York: Cambridge University Press, 1995), 195–226.

71. Daniel, *The Philosophy of Jonathan Edwards*.

72. Amy Plantinga Pauw, "'The Supreme Harmony of All': Jonathan Edwards and the Trinity" (Ph.D. diss., Yale University, 1990); Amy Plantinga Pauw, "'Heaven Is a World of Love': Edwards on Heaven and the Trinity," *Calvin Theological Journal* 30 (1995): 392–401. Pauw's dissertation was published as *The Supreme Harmony of All: The Trinitarian Theology of Jonathan Edwards* (Grand Rapids: Eerdmans, 2002).

73. Miklos Veto, "Spiritual Knowledge according to Jonathan Edwards," trans. Michael J. McClymond, *Calvin Theological Journal* 31 (1996): 161–81; McClymond, "Spiritual Perception in Jonathan Edwards," 195–216. See also Richard B. Steele, *"Gracious Affections" and "True Virtue" according to Jonathan Edwards and John Wesley* (Metuchen, N.J.: Scarecrow, 1994); and Gerald R. McDermott, "Jonathan Edwards on Revival, Spiritual Discernment, and God's Beauty," *Reformation and Revival* 6 (winter 1997): 103–14.

74. Ava Chamberlain, "Self-Deception as a Theological Problem in Jonathan Edwards's 'Treatise concerning Religious Affections,'" *Church History* 63 (1994): 541–56.

and freedom of the will also have drawn attention in the period surveyed. John Kearney, in "Jonathan Edwards' Account of Adam's First Sin," argues that Edwards provided a coherent and adequate account of Adam's fall.[75] On freedom of the will, Allen Guelzo compares the Northampton divine's Calvinist metaphysics to James Dana's Republican theory.[76]

Edwards scholars also seek to unravel his soteriology. Paul Hinlicky follows the development of the doctrine of the new birth from Henrich Bullinger to Jonathan Edwards in a journal article for *Missio Apostolica*.[77] Michael Jinkins broadens his scope by tracing the morphology of the conversion experience and providing a religious psychology through a close examination of Edwards' revival treatises.[78] Bruce Stephens traced the doctrine of the atonement in American Protestant thought from Edwards to the later Edwardsian, Edwards Amasa Park. Stephens also considered Edwardsian Christology in his study *The Prism of Time and Eternity* (1996).[79] And fittingly, for the preacher of "Sinners," theologians have explored Edwards' doctrine of hell to determine whether he offers any insight for contemporary reflections.[80]

Lesser-known areas of Edwards' theology also draw investigations. For example, Stephen Clark argues that *History of the Work of Redemption* was unique because it was an early form of biblical theology, a use of redemptive-historical method.[81] Amy Plantinga Pauw dealt with Edwards' view of angels and demons in an article for *Mod-*

75. John Kearney, "Jonathan Edwards' Account of Adam's First Sin," *Scottish Bulletin of Evangelical Theology* 15 (1997): 127–41.

76. Allen C. Guelzo, "From Calvinist Metaphysics to Republican Theory: Jonathan Edwards and James Dana on Freedom of the Will," *Journal of the History of Ideas* 56 (1995): 399–418.

77. Paul R. Hinlicky, "The Doctrine of the New Birth from Bullinger to Edwards," *Missio Apostolica* 7 (1999): 102–19.

78. Michael Jinkins, "The 'True Remedy': Jonathan Edwards' Soteriological Perspective as Observed in his Revival Treatises," *Scottish Journal of Theology* 48 (1995): 185–209.

79. Bruce M. Stephens, "An Appeal to the Universe: The Doctrine of the Atonement in American Protestant Thought from Jonathan Edwards to Edwards Amasa Park," *Encounter* 60 (winter 1999): 55–72; Bruce M. Stephens, *The Prism of Time and Eternity: Images of Christ in American Protestant Thought, from Jonathan Edwards to Horace Bushnell* (Metuchen, N.J.: Scarecrow, 1996).

80. Bruce W. Davidson, "Reasonable Damnation: How Jonathan Edwards Argued for the Rationality of Hell," *Journal of the Evangelical Theological Society* 38 (1995): 47–56; John E. Colwell, "The Glory of God's Justice and the Glory of God's Grace: Contemporary Reflections on the Doctrine of Hell in the Teaching of Jonathan Edwards," *Evangelical Quarterly* 67 (1995): 291–308.

81. Stephen M. Clark, "Jonathan Edwards: The History of the Work of Redemption," *Westminster Theological Journal* 56 (1994): 45–58.

ern Theology, and in a festschrift essay for Shirley Guthrie, Pauw faulted Edwards' for failing to stress the Reformed emphasis upon the church as nurturing mother and choosing instead to hold up the church as the purified bride awaiting Christ's return.[82] Scholars also have been attentive to Edwards' thought on the church and sacraments. Fredrick Youngs explored the place of spiritual union in Edwards' view of the church, while William Danaher Jr. focused on Edwards' sermons on the Lord's Supper.[83]

Edwards' revivalism has drawn recent attention. One of the more comprehensive studies of Edwards' revivalistic methodology was F. Allan Story Jr.'s dissertation, which concedes that Edwards used human means to promote revival but defends Edwardsian methodology as scripturally based, practical but not pragmatic, mechanical but not manipulative, ecclesiologically focused, and focused on God's glory.[84] Frank Lambert claims even more than Story.[85] He argues that the Great Awakening was "invented" in a twofold sense: participants believed that they were part of a widespread movement of God's Spirit, a discovery hidden from secularists and opponents of the revival; but these participants also furthered the work by employing new means, particularly the rising print media, to further the awakening. The awakenings, whatever else they may have been, were at least cultural productions that appealed to the new print-based culture. Edwards plays into Lambert's story through his *Faithful Narrative* as well as his other revival activities in the 1740s. Another useful treatment of the revival period and Edwards' role in it is Ava Chamberlain's examination of Edwards' sermon series on the parable of the sower. In this series, preached after George Whitefield's visit to Northampton, Edwards offers a critique of Whitefield's itinerant methods and charismatic leadership style.[86] In ad-

---

82. Amy Plantinga Pauw, "Where Theologians Fear to Tread," *Modern Theology* 16 (2000): 39–59; Amy Plantinga Pauw, "The Church as Mother and Bride in the Reformed Tradition: Challenge and Promise," in *Many Voices, One God: Being Faithful in a Pluralistic World*, ed. Walter Brueggemann and George W. Stroup (Louisville: Westminster John Knox, 1998), 122–36.

83. Fredrick W. Youngs, "The Place of Spiritual Union in Jonathan Edwards's Conception of the Church," *Fides et Historia* 28 (1996): 27–47; William J. Danaher Jr., "Jonathan Edwards' Sermons on the Lord's Supper," *Pro Ecclesia* 7 (1998): 261–87.

84. F. Allen Story Jr., "Promoting Revival: Jonathan Edwards and Preparation for Revival" (Ph.D. diss., Westminster Theological Seminary, 1994).

85. Frank Lambert, *Inventing the "Great Awakening"* (Princeton: Princeton University Press, 1999).

86. Ava Chamberlain, "The Grand Sower of the Seed: Jonathan Edwards's Critique of George Whitefield," *New England Quarterly* 70 (1997): 368–85. See also Richard B. Steele, "John Wesley's Synthesis of the Revival Practices of Jonathan Edwards, George Whitefield, and Nicholas von Zinzendorf," *Wesleyan Theological Journal* 30 (1995): 154–72; and Charles H. Goodwin, "John Wesley's Indebtedness to Jonathan Edwards," *Ep-*

dition, Keith Hardman traces the history of evangelism and revivals in *Seasons of Refreshing* (1994).[87] However, his chapter on Edwards was largely uncritical, tracing the familiar story of Edwards as the hero of revival against Charles Chauncy, the enemy of God's work in New England.[88]

Edwards' theological legacy has received several fine examinations. Joseph Conforti explores Edwards as a cultural artifact that went through various transformations in the nineteenth century. Increasingly, the claimants to the Edwardsian legacy created a religious tradition that revered Edwards while moving far from his original theological positions.[89] Mark Noll traces the contested legacy of Edwards by focusing attention on the debates between the New Divinity and Princeton theologians over who was most true to Edwards' Calvinism.[90] In addition, Edwards' prominent disciple, Joseph Bellamy, received a thorough treatment in a study from Mark Valeri.[91] Moreover, the entire historiography of the New England theology was surveyed by Douglas Sweeney in an essay for *New England Quarterly,* charting how various nineteenth-century theologians sought to claim Edwards' mantle and how twentieth-century historians have traced the lineage.[92]

Finally, two academics have used Edwards as a resource for public theology. First, Gerald McDermott believes that Edwards provided theoretical resources to assist in the construction of new public theologies because he was concerned to avoid privatization and to main-

---

worth Review 25 (1998): 89–96. On itinerancy, see also Timothy D. Hall, *Contested Boundaries: Itinerancy and the Reshaping of the Colonial American Religious World* (Durham: Duke University Press, 1994).

87. Keith Hardman, *Seasons of Refreshing: Evangelism and Revivals in America* (Grand Rapids: Baker, 1994).

88. See also Nancy Koester, "Enlightened Evangelicals: Benevolence in the Work of Jonathan Edwards, Charles Grandison Finney, and Samuel Simon Schmucker" (Th.D. diss., Luther Seminary, 1994).

89. Joseph A. Conforti, *Jonathan Edwards, Religious Tradition, and American Culture* (Chapel Hill: University of North Carolina Press, 1995).

90. Mark A. Noll, "The Contested Legacy of Jonathan Edwards in Antebellum Calvinism," in *Reckoning with the Past: Historical Essays on American Evangelicalism from the Institute for the Study of American Evangelicals,* ed. D. G. Hart (Grand Rapids: Baker, 1995), 200–217. This was a reprint of an article from *Canadian Review of American Studies* 19 (1988): 149–64.

91. Mark Valeri, *Law and Providence in Joseph Bellamy's New England: The Origins of the New Divinity in Revolutionary America* (New York: Oxford University Press, 1994).

92. Douglas A. Sweeney, "Edwards and His Mantle: The Historiography of the New England Theology," *New England Quarterly* 71 (1998): 97–119. See also Douglas A. Sweeney, "Nathaniel William Taylor and the Edwardsian Tradition: A Reassessment," in *Jonathan Edwards's Writings,* 139–58.

tain distance between church and state.[93] John Bolt also uses Edwards for public theology, comparing him to the late-nineteenth-century Dutch theologian-politician Abraham Kuyper, and claims that Edwards and Kuyper came perilously close to idolatry in equating America with God's kingdom.[94]

Clearly, the academy's fascination with Jonathan Edwards has not abated. Rather, Edwards continues to be the object of highly original and informative theological, philosophical, and cultural studies. Scholars continue to believe that Edwards might hold some key to assist in living the Christian life in this world while others continue to be fascinated with Edwards simply as a great historical figure. Needless to say, after the outpouring of studies sure to appear during the tercentenary of Edwards' birth, the study of Jonathan Edwards will continue to produce some of the most creative scholarship in American religious studies. It is to be hoped that this work will prove profitable for the church.

93. Gerald R. McDermott, "Jonathan Edwards and the Culture Wars: A New Resource for Public Theology and Philosophy," *Pro Ecclesia* 4 (1995): 268–81.

94. John Bolt, *A Free Church, A Holy Nation: Abraham Kuyper's American Public Theology* (Grand Rapids: Eerdmans, 2001), 187–225.

INDEX